KOSHERSOUL

ALSO BY MICHAEL W. TWITTY

The Cooking Gene

KOSHERSOUL

The Faith and Food Journey of
an African American Jew

MICHAEL W. TWITTY

AMISTAD

An Imprint of HarperCollins*Publishers*

HarperCollins books may be purchased for educational, business, or sales promotional use. For information, please email the Special Markets Department at SPsales@harpercollins.com.

FIRST EDITION

Library of Congress Cataloging-in-Publication Data

Names: Twitty, Michael, 1977– author.
Title: Koshersoul : the faith and food journey of an African American Jew / Michael W. Twitty.
Other titles: Kosher Soul
Description: First edition. | New York, NY : Amistad, an imprint of HarperCollins Publishers, [2022] | Includes bibliographical references.
Identifiers: LCCN 2021059767 (print) | LCCN 2021059768 (ebook) | ISBN 9780062891754 (hardcover) | ISBN 9780062891716 (trade paperback) | ISBN 9780062891723 (digital)
Subjects: LCSH: Jewish cooking. | African American cooking. | Twitty, Michael, 1977—Religion. | Jews—Food—History. | African Americans—Food—History. | LCGFT: Cookbooks.
Classification: LCC TX724 .T85 2022 (print) | LCC TX724 (ebook) | DDC 641.5/676—dc23/eng/20211213
LC record available at https://lccn.loc.gov/2021059767
LC ebook record available at https://lccn.loc.gov/2021059768

---

22 23 24 25 26   FRS   10 9 8 7 6 5 4 3 2 1

SHECHECHEYANU—

*For the people who kept me alive to reach
this day, and didn't even know it:*

Rabbi Hayyim Kassorla

Andrew Melzer

Mark Meyerhoff

Elissa Kaplan

Phyllis Greene

Judy Treby, z'tl and Family

Adrian Durlester

Arnold and Gayle Brodsky

Rabbi David Shneyer

Meirav and Elah Levenson and Family

Rabbi Michelle Fisher

Lisa Pressman

Lisa Goodman

Rabbi Johanna Potts

Avi West, z'tl

Hazzan Enrique Ozur Bass

Rabbi Deborah Cohen

Sidney Stark

Razi Yitchak z'tl

Dr. Marcie Cohen Ferris and Bill Ferris

Jennifer and Nathan Wender

CONTENTS

Part III: *Neshamah*: A Soul Suite

Part IV: Eruvim

Part V: The Prepared Table

KOSHERSOUL

PREFACE

◼

WHY IS THIS BOOK DIFFERENT FROM ALL OTHER BOOKS?

When I first started talking about developing this book, a fellow African American food writer asked what it was about, saying, "So you're not writing about Black [food], you're writing about Jewish [food]." My response was reflexive: "No, this is a book about a part of Black food that's also Jewish food; this is a book about Jewish food that's also Black food because it's a book about Black people who are Jewish and Jewish people who are Black." What you're holding is the second in a three-book trilogy about the intersections (thank you for the language to describe this, Dr. Kimberlé Crenshaw!) between food and identity. I never set out to write tomes of recipes that we could quickly lose among the many. I want to document the way food transforms the lives of people as people transform food.

I meant my first book, *The Cooking Gene*, to be an early birthday gift to America, but especially the African American people on the verge of the solemn birthday of (Anglo-mainland) Black America, four hundred years past the arrival of the *White Lion* at Jamestown. In the text were laid the seeds to talk about being Black, Jewish, of Southern heritage, and gay, while focusing on the journey to find out how the story of food shaped my family tree and how the food we produced, prepared, and consumed along the way defined us, soul by soul, down to me. The vulnerability was the gamble of putting myself under the microscope to ask readers to understand my American journey through a culinary lens. I didn't want to leave anything behind. It's my conviction that our plates are constantly shaped by everything we encounter and everything in us.

We were swallowed by four years of attempted repudiation of messages of change and hope carried in on an era of swift and distinct change. Despite an outrageously different eight years from anything we have known in our collective narrative, we never really have had a national recognition of the particular four-hundred-year commemoration we needed to have. The year 2019 was followed by a year that can only be described as a postmodern nadir of Black existence, one completely in need of the wisdom from the past few centuries that exposed all the underlying challenges from before and beyond us. However, I was quite chuffed that no matter what else my inaugural book meant, it stood proudly in defiance at the opening of the dark ages. We were here not only before the *Mayflower*; we were here before the Drumpfs, and that was not to be forgotten or overlooked.

That same era also helped to stall this project. To talk about *The Cooking Gene* was to remind people of the Black experience's harrowing journey, bring back an awareness of our accomplishments, and assert a distinctly ethnic branding to our food story over the oft-assumed racial gloss. Meanwhile, all hell was breaking loose, and the growing loss of sleep spoke to our unease. Political scandals came and went like a battery of storms, and many hoped to see the pillars come down. They didn't.

Every day was a new flashpoint in the story of Culture Wars III. Each twenty-four-hour media cycle saw an uptick of red-meat policies to punish marginalized, oppressed, and outlier communities. The rising hate crimes and suspicions and anger from one group to another were painful and exhausting. Worse yet, the cloud above us, the knowledge that only a disaster that would affect us all could loosen the grip, loomed, and indeed on poisoned breaths and invisible biological bombs came the nasty release of a promiscuous plague. At last, something was present that was crueler to us than we were to one another.

I had to absorb some of this energy and motion to render this book honestly without condemning it to the times. This book is not a prisoner of the discourse of the forty-fifth president's rages, or of his minions, and at the same time, it is not possible to be liberated entirely from that stain. Even in this reflective moment, the West's original sins of anti-Semitism and anti-Black racism, as well as other forms of white supremacy, used to stir up resentment and anger and fuel conspiracy theories, have merged with continuing impulses toward misogyny, the suppression of the rights of the disabled and mentally ill, the continued struggle of sexual minorities, and the undisguised contempt for those struggling financially and for the working poor. In that nexus, Blacks and Jews and their Venn diagram have seen considerable turmoil and pain, and this too is a fundamental ingredient.

No matter the national sociopolitical climate, we humans are condemned as long as we breathe to the urge to eat and, when we eat, to find pleasure in the act and define our personal foundation. The Jewish people of the West and the African Atlantic Diaspora did not start their journey with exhausting shared pains or weaponized joy in their days; millennia and centuries have gone by with ample practice. That they, and we, have all survived yet again is another testimony to whatever magic lies in our traditions. Even when we were starving, our imaginations and hopes for redemption formed a feast in our minds that kept us going. We, the outsiders, have time-honored practice at seeking refuge in our pots and peering inside to see ourselves in the days when the outside world erases us. We, the children of the patriarchs and matriarchs of Israel, the children of Mother Africa, are ever finding meaning in our kitchens and our plates to overcome the next chapter of *They tried to kill us, we won? Let's eat.* I guess.

If *The Cooking Gene* was a present to African America on the pulse of its birthday, *Koshersoul* is recovery food. *Koshersoul* is chicken soup for the soul of Jews of African descent, the American and global Jewish peoplehood, and the folks in between in a spirit of celebration of our endurance and as a motivation for our healing in the raw and tender moment in which we find ourselves. There are other works about the existence and practice of Jews of African descent, but this is not an academic journey, and it's purposely not a cookbook. *Koshersoul* is an eclectic recipe file of diverse and complex peoplehood. My goal is to go beyond the strict borders of what Black Jews eat or how Black Jews cook, or even how "mainstream" Jews (with "mainstream" being nothing more than a polite term for white) have absorbed Black food traditions not usually seen as "Jewish." It is the border-crossing story of how the ups and downs of daily existence as a Jew of color affect us from *kop* to *kishkes* as we sit down to partake in the soul-warming solace of our meals.

Much like the people within these pages who have shared something of their lives, *Koshersoul* is not to be taken at face value. It's not just the food traditions of Jews of color that matter—it's the people and their lives and the legacy they want to leave in two peoplehoods where tradition and the power of heritage loom large even when the choice is to cast off or change directions. The net is vast—from the experiences of Black non-Jews who cooked in Jewish households to the foodways of Black *frum* Jews and those in African and Western communities of some antiquity. It includes Jews who identify as white but Southern who are heirs to an Afri-Creole food tradition in Southern cuisine and the cousin traditions held by Black Muslims in America and traditions in Black Jewish congregations and communities that have been separate from the mainstream. Between these tabs are many border-crossers and combinations, a rainbow of people challenging our notion of not only the false antipodes of Black versus Jewish but American and human living beyond the bubbles and boxes we've assigned to assuage what we apprehend as normal and socially digestible.

Koshersoul is a chapter in the biography of a people and a food memoir with side journeys into what it means to be a person with multiple families. When I go into the kitchen to make my unique brand of koshersoul food, all of it goes with me: "race," as practiced in America and the West; Jewish learning and folk culture; Black cultural expression; the spiritual spectrum of both communities; and the spirit of queerness and impetus of gay liberation. Food has been my primary lens for navigating my citizenship within the Jewish people and my birthright as a Black man in America. Flashpoints amplifying conflict in Black-Jewish relationships, significant and attractive to our appetite for pain and argument, cannot take the place of individual narratives and authentic lives and the way people create themselves. These recipes for each human experience—which Talmudic rabbis poetically and metaphorically expressed as not only "worlds," but "the entire world"—are not replaceable and negotiable as sources.

Between the flashpoints and controversies are people living their lives, including going into the kitchen and cooking and then sitting down and breaking bread. Before and after historical calamities are human beings creating themselves and contributing to the larger flow of civilizations. Moments trickle into memories into trends into customs into traditions and flow in streams to become the sea of narrative and the mists of myth and lore. No matter our fantasies, all is not recorded; many stories get lost, many remarkable lives and communities disappear. Silence and extinction are real horrors.

And yet, the antidote is the record of the recipes of human lives as celebrations of cultures often oppressed and marginalized, taking absolute joy in being ourselves as members of worlds built on top of worlds. In food, we are more authentic than we know, more self-revelatory than we let on. This is why even though our food journey can reveal our weaknesses and our plagues, it feels so good here. Food is an unbelievably clear path to truth, and its best performance relies on hope as a critical ingredient—sharing, acknowledging other lives, offering up ourselves, revealing our boundaries. *Koshersoul* will, I do hope, join another deep and solemn moment of reflection that morning after when we rebuild and reimagine and share our tables again.

My greatest hope comes from the ingredients that Blacks and Jews bring to the table. I am the first to admit we are an incredibly exhausting set of people. We talk about the food we had before and the food we're going to eat next while eating the meal at hand. We beg of our loved ones to partake in food as if we actually need to eat our oppression. Our stereotypical foods have become shorthand for inside jokes we tell almost definitely at the deepest hatreds facing us. We sprinkle on our food traditions, sarcasm, and irony. Still, there is a lot of memory in our heads, and on our tables, lots of love from parent to child sighs of security when we realize our menus translate our means of survival across millennia.

We love to complain, and then we complain about that. We Blacks and Jews don't always speak the same language, but our spirits are mutually intelligible. Black shame and Jewish guilt—our collective mullings over the Maafa (the disaster of slavery and its global aftermaths and colonialism/Jim Crow/apartheid/systemic racism and mass incarceration) and Shoah (the Holocaust and the recurring themes of genocide and suspicious finger-pointing at Jews), rabbis who fancy themselves Borscht Belt comedians and Black comedians who preach a thunderous sermon, the Four Questions and Go Down Moses—sit side by side and have done so for a long enough time to tell a story. We have made cultural history and food history together, but nobody knows where that story really begins. All the while, we are surrounded by the miracle of why we are still here despite the many attempts to annihilate our annoying stubbornness, itself a consequence of courage married to humor.

I promise you: all of this background stuff matters for the next couple of hundred pages. This book is about how our food makes us, but it's also about the other stuff that gives the food *meaning*, the most Black-Jewish word of all. Sit down at my welcome table and eat and be satisfied; this is just the *mise en place*. Trust me, it's such "nourishmul," as my best friend Andrew's *bubbe* would say, or (as my late mom would put it), it will make you wanna slap somebody, but not that hard. B'Shalom, Michael.

Part I

———

BERACHAH

Jewish food is a matter of text expressed on the table. Entering the Jewish foodscape changed my life.

Jewish food and Black food crisscross each other throughout history. Both are cuisines where homeland and exile interplay. Ideas and emotions and ingredients—satire, irony, longing, resistance—and you have to eat the food to extract that meaning. The food of both diasporas depends on memory. One memory is the sweep of the people's journey, and the other is the little bits and the pieces of individual lives shaped by ancient paths and patterns. The food is an archive, a keeper of secrets.

—*The Cooking Gene*

1

FAMILY HISTORY

The most imperative Jewish word to me is *mishpocheh* (meesh-poh-keh). It's Yiddish, and just so you know, I'm not too Ashkenormative; the Hebrew is *mishpahchah*, and for centuries, it has meant "family, tribe, clan." Deeper than that, it means family beyond blood or boundaries or even centuries. A closely related word is "landsman," לאַנדסמאַן, the connotation being that someone is from your same town or point of origin, but the gloss of which means "kinsman," someone who comes from what you know and are. Playing "Jewish geography" means figuring out how *mishpocheh* is a landsman.

When you're Black and Southern, the word is "kinfolk." The first question I ask someone who is an African American landsman is, "Where your people from?" That way, I know that a fellow landsman is *mishpocheh*. It's a beautiful thing across the African Atlantic world, that is, Africa and its diaspora in the West: we come from languages and cultures that don't know how to distinguish family—everybody is potential family. We talk about "play cousins," people who are so close they are as good as blood. In West and Central Africa, cousins are described as siblings, and cousins, aunties and uncles, and elders are mashed up into one mass of family and kinship beyond borders. Among African Americans, Afro-Caribbean folk, Afro-Latin familia, and Afro-Brazilian and African—to be kinfolk is to be connected, and rooted by a deep understanding of intimacy and shared experience.

When you're gay, the word "family" is code for being a fellow "queer person." It's a way of saying "LGBTQ" out loud without giving away that you're talking about a fellow member of the tribe. That's a key word here: tribe. Even though it's not particularly appropriate to describe ethnic groups in Africa, part of the dream of New World African genealogy is to know the tribe your people came from. American Jews often call themselves "MOT," "Members of the Tribe." Gay and lesbian folks often talk about being part of "the tribe" to describe being part of the "family." Black people, who are part of the "Qmunity," sometimes say things like "Is he/she in the Life?" or "Is he/she/ze a sister?" We use the term "family" in a deep way—some of us have been rejected or have experienced rejection or had to form new families, and often we're trying to reclaim the notion that we can be family too.

A mean troll on social media once called me out as being mentally ill for existing in multiple identity spaces. It didn't last long; the tweeps came to my rescue. I knew who I was: I had crossed the entire American South; gone to Jerusalem twice; visited Africa seven times, going to eight different countries and going back generations; dealt with life and death, abuse and love; been in the condition of poverty; and been brought to tears by the possibility of success and living my dreams. Yet, in all those things, the one common thread was coming to clarity that I had always been and would always be surrounded by family.

When that's your worldview, the humans you share the world with become more intensely real as people you can be blood with, bond with, and potentially break bread with. One day, after having a million conversations and seeing millions of faces and sharing enmity and joy with others, it hit me that this is why we cook for one

another, share food and talk about food and beyond—we just want
to be family to one another. That desire is almost destiny, even when
we disagree and put one another in various states of pain. There is
some redemption in coming to peace over a moment of comfort and
satisfaction, and sometimes the comfort and satisfaction are precisely
what we need to sustain that peace.

Hospitality is bigger than a matter of etiquette, and it can happen
anywhere we let it—life is people, and sharing is the point. In the
words of the *Otzar Midrashim*, "Greater is welcoming guests than
receiving the countenance of the Divine Presence." We are here to
be family to one another, to exist for the sake of others, even as others
exist for our sake. Consider this musing an invitation to be my family.
You don't have to be Black, gay, or Jewish, but if you are, we have a
little something to kibbitz about before we nosh.

Keeping Kosher, Keeping Soul

I want people to know that being Black and being Jewish is not an
anomaly or a rare thing. I want people to know how these two identities have such a rich history that the lessons we've learned across
time and space complement each other and have so much to teach
us about community, self-determination, diaspora, nomadism, and
collective liberation. I want people to know the incredible wealth of
knowledge, mysticism, and spiritual power available to us. I want
people to know about the deep reverence for ancestry and tradition
I take pride in.

The teacher and writer Yavilah McCoy says:

For me "soul" is the wellspring of Blackness that comes to me
from the physical and spiritual DNA in my ancestral line. Soul
informs and shapes my being and expresses itself through me, of-
ten without words. It's in my food, my music, my laughter, my

rhythm and movement, my sense of awe and inspiration in all things living and that have lived on this earth. Kosher soul is the way that I live "soul" in connection to my practice of Judaism. I believe that once upon a time in my ancestral memory there was not a need to explain or affirm the organically braided relationship between "soul" and "Jewish" in practice. White Supremacy has robbed the Jewish people and the world of many things, including in many cases, our shared memory of "Jewish soul" and our shared experience of Jewish culture manifesting beyond the paradigm of European-ness and whiteness. Kosher soul is one way of expressing my unapologetic commitment to reclaiming what always was.

Here's the first koshersoul reality: neither one of these words is to be taken literally. "Kosher" is a standard of ritual fitness according to Jewish dietary laws and is sometimes applied to other parts of Jewish material culture and ritual observance. In vernacular English it references something that is acceptable, is solid, passes muster, or is genuine. "Soul" has its own connotations of soul food, soul music, soul people, soul dancing. However, soul food has come to mean both African American vernacular cuisine and the comfort food and core traditions of other folk cuisines. Soul means a certain vibe and feeling, an earthiness and peace with yourself and your people.

The word "soul" is an English gloss for a concept that came over with the transatlantic slave trade from Kongo-Angola. Consummate spiritual philosophers, the peoples of Kongo-Angola profoundly affected how African Atlantic cultures transmitted their culture in exile. "Moyo" is the Ki-Kongo term analogous to what we call soul, spiritual essence, and energy. You know the word it became in the American South: "mojo," as in "I got my mojo working." It means your vibrations are busy doing the job of representing you, putting things into alignment, shining. Soul is the untouchable power and quality that functions as a noun, adjective, and verb all at once.

Kosher practice morphs a little bit itself into the term "kosher style." For the past century, it has implied not exactly kosher—although it could kinda be—but to use a coinage: Jew-ish. It's having all the brunch and kiddush stars at the same meal, although technically, they were never meant to be at the same table. What's important here isn't purity, authority, or fitness but feeling. It's the "Old World," nostalgia, feelings of connection, owning a taste that connotes particularity and openness at the same time. After all, you don't have to be Jewish to eat Levy's rye.

Both "kosher" and "soul" are quasi-ethnic terms. We use these words to communicate the core stuff of each world to outsiders. It's the desirable, marketable part of us as undesirables in a world where anti-Jewishness and anti-Blackness still remain undercurrents. But for how long? These terms are from a specific twentieth-century moment and place in American life. The diasporas that produced them keep marching on into new realities, but they are comfortable baggage. They are words that do the economic work of telling the long story in shorthand.

Everybody always wants to know our origin stories—how, exactly, did we come to be Black and Jewish? People want narratives that are cute and pithy and understandable. Something that digests easily and slides down with absolutely nothing problematic and historically challenging. Heartwarming stories of something far from Black that somehow makes room for worthy Blacks to be Jews. Others want to know why Black isn't good enough for us or what we possibly could need or want with extra oppression—or the yoke of the Torah.

I know a Black Jewish woman, a veteran, a vegan Reconstructionist rabbi. I know a trans male Black Jewish rabbi. I know a Black woman who is a Reform rabbi. And I know a Black Jewish man raised Hasidic who is an Orthodox rabbi.

I know more than just rabbis. I know an African American Jew who sings traditional Yiddish songs. I know a Black woman whom you might never take as "mixed" with a white Ashkenazi Jewish mother who fearlessly carried a Torah scroll down the street during one of the largest protests in American history. I know a Jewish woman who wrote a beautiful and searing version of the *Al Chet prayer*—the confession of sins—to address racism and anti-Blackness in Jewish, especially observant, community life. I know a Black Jewish biracial and binational activist who lives in Toronto and in the same city a Black Jewish Canadian Jamaican principal.

We are Ethiopians and Eritreans—the saving remnant known to harrowing news stories and the biography of Tiffany Haddish.

For that matter, we are lots of celebrities and notables. We are used to hearing, "He/she/they are Jewish?" (upspeak on the JEWISH—and then a jaunty "huh/hmm/oh").

Sometimes, when we are lucky, as I have been, we are also, "He's Jewish just like us. We're all Jewish."

We are Yaphet Kotto, of blessed memory, whose Panamanian mother kept strict kosher and whose Cameroonian father reminded him of their deep Jewish roots as African royals.

We are British and Canadian and Dutch and German. We are certainly Israeli.

We are Ghanaians and Nigerians and Abayudaya Ugandans and Lemba South Africans and Cape Verdeans and Senegambians and Congolese with deep Portuguese Jewish roots.

Others were living Black and Jewish in the Sahel of West Africa, practicing Torah Judaism until the slave trade came along.

We are the people on the outskirts of the Black Jewish blood and bodies and brains of Afro-Brazilians, Jamaicans, Surinamese, and Afro-Cubans.

Some of our mothers and fathers are just some flavor of non-Jewish Black; some of our mothers and fathers are just some flavor of Jewish non-Black.

Others of us have two Black Jewish parents, and some of us Black

Jews have distant Ancestors who were Jews—often non-Black but sometimes others.

Some of us came from the bosom of what are now centuries-old synagogues in Harlem and beyond. Some of us worship in shuls on the South Side of Chicago; others in Virginia and North Carolina, Baltimore and Philadelphia. The Torah scrolls are Ashkenazic; the Hebrew is Mizrahi; the clapping, singing, and preaching are all African American. There are pictures of us gathering in the days of old and now—Hebrew lessons, bar and bat mitzvahs, gathering for *tashlich*, preparing for Passover with matzoh, wine, barbecue-style braised lamb, collard greens, and Go Down Moses.

Others are just Jews by choice; some say "just converts."

Some of us have a little bit of everything above in us. Most of us find some way to make sure we are valid on paper in the eyes of one movement or another. Some, like me, carry our papers with us so that everyone knows we are as legitimate as a paper will allow us to be. Sometimes I call them my freedom papers, with no small sense of sour smirk and cheek. When someone claims they can't see my Jewish soul, I can throw the papers in their face and tell them to get their soul checked.

We don't want conflict. We have a history, and we are still piecing it together. We just don't want to always give our origin stories before our names. Yes, we have Jewish journeys, but we have names first. These gestures toward true inclusion after being Black and Jewish for thousands of years in one shape or form go a longer way than constantly speculating whether we are real, trustworthy, desirable, or authentic.

We are a fairly close-knit community of thousands upon thousands; the internet has made us feel smaller and more compact than we really are. It doesn't take long to find us through each other, especially those who dare to not only stand out but own it. Every day, a new one of us is born. Every day, another one of us leaves—some anonymously Black and Jewish—resistant to engaging in the flash-points and crises of identity that other people have against us. Some of us exist, choosing to be Jewish by sneaking into the back row for Yom Kippur, never touching bacon, giggling privately to ourselves when someone within earshot says something culturally Jewish, and we know they think we don't or couldn't possibly understand.

We are complicated people. Koshersoul, to me, is making food and making material and ideational culture that, when consumed by others, requires digestion and isn't always easy to swallow. So here we are: the goal is not to prove how Jewish we are or how relat-able, or how Jewish or how Black; the end is proving that we are here, we cook and share and eat, and therefore *hineni*, we are present in our own making.

Put the collard green kreplach in your mouth, chew, listen, learn—repeat.

The Spoiler Alert

When I first dreamed up a book exploring my Black and Jewish iden-tities inside and outside the kitchen and how the collective cooked itself into existence, I swore I was going to open up an entire world of Black Jews mixing up foods from both worlds. Sometimes that happens, but most often, it's not on the radar of most people I've met.

At first, this caused me a bit of personal grief. What was I really writing about? What was I trying to document? Whose story was I trying to tell? The need to make "koshersoul" something bigger than me and tribal came from insecurity imposed from without; if every-body wasn't "doing it," how could I be sure it was real?

This is the twisted logic that started to live in me. If I couldn't find a minyan or more of Black Jews making Afro-Brazilian cholent with a side of biscuit kugel and jollof rice–stuffed cabbage (I just made that up), then the story I was trying to tell didn't matter. I needed

Black-up to make me real, other people to prove that what I was do-ing wasn't just a niche private obsession that could be tossed into the trivia bin. I needed someone cooler than me to make me cool. The need to be valid to the white gatekeeper gaze as someone who branded the discovery of an unrecognized cultural phenomenon wasn't healthy or smart; so this project changed when I realized I had nothing to prove to anyone, let alone someone who thought they had the power to make me real or valid.

I wanted to discover us, but really I had to discover myself and why my story mattered in the context of a constellation of other sto-ries. To paraphrase a frequently quoted rabbinic piece of wisdom: to save one story is to save the entire world. What mattered was not that our "koshersoul" had rules and boundaries and lines but that we each catered our culinary and cultural coping mechanisms to the unique journeys we faced as individuals. Trying to navigate two very rich traditions and melding or separating them when mood and message mattered—that was what koshersoul was really about. The goal of this book became to remove all the labels, not create another.

2

THE NUMBERS GAME, OR "WHERE THE KINFOLK AT?"

> If you want me to spell out who I am, I am a mixed-race
> Black Jewish woman, and that's who I am—if you want
> me to . . . I've had people question my identity my whole
> life—I give zero fucks about it. It's a them thing—it's
> not a me thing.
>
> —*Tema Smith*

There are so many complicated issues at the intersection of being Black and being Jewish. So many incredible people, particularly Black Jewish women, do this work day in and day out. They are single women, mothers, former military, rabbis, lawyers, wives, cis, and trans. They are converts, born to Black Jewish or other mothers of color, born to white-identified Jewish mothers, or are Jews of patrilineal descent. (And believe me, all of those categories matter to the life experience they bring to their work and everyday life.) Whether they plan on it or not, many are thrust into activism and advocacy.

Tema Smith is a great voice for these issues, and we've had the occasion to break bread in the kosher-style restaurants of her hometown of Toronto. We've done programs together and frequently are called on among the roster of friends and colleagues who can speak to unraveling what being Black and Jewish means and why our experience matters. It's a constant realization that education matters—especially in my and Tema's respective Jewish communities, where we have both served as teachers and done other communal professional work. Because being Jewish involves more than just religious activities, this work impacts not only intergroup relations but Jewish social work, Jewish education, and Jewish media, as well as having implications for Jewish ritual practice and communal organization.

"What we have to be careful about here," Tema begins one of our conversations over a Manischewitz-based cocktail on a warm Ontario afternoon, "is reifying the racial lines that have been drawn for about five or six centuries, racial lines that make racial categories firm and do the work of maintaining white supremacy."

I pipe up: "The biggest thing we face is being told that to be Jewish essentially is to be white, that being Middle Eastern is being some form of tan Caucasian, that these identities are one and the same. Or my personal favorite, that there is a Mediterranean branch of the Caucasian race to which Jews belong. It's exhausting."

Tema says, "There is this complicated relationship to diaspora and purity and oppression that brings out the best and worst in people. It's something oppressed people do; they get rubbed off on. Here, it's the oppressor's philosophy of who is in or out that creates conflict or makes more complex our internal conversations about who we are. Some people in our larger community don't believe in Nazi race science but come very close to applying those rules and understanding. We are beginning to have renewed interest in the insistence on matrilineal descent as a gauge or a test or anything that shows our obsession with purity when we know we are a mixed multitude."

"In the mindset you describe," Tema says, "Ashkenazi is seen as being closer to whiteness than being 'Middle Eastern,' whatever that means to people. In my other home, the United States, 'Middle Eastern' can mean white, but that's only because legal action was used to keep brownness in check."

"Tema, one of the most important parts of the Torah is called *Naso*, where we are literally commanded to stand up and be counted in a census. I'm always asked how many Black Jews there are. As someone who works in this space, why do you think our numbers matter?"

Tema sighs. "Well," and then she makes a big gutsy laugh. "There are a few different angles. Who are we even talking about? We're talking about people who are born to long lines of Jews who are Black from Africa and from the Caribbean; we are talking about people who have inherited Jewish tradition, people who are biracial, converted, adapted, and everything in between. We aren't talking about any one thing. We are talking about people who aren't necessarily active in any one community. Even and beyond that, we are talking about a marginalized community within a minority. We are talking about layer upon layer of complications. We know that minority groups get undercounted in any attempt to count populations. Getting statistically valid counts is harder the smaller the group being counted is.

"A lot of the communal surveys have not asked about race, or they mostly focus on white or not-white. You get 'White, non-Hispanic,' 'Black non-Hispanic,' 'Other non-Hispanic,' and 'Hispanic.' These questionnaires have no specificity in terms of what we are talking about when we say 'Black Jew.' We have no data about their denominations; we know nothing about Black Jews beyond anecdotal information. We are winging it at best. We have no idea about how many Black Jews are in Canada—the question has never been asked, but we are here, too. We are talking about the American Jewish Population Project [which researches the size and composition of the Jewish population in the United States] and it isn't enough.

"We are talking about roughly 142,000 souls—the count of Black non-Hispanic Jews in the United States. That's the best data that we have. How do I know if I'm counted in that or not—or you? There's no way to know." Tema's hands are in the air, and with a shrug, she laughs. She reiterates the need to know who the Jewish community is made of and to be flexible regarding its definitions.

Race is simultaneously socially constructed and very real, and yet immutable categories built to racial concepts and hierarchies are not. I liken racism to having very strong belief in a mythical creature. It can be very powerful, frightening, and complex, but race as a fixed biological reality is believing in the monster. Tema says, "Racism constantly changes, and it's completely contextual as people migrate, integrate, fight. But for us, all of those complicated things in a Diaspora group—they just don't fit. Even worse, we've now conflated the question of 'What's your DNA?' with 'Who are your people?'"

I remember seeing the ethnic/racial label "Hebrew" on a multicolored map from Ellis Island. In an era when the blood libel was still a thing in early twentieth-century America and quotas and gentlemen's agreements and clauses on who could live where were still very aggressive forms of anti-Jewish regulation, it was important to identify European Jews as separate from other people who might be seen as white. Some Ashkenazi Jews looked the part; others looked as if they had walked right out of the Middle East or Central Asia; and many Sephardi Jews looked no different from their Ashkenazi counterparts or favored Italian, Greek, or Slavic people whom they lived close to. "Hebrew" indeed.

"People want it to be simple," Tema continues, "but it's not and has never been. White Jews were anyone who didn't fit another ethnic category. Many Jews in colonial America were already "white" when the Constitution was signed. I think some white Jews are simultaneously correct and incorrect—about whiteness. There is still discrimination and racial anti-Semitism, and many WASP-y people think Jews aren't quite white. White context is also important here. Everything does not fit into these neat little boxes and binaries. We have to be comfortable with people's racial identity being and not being a thing.

"I feel like I play translator a lot. I spend most of my life in Jewish communal spaces and spend an enormous amount of time translating Black community issues to Jews and explaining and translating Black Jewish experiences to white Jews. This is a way of using my light-skinned privilege. People are thinking, 'This person looks like me: I can understand and believe what they tell me about Black people.' It's uncomfortable because it's a huge amount of responsibility."

I have a word for people like Tema and me: border-crosser. We are people who have always existed but have never really had a voice. We don't fit in boxes. We aren't the typical Black Jew. We are Black Jews who have something to say and mix it up with other Black Jews and hear their stories in order to introduce them to the world. We are here for something straightforward—communication across the very divide we live in.

Tema continues: "There are these big discrepancies. There isn't any way to talk about Judaism using the language of religion—because, in many ways, it's a Christian notion that Judaism is a religion. It's not that hard to understand peoplehood unless you're fighting against a wall that's been up for centuries."

"I feel the same way about being Black," I add. "Black peoplehood isn't a color or a phenotype. It's a very complex braid of how we look, where we ultimately originated from, the reason why we've moved, been exiled, enslaved, traveled. It's also the social category others put us in. If you're Jewish, you're a faith; if you're Black, you're a color, and at worst, Tema, a so-called race. I do believe both Jews and Blacks are peoples, just in different ways."

Tema looks down and over at the Manischewitz cocktails we slowly sip, and then says, "Different Diaspora stories but similar. As Jews, we were a nation and then got scattered and picked up some people on the way—we have an origin story—even converts have the same origin story. As Black people, we got our nationhood after we were scattered."

"Gender is also an important lens," Tema continues. "Black women have very different experiences with security in synagogues; the gender matters of which parent is biracial. Matrilineal descent determines who is Jewish in mainstream Orthodox and Conservative Judaism. In traditional Judaism, the moms drive the religious life of the household and its cultural identity. From what I've seen, the vast majority of mixed-race Jewish kids have Jewish moms. The mothers drive that engagement. But you see, this dynamic forces certain questions—especially if you are a Jewish woman of color—about legitimacy in some people's eyes, legitimacy-based race, and assumptions about race.

"But you know, there is a huge amount of cognitive dissonance. In general, the Jewish community values equality and justice and believes itself not to be racist. To quote Ilana Kaufman, 'We're not hermetically sealed.' We do a really good job at setting ourselves apart and when it comes to looking inside ourselves, people get defensive. It's normal to get defensive when people challenge you on something you're not used to being challenged on or ask questions you've never been asked. Shaming people does not make people change. This has to be fearless, persistent, but gentle and sincere work."

"But Tema," I say, "that's the hard part. We get shamed, we get put in situations where we can't cope, we have stressors other people don't have. The Jewish community is getting more diverse, and we have to make equality and justice a priority. It's not just about us; it's about the Jewish community as a whole. Our integrity as the Jewish people as a whole is at stake."

"That's why I want the people who haven't examined this for themselves to start to do the work," Tema says. "If this process makes you uneasy, there's a reason why. If you're feeling defensive, that's the door you have to push through to make the change. It's not on every Jew of color to help you through it. There are some out there to help you through it, but not everyone. That's not the job of every Jew of color. Judaism says, 'Get thyself a teacher,' so choose wisely."

There are those times when we are not in the mood to explain our identity to everyone. When I was a Hebrew school teacher, I did not have an out because I was the only Black teacher in the building. I had to teach kids and parents and fellow teachers alike how to deal with the next Black person they saw, let alone the next Black Jew. Sometimes what I said made a fantastic difference, and other times, nothing I said got through and it didn't matter anyway, not in the moment at least.

I chime in: "It's the narrative of Jewish success but Black stagnancy, although there are many poor Jews and many successful Black folks. Buzzwords get thrown around, like 'Pick yourself up by your bootstraps,' and people suggest that critical race theory is bad for Jews. Bad for Jews, or bad for Jews who rely on whiteness? If you're Black and Jewish on social media, you also get into this thing about, Are you real?, Are you loyal?, Are you valid?, Are you really one of us or suspect?"

"Yes, we deal with that *shandeh* [shame]," says Tema. "Like, can I have your whole fucking résumé? There is this real fear that there will be an influx of fake Jews—Black Jews who will delegitimize, or fake Jews who will turn everyone into a *mamzer* [illegitimate; literally, a bastard with no lineage]. Again, we are coming up against the idea of ruining purity. I mean, why on earth? Who are these armies of people? Why are they faking it? What intellectual purity test really exists to keep them out, and why do you want that?"

Tema's last statement stuck with me. How often had I felt like I didn't have the wherewithal to be myself and express myself and my feelings like any other Jew? How many times did I feel the need to prove that I was as knowledgeable, that I was legitimate or literally carried my *teudat gerut*—my conversion certificate—with me. Why did I let other people saturate my life with tests on my spirit? The term these days is "impostor syndrome," and even though I knew who I was, did they?

I cook and teach to be counted. I learn the history of every dish and ingredient and names and geographies to be counted, just like I study the history of the Ancestors to count the ones who came before us. I know how easy it is to obscure the culture makers, to erase the creators and say they never were. I do this work so that someone will look for my number among the censuses that don't know me by name and never asked. I create food so there will be a trail to find us by, something to start a legacy.

3

THE BUS RIDE, OR "FOR THE LAST TIME, THIS IS WHY I'M JEWISH!"

The number 5 bus ran from Silver Spring to Rockville, not only the heart of the suburban sprawl in Montgomery County, Maryland, but also basically from one side of the Jewish community to the other. At the time, in the early 2000s, the bulk of the national capital's Jews lived in Montgomery County. They ran the gamut from "ultra" Orthodox to members of Chabad Lubavitch to Modern Orthodox of all stripes and even a handful of traditionalist Conservatives who were nested in communities where you could take a walk on Shabbat but who would never consider hiring a woman as a rabbi. The bulk, however, were egalitarian congregations with a history of at least one woman rabbi or cantor and big sanctuaries with movable walls to accommodate the twice-a-year overflow on the High Holidays of Rosh Hashanah and Yom Kippur. If you wanted to be nondenominational with an interfaith family, there was a home for you. If you wanted to be a humanist Jew, the area accommodated, and Jewish renewal thrived alongside, independent *havurot*. The number 5 bus took you from one edge of the American Jewish Madagascar to the next. On the route, you could see each of those communities enact their own version of Judaism, each one a satellite of different cultures and ideologies writ large in the Diaspora.

Suburban Jews in the DMV (District of Columbia–Maryland–Virginia) were formerly based largely in the city of Washington, DC, with the oldest congregation being Kesher Israel in Georgetown, with adjacent old congregations in Alexandria, Virginia, and later in Maryland. This population of suburban Jews would swell after the uprising of 1968, after the assassination of Dr. Martin Luther King Jr., because, like many metropolitan areas, race and redlining had deep impacts on the ways the "Jewish community" and "African American community" interacted. Not far from my former second home on Kennedy Street were covenants on 16th Street stating that no "dogs, Jews, Negroes or Hindus" be allowed to buy or rent housing. The DMV's relationship with race is even more complicated by the fact that it was legally segregated, and all three jurisdictions were under Jim Crow laws, until the mid- to late 1960s. Apart from a significant attempt to integrate Glen Echo Park, the racism where I lived was grumbly and that of social indigestion, largely not the burning-cross type, even though Maryland as a whole cannot exempt itself from that kind of activity.

Many of these migrating congregations navigated land value and access to previously established buildings as they climbed upward. Some built the typical suburban '70s shul with a social area, a kitchen, a sanctuary, and spare rooms for meetings and classrooms. Over time these would be abandoned to Hispanic evangelical churches and Korean Methodists. The synagogue I attended had several homes since leaving DC; the one that was the most significant was on the former land of Isaac Riley, the tobacco plantation owner and slaveholder who held Josiah Henson in bondage. For many years the maps clearly stated "Uncle Tom's Cabin" since Henson was the inspiration for Harriet Beecher Stowe's novel of the same name.

Henson was born and raised in Maryland, taken to Kentucky with

Riley, and from there escaped to Canada. However, his descriptions of his enslavement on Riley's property are ample and vivid enough to indict every foot of the land in his acreage that became part of Jewish Montgomery County. It's an inescapable layering. This was one place among many where the words of the Passover seder were intoned over generations many feet above the bodies of enslaved Blacks deep in the soil surrounding them. America was one people's Goldene Medina, but for another, it was not.

Not every Jew in Montgomery County was or is affiliated with a congregation or is religious. Some people still live there because it's close to family and work or because they went to school in the DC area and never left. The suburbs are increasingly switching places with urban centers as gentrification reshapes the landscape. Young urban professionals with families and younger religiously and culturally engaged Jews are settling in the city and reinvigorating newer forms of Jewish life that are outside the traditional mainstream while supporting base institutions such as schools and new kosher restaurants—largely vegan and vegetarian. Some just do their own thing, expressing their Jewishness through their progressive values and lifestyle.

It's summer 2002. Enter into the scenario a man of that ilk and myself. I was wearing my suit and best *kippa s'ruga*—knitted and fitted—not the kind you get in the bar or bat mitzvah bin. I was headed to services on the bus and saw the thirtysomething-year-old man with his ample basket of vegetables, sandals lined in Montgomery County's finest red dirt, and smudgy glasses and straw hat. He was pleasant and engaged me with a "Hi!" and inquired if I was going to synagogue. I was getting used to this pattern. Visibility as a Jew, some might force themselves to use the word "Black" in front of "Jew," meant that nice or not, I was going to have to choose whether or not I wanted to engage everyday people on the question of my identity in the way others would not.

Jewish Geography is one of the first games we play when we meet each other as Jews in public. It's similar to Black folks playing "Who are you kin to?" However, it's also far and beyond kinship and lo- cality. Jewish Geography is a not-so-subtle verification system es- tablishing one's place in the networking system of American Jewish identity. It can also be a very tricky place to be as a Jew of color; your perceived inability to answer certain questions within traditional lines—like "Where did you have your bar or bat mitzvah?" or "Who was your rabbi growing up?" or "Did you go to _____ camp?" or "Did you pledge ____? or "Have you been to Israel, and when did you go?"—is a marker of the lack of a typical American Jewish lifestyle with a large degree of privilege to someone born inside the culture.

And this is what I mean by tricky. Being able to hold a conversa- tion as a Jew with another Jew at its most positive can lead to several different wonderful opportunities and further conversations, connec- tions, and a heavy slice of comfort. Being able to be "just Jewish" and not an outlier puts you at ease and removes the element of interro- gation. But when these conversations happen across a chasm of per- ceived whiteness or prejudged Blackness, they can be prickly, if not uncomfortable. Of course, "race" isn't the only thing that can shape these conversations—keeping kosher, Israel/Palestine relations, egalitarianism, observance, or political party membership can also shape whether *mechitzah* will go up between two people or whether it will be a match.

That day I was lucky. Nobody wants to wear the word "convert" on their sleeve, let alone their face. I shouldn't have to say that not all Black Jews are converts, but someone needs to read that again, so I just wrote it. I don't like saying that or defending that in public conversation, but I often do. As pleasant as our banter was on that twenty-minute stretch of bus stops, as unremarkable as that conver- sation was, it did leave me with one typically Jewish sweet-and-sour moment.

"Are you in the right place?" he asked me. "I mean, are you okay? Do people treat you differently?"

"Sometimes, I guess. I don't always know what to say or how to respond, but it's my job to love the Torah."

He squinted at me and rubbed his smudgy glasses with his sweaty garden shirt.

"Do you love the people?" he asked.

"I love my neighbor as myself, and if not me, who? If not now, when?"

I was proud of myself. I sounded Jewish enough. But he wasn't there for that.

"I think you're in the right place," he said. "But you'll know you're in the right place when other Jews get on your nerves, they frustrate the hell out of you, annoy you, make you feel shitty, but they are still your people, and you love them back and just as stubbornly. That makes you a Jew, as much as the *mikvah*."

He wasn't wrong. I had lived that in my Blackness. I had lived it in my gayness. I had not yet fully lived it in my Jewishness. I was new, and the *mikvah* water was still behind my ears. I was still dealing with the layers, the levels, the ladder steps that communicated my unique place in the Jewish people.

The conversation never left my mind. "Jewish" was the negotiation of feelings, personal and spiritual, and social investment—not just what I wore or how I prayed or whether I had gone to Camp So-and-So, knew Rabbi Such-and-Such, and adhered to these or those teachings or kept Shabbat a certain amount of minutes past sunset. No, Judaism was first and foremost one part of the culture of Jewish people. Your place in the *mishpocheh*, the family, and how you navigate that place, not just with others but within yourself—this is the boot camp of identity, especially intersectional identity, and it's where you find your special truth that only you can bring to the table.

Earlier that morning, I had made beautiful golden challah, the Beigel Family Challah from Joan Nathan's *The Foods of Israel Today*. The recipe survived the Shoah even if some of the people who baked it did not. I had to think about my relationship to the history of those two loaves of bread and all that came before and after it as my hands shaped the ropes and manipulated the dough and painted them with the liquid gold of beaten organic egg yolks. I didn't just know the story; I felt it in flashbacks, and all of that was part of my being in this community, this family, for life. It dawned on me as I got off the bus that I entered Jewish culture and religion through food, my favorite medium. It would be through the toolbox of food and conversations around food that much of that navigation to find my Jewish self would take place.

Mayseh:

A BLESSING ON STRANGE CREATURES

בָּרוּךְ אַתָּה יהוה אֱלֹהֵינוּ מֶלֶךְ הָעוֹלָם משנה הבריות

Baruch ata Adonai, Eloheinu melech ha-olam,
m'shaneh habriyot.

Blessed are You, LORD, our God, King of the Universe,
who makes creatures different / creates strange creatures / varies the creation.

Let's do a text study:

Schulchan Aruch in Orach Chaim *225:8–9 writes that for seeing a person with a dark, albino red, or white complexion, a person who is bent over because of obesity, a midget, a person with
a lot of warts, a person with hair that's attached should make the*
Bracha *of* Meshaneh HaBriyot.

Kitzur Shulchan Aruch *60:13–14 says to say* Meshaneh
HaBriyot *on a black person, a ginger, an albino, a midget, an
extremely tall person, a retarded person, an amputee, a blind person, a person with boils, a monkey, and an elephant.*

Rabbi Joshua ben Levi said: "On seeing pockmarked persons, one says: 'Blessed be He who makes strange creatures.'" An objection was raised: "If one sees a negro . . . he says: 'Blessed be He who makes strange creatures.'" . . . Our Rabbis taught: On seeing an elephant, an ape, or a long-tailed ape, one says: 'Blessed is He who makes strange creatures.'

There is a big difference between reading something at face value and studying it. There is also a big difference between the lens of one person studying a text and another. "You see," says my friend Rabbi Shais Rishon, who also goes by the moniker MaNishtana, "this is why we need to have not just white people and their lens when looking at a Jewish text. This part of the tractate Berakhot, which deals with the very important area of blessings in Judaism, is all about how we experience life and the things that G-d has made." MaNishtana is an African American Jew, born and raised to Black Jewish parents with a Jewish lineage going back generations. A Jew is supposed to say one hundred blessings a day—doable if you say the three main prayers and say the blessing after meals several times a day and open your eyes and bless about thirty more things or experiences—then the custom has been fulfilled.

"The text is looking at someone who is very dark or very light," MaNishtana says, "so someone who has melanism or albinism, it's not honing in on phenotypical variation, or notions of what we might call race. But if you're commenting on this text from the viewpoint of a certain era or place, much like many texts in Judaism, you can find a way to argue it into a certain space shaped by your worldview."

I was nineteen when I first brought home the gold-lettered English translation of the tractate Berakhot of the *Bavli*—the Babylonian Talmud. No collection of rabbinic work has been more probed for evidence of Jewish prejudice and spiritual chauvinism than the *Bavli*; it is a collection so maligned that Martin Luther himself wanted it burned to stamp out Judaism. It is not one book but a vast encyclopedic un-encyclopedia of conversations, arguments, legal pronouncements, and lore woven together from the Oral Torah (oral tradition). Its text is a sandwich of different eras. Its architectural look on the pages—which center the Mishnah and Gemara, surrounded by the texts of great rabbinic scholars across the next fifteen hundred years—is not a straightforward scripture by any means but what could be seen as the first transcribed webchat that just happened to spread out over time and space. Many of the arguments and conversations have no authoritative conclusion.

To read or study any rabbinic literature is to note that the emphasis is on the questions asked, not the answers given. To enter those pages is to become an asker of questions, a maker of arguments, a student and a speaker, a voice, and a listener all at once. It's exciting because it's challenging, chaotic, and bewildering and, by its very nature, speaks to the building blocks of Jewish civilization as text and response to text and argument over meaning, values, justice, and the import of lived experience. Besides a matter-of-fact vision of fulfilling commandments and customs, the *Bavli* is an overwhelmingly male, Middle Eastern, patriarchal voice to a world of migration and call-and-response between what was then Eastern and Western (read Greco-Roman, from the Hellenists to the Roman Empire) and ancient rural and increasingly urban realities. It also has a sense of poetry, humor, and wisdom literature bound together with whatever in botany, medicine, mathematics, zoology, astrology, and astronomy will amplify following the Torah and expanding that obedience to the era one finds oneself in.

The blessings in Judaism are varied and are a product of the poetic in rabbinic think. They are intense and seem to address every aspect of the human condition. There is a blessing for leaving the bathroom that recognizes the complexity of the human body. Other blessings discuss the flowers or rainbows or storms or wine, bread, vegetables and fruit, and "other foods," a polite way to skirt sanctioning blessings on meat, fish, or liquids that aren't wine. There are blessings of thanksgiving that men say about not having been made women, and there are blessings that were later innovated to push back against that blessing—starting in the Renaissance. There are blessings that have been created to answer voids in the tradition, and there are ancient blessings that have been reinterpreted to fit different times.

So, imagine my surprise when I opened this volume among many and read in 1960s English, "if one sees a negro." What does that mean for me? I looked at the date the book was published, but not being an Aramaic or Hebrew scholar, I was locked out. I constructed a gate in my mind between myself and the text. I was disappointed and alone. Could I be in this flock or not, since I was already dealing with a language I was born into where the word "black" holds a mountain of negative connotations? I felt trapped.

This is where we do some real talk. Judaism, the religious culture or civilization of the Jewish people, requires us to think outside the box regarding our thoughts about "religion," especially when that word often simply is code for Western Christian worldview. Whether people like it or not, Judaism has always evolved, even in its relationship with itself. The story of the Akedah—Abraham's binding and near-sacrifice of Isaac—is a great example. The request to sacrifice one's child—and Isaac is no little kid when this happens—is not the bizarre part despite our Hallmark vision of biblical-era religion. The odd part is when Isaac is unbound, and a ram in the brambles takes his place, in a complete break with other surrounding traditions that practiced human sacrifice.

"Two Jews, three opinions," we say. We are more than the answer; we are the arguments that lead there, the journey, not just the destination. It fits Jewish history, the search, the path, the migration from narrowness to wide expansiveness, from the margins to the center, and opportunity. This is not akin to wandering—a very anti-Semitic notion by lore—but rather a search for meaning moved by the vastness of meaninglessness so apparent in the world.

If the interpretation of the text above makes you uncomfortable, you're having a Jewish moment. That feeling you're getting doesn't exempt you; it means you are engaged. The fact that as you read this, we are studying the tradition together, is a Jewish moment. That feeling you're getting as your synapses fire and you "have so many questions" is Jewish. The fact that there are no easy answers here is very Jewish and why ultimately I love Judaism, as it searches for truth and justice and has no problem confessing its ancestral problematic-ness.

My former supervisor and mentor, Adrian Durlester, affectionately known as Mr. D, had another take. Some people have used the text to marginalize men of short stature. Mr. D never identified as a "midget" and technically is not, but he is a very short-statured man at 4 feet, 10 inches. He never had anything but good humor about it despite moments when he noted with pain the ways he has been discriminated against or taken advantage of because of how people read his height.

Mr. D. once said, "When I was in second grade, everyone in the class got a chance to put the American flag into its holder. When my turn came, the teacher passed me by. So I marched right up to her, took the flag from her hands, pulled her chair out from behind her desk, moved it over to the blackboard, climbed upon it, and put the flag in its holder. I don't recall what, if any, repercussions there were from this incident, but I do vividly remember what I did and how angry I was at being skipped over because of the "defect" of my height.

Mr. D is a Jewish educator in love with Jewish music and learning, so this text of Meshaneh Ha'Briyot gives him pause too, and it connects with verses in the Torah that might exclude him from religious service—or from his entire career. We sat together—a short man and a Black man munching on bagels—and examined Meshaneh Ha'Briyot. I remember him saying, "The Rabbis don't have our vision or values here, and we can't expect them to, but it's deeper than that. How do we see ourselves? Are we expected to look in the mirror and say this blessing? Or do we look at people like us and say it? Is this blessing about being odd, or is it about appreciating difference? I see it as appreciating all the variety of human beings that are ultimately made *betzelem Elokim*—made in G-d's image. Ultimately, however, you have to go into the language and apply the best of our values to reason out what this text means and why it is there."

Gold letters on binding make me still. So formal, so official, so strong and finite, but those gold letters don't bind me any more than the rope that bound Isaac or the opinions of others. I am still in the act of self-definition and understanding my own power as self-defined. I am here—*hineni*—the very word of Abraham, my ancient father, always on the verge of a new journey. What a strange creature I am, true—Black, Jewish, gay, and invested and imbued in my Southern and African heritages, made in the image of G-d like every other member of the human family. From *mechiyah* (joy) to *tsuris* (troubles) in pain and in power, I happen to believe my life is a blessing because I deny it is a curse to be something other than "normal." I am happily different.

4

YICHUS:
WHY I LOVE JEWISH FOOD—
THE HONEY ON THE SLATE

When I was a Hebrew school teacher, my favorite film I used to show was *A Life Apart*, a documentary about the Hasidic communities of New York City narrated by Leonard Nimoy and Sarah Jessica Parker. Why? Because it showed certain Jewish customs that my mostly Conservative and Reform students might never be exposed to otherwise. Besides, they usually went on a field trip during their confirmation year (tenth grade) to New York, where they would be dropped dumfounded, usually in the bosom of Crown Heights, and where they would equally be stared at with exotic wonder as they did their best to appear G-d fearing and *tznius*—modest, at least to the dress code of their hosts. I always thought the best cure for *sinat hinam*—baseless hatred and conflict—was we as Jews knowing each other, feeling at home when we were far from home.

The documentary has aged around the edges, but it remains like charoset in my soul because it captures some timeless customs tucked in the nooks and crannies of Jewish civilization. The filmmakers managed to gain access to a world where most rituals do not get recorded but are lived as if they were meant to exist in vibrant defiance of documentation. The work turns to education in the Hasidic world where it captures a boy receiving his first haircut, or *upsherin*, after which he is covered in a *tallit*, or prayer shawl, and whisked off by his father in a car to join a class in session where his teacher reinforces his understanding of the Hebrew alphabet, or *aleph-beis*, by placing a candy on each letter as he proudly repeats them, sound by sound.

Each time, I would stop the tape and pull out several books with images from the Middle Ages, most notably the so-called Birds' Head Haggadah, where the prohibition against graven images is taken so seriously that Jews are depicted with the heads of raptors—but with beards and the *Judenhut*, or Jewish hat, that would further mark them as outsiders. Here in nearly a mirror image, minus the car and candies, is a boy on the knee of his teacher, slate of the alphabet adjacent, plied with sweet cakes and snacks, even as we presume according to custom that a drop of honey was applied to the slate so the boy could lick each letter, further endearing him to the sweetness of learning and of mastering the building blocks that will unlock his ability to study the Holy Torah, the Five Books of Moses.

Learning is sweet; that's the message. Knowledge here in drag as honey, like the fruit of its very tree at the beginning of history, is the consumption of something delectable and irresistible, and problematic. There are consequences and curses. In the post-Lilith narrative, Chava (Eve) finds herself shouldering the burdens of all the world's sins with the punishment of childbirth just for good measure. All she got was to be created out of a lousy rib—and now I want you to know that's not the story I choose to believe.

For the person indoctrinated in this way, learning will not always be candies and sugar cakes and honey and dainties. It will reveal itself as the gateway to further otherness and marginalization and the inability to live without a life lens that will consistently make one feel as though one is on "the other side" (*Ha-Iver*—the root of the Hebrew word). The boy will learn that for the sake of this text and its traditions and customs and culture, he should be willing to forfeit freedom and even life itself should his enemies ask him to abandon it. Even the horror of giving Jerusalem over to amnesia carries with it the curse of the tongue, forgetting how to speak, sing, and eat. No wonder those angry bird Jews permanently locked in frame snarl at the goodies.

Let's be clear: In Judaism, prayer is work (*avodah*), not begging. Study and asking questions are baked into Jewish identity's DNA. Wrestling like Yaa'kov (Jacob) once did with the angel—with our impulses, with what is the right thing to do by our neighbors, with how to merit honor and respect for our Ancestors and just barely to make it out alive with our wrestling with G-d—is the key ingredient in Jewish food and learning because in Jewish peoplehood, "cookery" isn't just a form of personal, cultural, historical, regional, or class distinction or expression; it is a form of wrestling itself and of learning. It makes you *shvitz*, and I have to admit, I love that.

Jewish food is born in a challenge, and it likes it that way. Lox is not so lofty, nor is cream cheese; they masquerade as if Moses or Miriam ever saw, touched, or tasted them. They didn't. Many changes have been made since that first humble offering of wheat, barley, rye, spelt, and oats with a side of grapes, figs, dates, and pomegranates, and olives—who can forget olives? There were onions and leeks and melons and probably tilapia and Nile perch the size of a man in the land of Egypt. There were Mesopotamian beers and stews and spices and herbs from the Judean hills, but despite the idea that Jewish culture is a relic frozen in time, the minute Sara and Avraham started moving, the Jewish plate began to change.

That plate has been shaped by millennia of conversations about the foods that define us as Jews *kashrut*; the dietary laws that range from revelation to reconsidered reflection take up real estate in the mind of every Jewish person, whether they observe its dictates or not. Jewish eating spaces are where we have to negotiate not just the past but contemporary food politics of origin, ecological and social responsibility, and the curious braid of justice and righteousness, with a tiny bit of caritas that we sum up in one word—*tzedek*. Values are baked into our matzot, our honey cake, our borekas, and our boyos. Without fail, so are our conflicts and terrors—rocky myths about purity, attribution issues, unresolved struggles, classism, and racial flashpoints. That's where, one hopes, the passionate argumentation comes in, the striving toward something better, the self and group correction.

Jewish food has a textual character; it turns words into food. The weight of meaning and history and narrative sits behind nearly every dish and the ingredients that make up those dishes. And if you don't believe me, trust the late Rabbi Gil Marks or Claudia Roden, Joan Nathan, Faye Levy, Dr. Marcie Cohen Ferris, Dr. Ted Merwin, Dr. Hasia Diner, or Jane Ziegelman—stars in a constellation of Jewish culinary academics and authors. Jewish food has its own knowledge base, its own thrilling stories, and for more than twenty-five years it has set my imagination on fire. The study of Jewish food even gave me the ability to reach the language and ideas I needed to resurrect part of African American foodways from the grave of slavery. It makes sense that the people who gave the world Passover would have the keys to unlock the buried tombs created by America's original sin.

This penchant for Jewish food as a time machine makes the experience of Jewish food feel as though you've entered historical moments and captured them with your senses—even if you really haven't. It's the perception of time travel that counts. If that doesn't grab you, it's the references drawn from scripture to Midrash, or retellings—like the apple trees under which the midwives Shifrah and Pu'ah held the Israelite males or the mystical numerical value, or gematria, of dill or the grandmother wisdom that walked to the market to acquire a chicken or a carp or picked wild rocket or za'atar from the Judean hills. The beat goes on, and it didn't stop in ancient times or the Middle Ages. The new narratives spring not from *shtetlach* (Jewish villages or enclaves as in *Fiddler on the Roof*) or the *mellahs* (Jewish quarters of North Africa) of old but midrash made of nostalgia and critique for the food on the table behind the confirmation pictures of the '70s, '80s, '90s, and '00s. Jewish farms staffed with young people looking for alternatives to prescribed destinies, Queer Soup Night attendees, and DIY deli machers are changing the next chapter that's being written.

Jewish cuisine is fed by the seasons and sanctified days as well as by history. The ancient Jewish agricultural cycle, as well as the seasons of homeland and Diaspora, is still very present in Jewish food. Demands are made of the cook of Jewish food—that Sabbath food is ready to eat on time or that a special bread is baked and consumed fresh or that dairy is for Shavuot and fall fruit for Rosh Hashanah. There are times when we are instructed not to eat and to understand eating as part of our temporary corporeal prison. There are also times when we relive grape harvests and barley cuttings, mass exoduses, and sacrifices.

Jewish food is just like the Jewish people—it looks like wherever we've been and whoever we've been with. Jewish food is just as orange and purple and green and blue as it is brown and gray and white, which many people woefully assume is the crux of Jewish food—based on a food space somewhere between the food of the tenements and the *hechshered* (rabbinically approved) processed foods of the nuclear era. Jewish food is sabich, kneydlakh, chremslach, z'hug, dabo, challah, kubbeh, hamin, cholent, sweet and sour carp, fesenjan, injera, doro wat, stir-fries and frittatas, Jerusalem mixed grill, harissa, "Miami" ribs—the list goes on as far and wide as the map of Jewish movement and commitment, and somewhere in all of that incredible culinary diversity, I locate myself.

Religiously Gourmand

Fressfumkeit—my absolute favorite Yiddish word. It means being a Jew through your stomach, being committed to Jewish peoplehood through its flavors and tastes, and being devoted to it as a gourmand. Jewish food is the source of my devoted deep dive into culinary history and food as folklore—the lived text that often gets ignored. Jewish food can be and is me; it has room for me. It has room for my collard greens in kreplach, for Nigerian suya in my brisket, for Jamaican peas and rice on the High Holidays, and for matzoh meal fried chicken at Pesach. The place at the table has not always been made for me, but here I am—this is the party I wanted to get into and where I'll stay. I'm here for the arguments about recipes and the pains in the *tuchus*, for the endless questions and reconsiderations and exhausting conversations that end with sighs and no resolutions. This is what I signed up for.

I'm also here to make challah and chicken soup as golden as possible and meat cigars—a Moroccan answer to a spring roll, I guess—that make your mouth water. I am keenly aware of the role I play in history every time I make Jewish food or expand what Jewish food can be, every time I set my hands to participate in the tradition. That tradition is relentless, including each weekend with Shabbat—the weekly commemoration of G-d as resting Creator and the most important holiday in Judaism. There are holy days, feast days, new moons, lifecycle events—each an opportunity to express my relationship to the eternal through food. Here, in Jewish life, I always have something to do.

Four thousand years later, I am present, and when I am not, I hope that what I do and what other Jews of color, in particular, will register in their Jewish journeys—both because of their difference and because of their commitment to our tradition—is this connection. And beyond that, Jewish food is where we can flourish because of the centrality of humor and joy in both traditions—African and Jewish Diasporas—of beating back trauma through brave happiness. Nothing is like being in this specific, crazy, busy intersection. It is maddening, and it is lovely. *Hineni*—I am here.

5

SIT AT THE WELCOME TABLE AND EAT AND BE SATISFIED: BLACK FOOD AS JEWISH FOOD

"Negroes are all Jews . . ."

Dig: I'm Jewish—Count Basie's Jewish. Ray Charles is Jewish. Eddie Cantor's goyish. B'nai B'rith is goyish; Hadassah, Jewish. Marine corps—heavy goyim, dangerous.

If you live in New York or any other big city, you are Jewish. It doesn't matter even if you're Catholic; if you live in New York, you're Jewish. If you live in Butte, Montana, you're going to be goyish even if you're Jewish.

Kool-Aid is goyish. Evaporated milk is goyish even if the Jews invented it. Chocolate is Jewish, and fudge is goyish. Fruit salad is Jewish. Lime Jello is goyish. Lime soda is very goyish.

All Drake's Cakes are goyish. Pumpernickel is Jewish and, as you know, white bread is very goyish. Instant potatoes, goyish. Black cherry soda's very Jewish; macaroons are very Jewish.

Trailer parks are so goyish that Jews won't go near them. Jack Paar Show is very goyish.

Negroes are all Jews . . .

—*Lenny Bruce*

Lenny Bruce was a rebel comedian, a tester of obscenity laws, with a lot of absurdity, wit, acerbic darkness, and, frankly, hidden truth. This famous bit is permanently lodged inside of me. Unpacking it would take too much time, but the feeling of this bit grabs you by the ears as he describes an America two generations at most beyond Ellis Island and the first two waves of the Great Migration—post–world wars, post–Great Depression, post-boom, with ethnic particularities melting into a milquetoast lie agreed upon. Here, Jewish isn't some exact formula based on ancient codes, separated and sacrosanct; it's an entire approach to being American, a style, a sophistication, another way to read the world. Jewish is the authenticity of flavor, realness, funk in all its permutations—emotional to grooviness, depth, complexity. "Negroes are all Jews," Bruce says, and as the routine continues, he includes formerly marginalized Italians and apostate Irish in a new telling of the world and its categories.

In a 2012 essay titled "Oh My America: Lenny Bruce and the Golden Age," Lawrence Bush shines some light on Bruce's references to Black America:

> *Let's briefly study the text. It begins with Count Basie and Ray Charles being Jewish. Why are they Jewish? Because Benny Goodman is, George and Ira Gershwin are, Artie Shaw is, Stan Getz is, and Paul Desmond, too. Jews embraced and appropriated jazz, and jazz helped define the new Jewish consensus. Besides which, said Lenny Bruce, "Negroes are all Jewish." Of course, they were. Negroes were slaves unto Pharaoh. They were the Chosen People of America. America would know itself and be redeemed only when it embraced its Negritude. And they were the white people who knew that. This is why close to half the white Freedom Riders who went South in the early 1960s were Jewish—all with worried Jewish mothers.*

The key word here is "white." This is a moment of American Jews finally ceasing to be "Hebrews" in the turn-of-the-century Ellis Island racial parlance and starting to be white folks, as in the critical work by Karen Brodkin, *How Jews Became White Folks: And What That Says About Race in America* (1998). Covenant laws and gentlemen's agreements notwithstanding, Ashkenazi Jews, after the Western international embarrassment and tragedy of the Holocaust / Shoah through to the establishment of the state of Israel, were in a very different place from those who lived in a world centered at the margins of Western identity. Bruce is talking about navigating a creeping goyishness that is actually the purgatory of white American culture. It was idealized in the mid-twentieth century—less exciting and challenging than what came before it and certainly what came after it. These American Jews had new choices and new dilemmas, and in grappling with the new realities—the genocide faced by world Jewry was undetachable from the nexus of colonialism, imperialism, and nationalism—in the Diaspora space where they would flourish the most and in the state that had just become their new hopeful glory, new lines were drawn about who was "us" and who was "them."

The other way to look at it, at least from my perspective, is that Lenny Bruce draws the same lines of distinction that many groups do to delineate friend and foe, accomplice and ally, and even kinfolk and family. When one is brought from the margins to the center, this process helps one navigate being an insider and an outsider. African Americans have done it for quite some time; it's part of our safety check—who is Black and who is white? We know what we mean when we say "Black people of . . ." and "they just like white folks," or even just "they Black." This is all very quaint if it weren't for the fact that alongside all of these mental allegiances are serious divides in both Black and Jewish communities among members of the same group who obviously have more in common than not.

Lenny Bruce's new reading of Israel Zangwill's melting pot is instructive because it has already become way more complicated in the twenty-first century than he or Israel ever could have dreamed—for America and American Jews as well as for us "Negroes." Our flashpoints, conversations, and arguments have eroded some of Bruce's binary and amplified other elements of it. Do the appropriated parts, like jazz, need to be given back? What if klezmer is now inherently jazzy? If Kool-Aid is very Blackish, is it still very goyish if "Negroes are all Jews"? As more societal comforts and compromises rise and fall and the old boundaries and borders of power shift, how do any of us cope with our tortured histories and enduring legacies of pain and still create from a place of discovery, resistance, recovery, or rebellion?

It's a lot.

To put it another way: Many of the more sublime and important cultural pieces come out of our responses as people on the margins to the original Western sins of anti-Semitism and anti-Blackness. These sibling evils have forced us to really understand ourselves with our backs up against the wall in defense mode. It's jazz innovated in red-light districts and brothels and wounded or starving Jews and Roma and Tatars playing the music that becomes klezmer on the outskirts of areas in Eastern Europe where such people were not welcome. It's Marc Chagall and Sholom Aleichem and the brothers Singer drawing on the shtetl and ghetto; or Romare Bearden, Jean Toomer, Zora Neale Hurston, and Richard Wright painting portraits of rural and urban life under Jim Crow. Oppression and marginalization are horrible, but they are fertile ground to create cuisines, languages, aesthetics, sexual diversity, ecstatic religious movements, political theories, resistance politics, and beyond.

Over time it's also Al Jolson straddling the last days of minstrelsy while introducing America to Eastern European Jewish cantorial art, and African Americans who performed Jewish cantorial pieces at concerts. It's Aretha Franklin and Carole King making musical classics and Richard Pryor (the father of Jewish children) and Gene Wilder making us laugh at the corner of shtetl and ghetto.

Will Smith and Jeff Goldblum save the world, just so subtly symbolic, and Willie "The Lion" Smith and Louis Armstrong were no strangers to Yiddish. Julius Rosenwald built those schools when the South refused, and Black communities were grateful; meanwhile, Black newspapers sounded the alarm about Hitler, anti-Semitism, and white supremacy while others didn't care. Every single drop of this is part of me and our journey as Blacks and Jews and Jews who are Black.

Black Is, Black Ain't, Soul Is, Soul Ain't

Nomenclature and self-definition do not constantly change among marginalized and oppressed people for fun—they are there for safety, power, and comfort. What you call yourself and others matters; it isn't creating labels to be a pain in the *tuchus*—it's redefining the spaces in your world that have already been defined for you, by the Others—capital *O*. For example, I tire of having to explain that "African American" is not my label to catch all types of "Black," since not all Black Americans are African Americans. I realize that's confusing—but in my dictionary, "African American," a term that was first put in print in the eighteenth century in Revolution-era Philadelphia, is there to describe the people who came to this country predominantly on slave ships in the seventeenth to nineteenth centuries and then built an evolving culture and legacy in the aftermath. Afro-Caribbeans, African immigrants, and Afro-Latin descendants have adjacent histories to other parts of Black America, and none of those nearby cultures is actually new to the scene but have been here since the beginning.

To be Jewish is to be inside and outside of whiteness in America, to straddle the territories of culture, "race," peoplehood, and, most problematic, religion. Jewish languages have several terms to describe levels of spiritual piety and religious commitment, engagement, and detachment, and none of those terms and ideas has much of anything to do with actually being "Jewish," in the all-encompassing sense. To be African American is to do something similar—to have a culture or a collectivity of cultures, certainly, to be a people—and to be in the minds of many imprisoned by phenotype and a blend of evolving and antique versions of our really lousy concepts of "race." Black people didn't invent their caste—it was invented for them, and it has taken up the role of being a unifying factor for all Black people around the globe, defining how cast(ing) and caste define our collective and personal experiences. Isabel Wilkerson, in her book *Caste: The Origins of Our Discontents*, elegantly makes that connection for us between the world of performance (a cast or casting) and that of socioeconomic and cultural hierarchies (caste), and here we are with centuries of bias through which we create the lens to have these conversations and judge people the minute we set eyes on them.

That stark reality does not stop at the kitchen or restaurant door or at the table. Uninformed people really do struggle with the terms "African American foodways" or "Black food" or "soul food" or "Jewish food," and of particular note in geopolitics, the notion of "Israeli food." This conversation is already headache-inducing if you aren't familiar with the drill. "Why can't we just eat and enjoy food?" you might ask. Why not, indeed? Because even if we try to deracinate the food of the oppressed, marginalized, and dispersed to make it comfier, more *heimish*, more casual, for the people into whom that food and cuisine are woven, it will always be fraught with the narratives and understandings that don't allow for the convenient detachment of those who just want cheap eats and cheap cultural thrills.

Soul food, for example, isn't really defined by the slaveholder, although many people try to start the story there (you see, there were some slaves [enslaved Africans], and they were given only the scraps by the slave master, and they were creative and invented soul food), and it doesn't start with Columbus's ass either. (Apparently, he personally invented the food courier service by giving Africans corn, tomatoes, peppers, pineapples, and peanuts.) The insidious food lore that surrounds us doesn't take a vacation from assumptions of inferiority or limitedness, stereotypes or prejudices about other cultures, and yet we who have to deal with the result of centuries of nonsense have people getting in our face asking us to give up the chip on our shoulder. Soul food is the memory cuisine of the great-great- and great-grandchildren of enslaved people; it is not "slave food" but rather is the result of accumulated culinary ideas from migrations across time and space; and it was created and conceived as a construct during the same time Lenny Bruce (see above) and company were reconfiguring what "Jewish" means in a multicultural society.

As my wonderful friend and chef Therese Nelson put it: There is soul food, the construct, and soul food, the canon—kinda like for Lenny Bruce there was Jewish, the canon, and Jewish, the construct, and in his routine, he focused on the latter. Food is not inconsequential when you want to look at the construct of a culture and understand what makes it tick and how its rules play out. You walk into food spaces with all of these matters swirling in your head and around you and in the people you encounter. It's adorable that we think that we are beyond something so pervasive and human and old. This is one of the many passive realities inherited from all of our Ancestors—judgment and assessment through meals, ingredients, flavors, and tastes. Few escape it.

Jews Are All Negroes

It's a common joke to try to make Blacks and Jews the human antipodes of the West or America. Antipodes: two points on the globe that are the farthest away from each other. To see the Blacks and the Jews—never seen as the same entity—as separate and light-years away from each other is the joke, the reassurance, the idea that those with similar and common sufferings at the hands of some of the same perpetrators will at best be workers together at the foot of the Tower of Babel. The reverse, the nightmare of white supremacists, still very much in fashion, is the idea of nefarious Blacks and Jews—again, never seen as the same entity—as unified in an attempt to destroy the West, America, or whiteness. In between these are the notions that we hate each other, we tolerate each other, we love each other, or that we don't know what to do with each other—and yet again, we are not the same entity. Many people just don't know how to handle that.

Food, of course, makes this all more complex. The solution is not to impose the notion of cuisine without borders, to throw our hands up and gleefully proclaim "Whatever!" We don't need to erase obvious boundaries, the differentiation of histories and personalities, and the circumstances that each group brings to the table just because it might make it easier. We can resolve to make an effort to compare and contrast all of the pieces to comprehend where people intersect and find common ground. "Food brings people together" is a tired-ass cliché, and it doesn't begin to hint at the hard work it takes to have conversations about how food can take us on emotional and intellectual journeys in the efforts of self-understanding, healing intergroup conflict, or informing us about the ways our paths necessarily intersect or diverge.

It doesn't do the work unless you want it to. Seeing only the culinary canon—the clichés, the common knowledge, the stereotypes—takes you nowhere. It is the construct—where a food culture can and must go when the canon can give only suggestions on direction—that gets us to the crux of the foodways and also the space where we can know where that food culture can, along with other elements of the culture, really have a "conversation" with another. Sometimes two food traditions have nothing to say to each other and are so different that only exotic appreciation and timid distancing occur. Other times, they cannot shut up as they make love and, simultaneously, argue.

We are where both streets meet.

Shtetl to Soul

It was partly by using food to teach seventh-graders about the Shoah and trying to communicate the deeper ways to understand loss, memory, and a retained culture that I began to appreciate how much the cuisines of Black and Jewish Diasporas had in common. Civilizations without borders re-create themselves after tragedies and traumas, and they migrate and mutate in response. Just as important, and maybe more important, as what their canons dictate is how their constructs grow and push the culture and its cuisines forward. In particular, the legacies of African Atlantic/African American and Ashkenazi Jewish cultures in the West are important, given the rich dialogue generated by two hundred or so years of common concerns and evolving co-operation and conflict in the United States. Above all is the familiar guest, trauma, and its best friend, want.

Yiddish foodways are extremely beautiful because there are so many similar issues with their cultural interpretation of African American foodways. They even have the same kind of language transmission—the recipes were passed to the next generation in a terse vernacular that bridged ancient homelands and new realities. (Yiddish wasn't "bad German," and AAVE [African American Vernacular English, or Ebonics] wasn't bad English; they were languages born in their place to facilitate specific communal transitions.) In my opinion, people ascribe way too much to ingenuity and poverty; "that's all they had" gets said, and then a shrug, a look, a dismissal. No, that's not enough. What does it mean to see these others and how they eat and know what you eat and what you *have to have* and translate everything in a vernacular born in exile, mixing ideas from all the places you've been?

What's most galling is that we've generally missed the mood that looms over both Yiddish food and soul food traditions. They are exploited and extolled for their comfort but demeaned for their lack of health benefits or damned as irrelevant. There is a familiar feeling of shame among some: Yiddish food was pre-Shoah/Holocaust food, the food of *balobostehs* (homemakers) and weakened, starving, pious yeshivah boys compared with Newish-Jewish (Israeli-Mediterranean food—the food of the sabra). Soul food was that of ignorant "slaves" fed a diet to match their bonds in other ways, something to keep them in physical chains that did not require shackles. One recent news story spoke of an employee at Ikea who was offended that his manager served watermelon because "the masters gave that to the slaves," a complete fallacy.

In both cases, the foods of Ashkenazi Jews and Black Americans have been maligned and marginalized right along with the people. If the food was corrupt, so was the beleaguered, antiquated way of life we no longer have a taste for because it embarrasses us. However, these were survivors; they were hyperaware of the seasons, frugal and attentive, and most of all, they used their food to show transgenerational love. The idea that something somehow lacked in their gastronomy or worldview came from without, not from within. When people feel that connection between Jews and Blacks in America, it's not just in struggle, or in satire or survival; it's in the very soul of the cooking itself.

When people ask me about my favorite "Jewish" food, I say kasha varnishkes. I understand it. It's the best of the earth in one bowl. The barley that people saw in fields, the pasta it took G-d and miller and mother to partner in making, and onions—the soul of any soul cuisine, brown and sweet and savory and present—are all in one dish with butter or schmaltz and salt. What more do you need? I see all the people and the feelings they had about their food and their position in life, their pride despite their degradation, and the sense of relief when they got to enjoy just one more thing in life.

As I write this bricolage narrative, it becomes clear that a linear account of Jews and Blacks eating and cooking together or for each other is thorny because we are so often oppressed and marginalized and pushed to the edges. So much is missing, but worse yet, the generations descended from the survivors sometimes do not know how to feel about or comprehend their Ancestors. And yet, our job is to bridge the chasms and feel our way back to a place where we can see beyond imposed lenses that regard us as earth-shatteringly oppositional and then to seek out history. Those accounts, where we find common ground in spirit and purpose, do exist. Food was where these common Ancestors of mine tucked away secrets, hopes, and tactics for overcoming being forgotten and telling a story in which all humans could see themselves reflected.

Mayseh:
THE EXCHANGE

Marc Steiner is a well-known radio personality and social justice activist born and raised in Baltimore. His father was a Jewish Marylander of German origin; his mother, a convert from Great Britain. He was born and raised in a very complicated but vibrant city caught between its last days as a thriving border state port and a post-1968 shadow of a fallen dream, and his adventures in and out of Charm City have shaped his outlook on Black and Jewish relations. He is one of the surviving voices of a unique generation in a time when integration held great promise for both communities.

Baltimore emerged in the 1720s as a port with ties to the trade in African bodies and tobacco, those same bodies cultivated around the budding city. Although it became a haven for free Blacks, this status emerged only when north and central Maryland planters abandoned tobacco for wheat, rye, and corn and wanted to thin their chattel holdings. Those who were not emancipated in the interest of avarice were sold to the highest bidder, providing the Lower South with thousands upon thousands of new workers for King Cotton.

While tobacco and large plantation slavery would persist in

southern Maryland and parts of the Eastern Shore, Baltimore and the immediate area surrounding the city became increasingly tied to trade, industry (one of the few industrial centers in the antebellum South), and immigration from Europe. Before the American Revolution, trade from the West Indies brought enslaved people and goodies for the grandees, including exotic spices and foodstuffs, straight to the Chesapeake through the wharves of Baltimore's early harbor. Jewish traders and businessmen with connections in the West Indies were active in the city, working largely in island plantation provision and the food and spice trade since at least the 1760s. The mixture of Sephardic and Ashkenazi Jews became predominantly German Jewish during the waves of immigration in the 1820s. With a larger Jewish population came a burial ground and questions of expanded rights and opportunities. Maryland's groundbreaking "Jew Bill" of 1826 gave Jews the right to hold public office in the state, formerly America's sole Catholic colony located solidly in the nineteenth-century South.

Baltimore's Jewish community continued to grow, and with the Civil War had divided loyalties. In 1855, Rabbi David Einhorn, a Bavarian Jew, was appointed to Har Sinai, the oldest synagogue associated with the Reform movement, but he was run out of town in 1861 after delivering a fiery sermon in German against the institution of slavery. Calls to tar and feather Rabbi Einhorn sent him fleeing to Philadelphia, where he was no less dedicated to his fervent belief that enslavement was an unjustifiable evil. Despite being the largest center of free Black life, Baltimore was also perhaps the largest open prison for the same population, who had to constantly be on guard against being captured and sold into slavery or seeing the capture of those among them who had run away to hide in the oasis. Rabbi Einhorn probably saw all of this with his own eyes: the sales, the pursuits, the whippings, and the daily demeaning of Black Baltimoreans by a defined racial code.

After emancipation in late 1864, moving toward the end of the Civil War, slavery began to shift into Maryland's approach to Reconstruction and Jim Crow. By the time Jim Crow became entrenched south of the Mason-Dixon Line, Jewish immigration had shifted from German Jews to Jews from Eastern Europe, including Poland, Galicia, Hungary, and the Pale of Settlement bordering Russia. The 1880s to the 1920s, with its mushrooming shuls, mostly Orthodox, then Conservative mixed with Reform, was the birth of filmmaker Barry Levinson's celluloid Baltimore; pop culture enthusiasts will remember Grandpa (decidedly not Zayde) regaling his grandchildren with stories of his immigration to America and a Baltimore row house. It was a unique community in a Southern border state in a city where large Polish and Ukrainian, Irish, Italian, German, and Greek populations set it apart from its neighbors to the South that were shaped by the Lost Cause and the affirmation of the cult and culture of the Old South.

Blacks and Jews had lived side by side in Baltimore for two centuries by the time Marc Steiner was a Boy Scout in the late 1950s. Many Eastern European Jews moved up in society, benefiting from built-in racial imbalances and adjacent whiteness as much as from a commitment to learning the language and education. Black women worked in Jewish homes as cooks and domestics, and Black men worked in stores and factories owned by Jews. African Americans in Baltimore patronized and learned to relish Jewish deli food. The menu of Attman's Delicatessen on Lombard Street, where crates of squawking chickens were stacked, introduced world-famous corned beef sandwiches, sauerkraut, kosher dill pickles, and pastrami to the urban food scene of new migrants coming from the rural South. The new Baltimoreans came mainly from the countryside of the Chesapeake and Tidewater of Maryland and Virginia, with others migrating from the tobacco- and cotton-growing areas of the Carolinas.

Yiddish and Yinglish mixed freely with the watermelon, strawberry, and peach songs of the A-rabbers (Black fruit and vegetable peddlers who used horse and buggy). Jewish kids noshed on coddies (potato cakes) and slurped snowballs and loved hotly spiced crab (eaten outside the house by many, but not all), like any Baltimorean. It was not a utopia, and its racial issues certainly impacted interactions between groups, but it was also its own special thing—neither the shifting neighborhood politics of New York nor the performance of Deep South racial hierarchies of Atlanta. This, against the background of persisting anti-Blackness and anti-Jewish attitudes and residential covenants made for white gentiles, gave the whole city a stifling fruitfulness for both groups apart and in conjunction with each other.

Marc told me a story that reflected this tightrope:

"In 1957, Baltimore was very segregated. My uncle sent me the *Boy Scout Handbook* from England, and I devoured it. When I was eleven, there was nothing I wanted to be more than a Boy Scout. Mrs. Mozelle Jackson worked for my family as a cook and domestic, and her nephew, Mr. Dennis Foster, was a longshoreman. They would have coffee and tea and cake with my mother before she left for the day. I called her Mozelle, I called him Dennis, I called Mrs. Jackson's husband Andrew. It wasn't until I went to the basement of the church on a Monday night—Faith Baptist Church on North Bond Avenue—and heard him called Mr. Foster that I realized these adults were Mr. and Mrs., just like the Jewish adults I grew up with and not just people older than me that I could call by their first names.

"From eleven to thirteen, I was in this troop. I wanted to be around many different kinds of people, not just white Jews from Forest Park. All the guys piled out of the Mr. Doughnut shop near Broadway, below Hopkins and above Fells Point, which was a Black neighborhood. I wouldn't get out. Mr. Foster said, "Anywhere we go, you can go." I got a few stares, but nobody did anything to me, and I got used to being the only white boy, and most often, the only Jew.

"We had our first campout in Maryland at Broad Creek; my mom packed my dinner, which included these two thick-ass lamb chops. I was paired with Edwin Johnson. He looked at them and pulled out these two skinny-ass Esskay hot dogs. We didn't say a word. I handed him a lamb chop, and he handed me a hot dog, and we cooked them together and ate them together. I had nothing like that before, and I'm sure he had never had a lamb chop!

"Edwin would come to my house, but none of the other kids would play with us. When I went to his house, everyone would play with me. They thought I was odd because I was white, but they thought it was cool, and I got along with everybody, and everybody got along with me. In most places in Baltimore, unless it was a Black-owned restaurant or bar, if you were Black, you couldn't sit down. Nate's and Leon's were Jewish-owned, and you could sit down and eat—there were very few places like that. Paul's Restaurant in Forest Park was Jewish-owned, but they wouldn't serve us because Edwin was with us, but my mother would not move until they served us. That's how we integrated Paul's.

"When we were at a camp gathering, there was only one black Boy Scout group—and that was us. We got our little medals and awards, but afterward, this white goyish kid came up to me. I didn't know him. He looked at me dead in the eyes, and his look seared into me. 'What in the hell are you doing in this troop with all them niggers?' That was the Baltimore I grew up in. It never let up."

Mayseh:

THE BRIS, OR "I THINK I HAVE
THE WRONG HOUSE!"

Thus also spoke Marc Steiner:

"My first wife was African American, our oldest grandson, Avi, was born some twenty-seven years ago. It was a big deal, my father *kvelled*, and Chelsea, our daughter, Avi's mother, wanted to have a bris. So, my father got the mohel, who was a patient of his. We were over on Bland Avenue on the Westside. It's our family, so it was a very highly interracial bris ceremony, guests from all over, and every walk of life in Baltimore.

"The mohel arrives, he walks up to the door, he sees three tall Black men, two with long dreads and one with a huge Afro. His eyes got all big, and he said loudly, 'Oh, I'm sorry, I think I have the wrong house!' He starts running down the steps—but then my father, the track star, came running down the street, and he was like, "No, wait, come back!" The mohel is freaking out because he had never been around so many Black people, and the non-Jewish Black men were freaking out because of the circumcision. It was a real hocks and lox comedy of errors. It was funny as hell.

"You know my first picket line was at age fourteen at Mondawmin Shopping Center. Black college students from Hopkins and City College were picketing the White Coffee Pot. I remember they were a branch of SNCC, and I asked my mother if I could go join them; she nodded, and I asked for a sign, and I was the white boy on the picket line. Everybody staring, but my mother was proud. The Jewish community in Baltimore was very mixed when it came to civil rights. Baltimore's Jewish community in the 1950s, when I was a kid, was a middle-class community. A lot of people had Black women working in their homes. We went to segregated schools. My elementary school wasn't just all white but 90 percent Jewish. Your neighborhood was where you were. It was who you were.

"When I was a kid, there used to be these Easter parades. One went up Charles Street, and the other went up Pennsylvania Avenue; I don't have to explain to you why there were two. I remember being struck by how much I fell in love that day with Penn Avenue. We look at Baltimore today, and it's dystopian, the way people have to live in the communities most affected by blight, drugs and violence, and police brutality. When I was a kid, there were no abandoned houses; there were no boarded-up homes. These homes had working families, extended families.

"The Poles and Ukrainians hated us the most. They used to call my father 'Jew' in Polish and Ukrainian (*żydy*) and called him "Christ killer." But my Pop was a track star, so they never caught him with their rusty knives. Of all the European immigrant communities, the Italians got on best with the Jews, the Greeks too, I guess. Baltimore was a city of allies, especially for Black people and Jews.

"On the west side of town, the Black community came up as far as Gwynns Falls Parkway. That's where Liberty Heights, Park Heights, and Reisterstown Road all meet at Druid Hill Park. That was the dividing line. The German Jews lived around Druid Lake Drive and Eutaw Place. The Eastern European Jews lived in East Baltimore and then lived in Forest Park. As Black people moved in, Jews moved out. But my generation went to interracial schools, including City College and Western and Eastern; about a third of the school was Black. There was a brief moment when interracial hope was real, but it died.

"The Black and Jewish worlds have always had this really strange relationship. To some Black people, the Jew was the slumlord, the corner store guy who rips you off—or could be the guy who helps you out, the only white person who cared. If you were Jewish, you may have been white, but there were quotas, boundaries that you couldn't cross; you might get your ass whopped by somebody who thought you were white before anything else. It's a very complicated story. Both anti-Semitism and racism are so embedded in Western civilization. But it's easy for anybody's group to go from oppressed to oppressor; it doesn't take much to flip the switch. That's why I'm so mad about the situation with Israel and the Palestinians.

"This is part of our tradition: to fight for the other oppressed. The majority of white members of Mandela's African National Congress in South Africa were Jews. Seventy percent of the white Freedom Riders were Jews. That's not an accident; we as Jews of that generation who wanted something different in society really seemed to understand what it meant to be the other, to have family that went through the Holocaust and were disliked and distrusted by the goyim. The closest people who we were different from in America were African Americans. All these stories, Jewish and Black, were crossing paths in my life. When I was thirteen, the most important book I had was a history of Black people in America called *Every Tenth Man*, and that book and what I saw around me prepared me for the picket line and everything after that—arrests, protests, boycotts, anything to never go back."

Mayseh:
"WHAT EVEN ARE THESE THINGS?"

Nothing is as awkward as the moment you find out someone is not your ally, your acquaintance, or even your friend. The moment when you discover real distrust and antipathy. It gets worse when it's your culture, your identity, and your place that are on trial. You question all of who you are. It isn't any fun to commit to being a native and being treated like an alien.

One of my first big catering gigs was for someone I can no longer call a friend—although our separation was not based solely on the incident I talk about here, but it definitely left an impression. He was a rabbi, and for the small community he served, he asked me to make a meal at his home for about seventy-five people, based on my koshersoul style of cooking. I agreed for a fee I would later laugh at, but I took the job because we had a friendly understanding. His wife was understandably nervous about a stranger in her tightly kept kosher kitchen and had her misgivings, but by the minute, I got more and more of a feeling that it was less my method of cooking than its material that turned her off. The final straw for the Yankee wife of the Southern rabbi was collard greens.

Collard greens. *Brassica oleracea var. viridis.* Collard greens are on my African American seder plate, which I use the last two days of Passover as a symbolic piece. Collards are the *maror*, the bitter greens, representing the bitterness of American chattel slavery. True to the season of Passover, spring collards are increasing in bitterness while winter collards mellow and sweeten. They were once endemic to the gardens of enslaved African Americans, a replacement for the many leafy greens our Ancestors ate in West and Central Africa.

My ex-friend's wife stumbled into their apartment, stressed and angry. Her husband had put her on the spot, asking her to go shopping for unfamiliar ingredients while he minded their baby girl. She left with my esoteric list of soul food products destined for that evening's Shabbat *oneg*, catered by me. Collard green kreplach was the dish. Kreplach, Judaism's opposite side of the Silk Road's relationship to wontons, are traditionally stuffed with bits and pieces of this and that—leftover meat from soup or brisket, bits of veggies.

She did not look at her husband. All the rage was centered on me. "What even are these things?" I was hoping that it was fake rage meant to stage a joke.

"Collard greens?" I said, trying to deflect with a smile. "They're good for you. My grandmother and mother and I used to make them all the time. You'll love them."

"I'm not touching them. How can these things even be kosher?" she raged. "Probably full of bugs. Whatever they are, they are gritty and dirty, and it got all over me, and now they are in my house and my kitchen. I hope you're prepared to clean up after yourself because I can't deal with this." Grocery bags went into the kitchen. Cue slams. Muffled voices behind a bedroom door—not an argument but a disagreement and a series of hushings. I felt humiliated.

In truth, my mother and grandmother were just about better than any *mashgiach* in ensuring the collards were clean. We would examine each leaf up to five times, washing and rewashing, even using a drop of mild detergent in the second rinse to clear out any remaining bugs or dirt before rinsing another two times until the water ran clear. We looked at every hole, at the stalks, and in the bottom of the big bowl for grit like miners looking for gold. The greens were rolled and cut into ribbons and rinsed again. Only when the matriarch pronounced them clean did they go into a rolling, boiling pot of broth-driven pot liquor seasoned with smoked turkey and onion, seasoned salt, and red pepper.

My fervent fantasy was to have a life of constant Black-(white) Jewish moments of mutual understanding. We would all sit side by side, learning about each other's families, and I would teach them everything I knew about collards and learn their grandmother's favorite recipe for (name that dish). This moment was where I learned to let that go. This scene was not a Hallmark movie or after-school special. I was at the wrong place, apparently doing the wrong thing for the right reasons. My ego could not let me break Shabbat.

My mind immediately went to the dark place of the lives of so many Black women and a good number of Black men who worked as domestics and cooks for white people. That was also a history being enacted here in a very different way. I had no excuses to frown. Thousands of others had survived tens of thousands of moments like this microaggression—assumptions of inadequacy, suspicions of contamination. Looking back on it, it was a good reminder that I was not special and that history had more to teach me than anecdotes; this was a lesson in survival of the spirit.

I worked my way through the methodical ritual of cleaning the greens, and every few minutes, I felt the rabbi's wife's head over my shoulder from the door, throwing scowls. They had lived in Asia, traveled widely, seen actual *treyf* and temptations, but it was my greens that somehow embodied the scary world of the unfamiliar. I reminded myself that this very American food was here before their Ancestors had disembarked from the far east of the Pale of Settlement. Soon, their home began to smell as endearingly familiar to me as it was uncomfortably exotic to her. In a very tense afternoon, I learned what made me and what it would mean to stand up for my Black-Jewish self.

Under threat of snow, I worked with a fever to get Moroccan carrot salad, za'atar chicken wings, barbecue seasoned roasted potatoes, and collard green kreplach ready before sunset. The greens simmered away without the benefit of the smoked turkey, but the pan bubbled with yellow, red, and orange peppers; red onions and garlic; and smoked paprika and kosher chicken bouillon. With time not on my side, I worked that little triangular kreplach and sealed them off with egg wash and set them to bake like spanakopita as the clock ticked down, and I set myself to washing the dishes so I wouldn't catch more hell.

An hour before Shabbat came in, the food was carted away. I showered and dressed, got dropped off to give a special talk at Friday night services. The assembled crowd for the *oneg* didn't leave a wing or bit of potato behind, and that night the one thing that everyone asked me the recipe for was the collard green kreplach. Before I said a single word about how much of this or that was thrown in the pot, I told the onlookers and eavesdroppers all about the green savior of the enslaved people's quarters that nourished our people in their journey toward freedom while maintaining a key healthy component of our African dietary roots. Before the candles burned out, a merciful G-d gave me my moment to be an alien no more.

Mayseh:
"IT'S CHICKEN!"

Suspicion is an important ingredient in the food culture of the oppressed and marginalized. Food operates as a way to promote cohesion and incorporation in the group, and the dictates of tradition, access, and folklore set the menu. However, the food of the other, especially those who might harm people in the group or those things eaten by groups alien to them, is often viewed with a measure of suspicion. Racial and ethnic and religious food stereotypes manifest themselves as lazy shorthand for how corrupt the cultures outside of our worldview are or how revolting the other is. Maybe some part of us, a vestigial part of our minds, associates consumption with becoming the other, the outsider, the marauder, the exotic villain.

We human beings often protect our feelings of being right within ourselves and our people by identifying with a certain set of foods. We also poke fun at people who don't eat like us. We often define our boundaries with the rest of the world by how we think food should taste or smell or what constitutes appropriate ingredients or ways of preparing or serving foods in a distinct order or within specific time frames. Sometimes we can have the same foods but prepare them so differently that they seem alien or incorrectly prepared to others. Other times we exploit the traumas and historical relationships between groups and their foods to weaponize that lazy shorthand of food stereotypes to wound and diminish. We as a species don't make it easy to sit down at the table of brotherhood and sisterhood.

For example, "White people don't season their food" is an old trope used to underline and highlight the idea that WASP culture or the aspiration to be a WASP isn't what it's cracked up to be. It's a subtle but stinging—no pun intended—cultural commentary on the way many descendants of European immigrant cultures in America have thrown themselves into an amorphous heap of whiteness in exchange for the privileges and benefits of not being of color in a society full of institutional racism. The "assimilation" we on the other side of the racial divide always heard about was the recipe for social acceptance. It wasn't quite assimilation for some of us; it was engagement with a developing idea of whiteness that we failed at miserably because we weren't phenotypically white and didn't have the same cultural orientation or historical references.

Woe are they, the WASPs and the WASP adjacent, but woe is us—and many others. Woe are the MSG bringers, woe are the dog and cat eaters, the gassy obsessed beaners, pity the spaghetti shovelers and potato and cabbage and corned beef people, the roadkill gourmands and other alien tasters. Mourn, however, for the Blacks—the most vicious cannibalistic eaters of man and pitiful soul food junkies, addicts of the fried, the greasy junk and sugary with their unfortunate palates and animal stomachs. Oh, don't forget about the Jews, whose legend has them drain the blood of Christian children to drink and knead into the Passover matzoh. Mind their pots, since they eat like witches. Their pots once held the secret that they were hiding their demonic devotion to their broken covenant with a Supreme Being that no longer wanted them.

Sounds harsh? That's not me talking, just centuries of history's nastiest gastronomic racism. Food is not only personal, it's used to indict. In *A Drizzle of Honey: The Lives and Recipes of Spain's Secret Jews*, authors David M. Gitlitz and Linda Kay Davidson take the reader through a tour of Inquisition-era Spain and Portugal. They reconstruct the story of food and drink in Reconquista Iberia by delving into the court cases of *conversos*—Jews who attempted to maintain ties to the land and their property by pretending to be New Christians. However, a network of spies and informants— not-Jewish and formerly Jewish—did their best to tell on who wasn't eating pork or who was seasoning their food with too much garlic, allegedly a Jewish trait. On the way through moldy cells and cries of the tortured, the authors uncovered a whole pantry of a people in a liminal existence. They were prisoners of a system built on revenge and anti-Semitism appropriating the culture of the Middle East, North Africa, and West Africa while beginning the next phase of Western culture by abusing the gifts and people that brought them to a new dance.

Black pride in soul food and the celebration of other forms of Black vernacular cuisine are part of a joyful repair from the damages of all the canards used to salt the wounds of systemic racism. And yet, it doesn't stop people from making inappropriate comments or medical professionals from making uncritical assumptions about African American patients' health and dietary practices. The real ailments don't come from following the mostly plant, seafood, poultry, and whole-animal seasonal, occasionally celebratory, diet of their Ancestors; they come from a post–Great Migration modernizing diet of processed foods. This spiteful reading of yet another element of Black culture has a pathology that adds to a cesspool erasing the Black creative element that shaped much of American cooking and the cooking of many places in the Western Hemisphere where slavery shaped the plates.

In return, white people were not only believed to be the bearers of unseasoned food, but they also were less clean and less scrupulous in their techniques and methods of making food taste good. Exchanging slight barbs through food was one quiet way of both resisting and participating in the internalized power play of pushing back against racism. Much like with Jews and anti-Semitism, jokes and hard-held beliefs about outsider villains and their foods reaffirmed a deeper belief that through their cruelty and denials, the others were morally deficient, from their hatreds to their communal and culinary practices. Food provided us others a means to look down on the palates and personalities of those who looked down on us. SNL jokes of Karen's potato salad with raisins was novel bigotry to bemused white folks but had a pedigree that was born the moment European and African cultures began to collide in West and Central Africa: Africans thought the Portuguese were the cannibals, using African blood for wine, brains for cheese, and pressed skins for oil.

Jews didn't escape some of the medieval archetypes surrounding their real and imagined foodways. The blood libel followed Jews to 1928 Massena, New York, where a rabbi was held for questioning when a local white Christian child went missing (but was later found). In *97 Orchard: An Edible History of Five Immigrant Families in One New York Tenement*, Jane Ziegelman recounts how immigration reformers were critical of Eastern European Jews for their garlic and pickled vegetable eating habits and how they sent their children to school with giant garlic dill pickles for or with their lunch. Again, moral and cultural beliefs were associated with food. Kosher butchering got a side-eye from many, with assumptions of animal cruelty and stereotypes of Jews being "bloodthirsty."

Kashrut is not without some reverse of this complicated lore. Jews over the centuries held fast to the idea that keeping kosher was so just because "G-d said so." Beyond that, there was the sneaking suspicion that a divine diet had been prescribed for health reasons, with notions of *treyf* food being poisonous to the body and soul. Or, far more serious, it was to keep Jews away from the foods and traditions of those who worshipped idols or as a preventative measure to keep them away from being seduced into marriage with others who did not follow the Torah. Much ink has spilled over why these ancient food taboos were born and why they persisted, but it's the suspicion of the food of the other that interests me.

Over time, *kashrut*'s communal and personal practice melded with regional and cultural preferences to create a guest list of tastes and flavors, an in and out list of what tasted or smelled "Jewish" and what didn't. In America, a shortlist of goyishe food sat along *treif* foods to affirm Jewishness in the "*treyfeneh* Medina" (the non-kosher land). White bread, mayonnaise on pastrami sandwiches, the lack of garlic and onion, and golden unctuous fat and sugar as a sweetener but no seasoning was just the beginning of a collection of shibboleths that set apart American Jewish food from that of the others. To be Jewish, much like to be Black, meant to eat certain foods, *at least some of them*, to practice and perform aspects of a rich, ancient culture.

The *mayseh* almost got lost here, but it's a short story and a simple one that needed the context. I found myself in a very tense and weird spot at a Black-Jewish relations event, a Shabbat dinner to which a Black church had been invited. I was one of two or three Jews who were Black in a college/Hillel space. The room smelled Jewish—the wine, the chicken broth, the challah, the kugels, the onions, the garlic, the lack of dairy—all the smells of Shabbat. And yet the terror on the faces of the non-Jewish Black folks was pretty plain; they were worried about what they would be eating.

When the Kabbalat Shabbat service and speech were over, everyone went to their tables. My table, mostly Black and not Jewish, along with the speaker, the former rebbetzin of Atlanta's famed Temple congregation, was eager to eat, but my cousins were suspicious. Matzoh balls were immediately suspicious, with the unwitting joke inherent—

"What part of the matzoh are they *made* from?" The fear grew until the main entrée arrived at the table.

"It's chicken!"

The elder sitting across from me and her grandchildren sighed heavily but happily.

Everybody likes salad, potatoes, chicken, and homemade bread, right? Not really, but that night it worked.

Part II

THE TABLECLOTH

6

MY HEART IS IN THE EAST

You will often hear or see the acronym MENA as regards Jews of color. It stands for the Middle East and North Africa. There is a draw to the cultures and areas of the Jewish world that are the brownest. The Sephardic community in America, which often mixes Sephardic and Mizrahi populations and elements, has tucked away in its folk practices and aesthetics something more approachable and appealing to Black folks coming into Judaism. For many of us, it's the bright colors, the deep mysticism baked into Sephardi and Mizrahi ways, the spicier food with warm-weather vegetables and rice, and the percussive music that appeal to something deep in our hearts. Maybe it's because the caress of Africa is visible, the relative adjacency to the Islamic world is present, and it is not, by default, the American version of "white." To be Jewish, for me in many ways, has been like holding multiple citizenships.

I am a Jew. I am Jewish, with no labels, but I am also very familiar and comfortable with Sephardiut and Yiddishkeit. I am actively on a search to create elements of a pan-Diaspora Black Jewish *mesorah*, or tradition. I use "Afro-Ashkefardi" and "Conservadox" to locate myself somewhere in a spectrum that doesn't always make room for anomalies like me.

Being in food spaces brings other challenges because of serious concerns about ownership, agency, context, appropriateness, and appropriation. Multiple narratives can exist at the same time and be painfully vibrant. People from the MENA region are a blend of Africa, the Near East, and Europe. For millennia, their genes, histories, destinies, and cultures have been mixing, retracting, warring, and marrying. That would include food as a necessary social lubricant. It is both a human necessity and a deep part of the culture of hospitality and generosity and is also a central part of the trade networks that made civilizations possible. Everybody claims that they are the creators of "salad," be it Greek, Turkish, Israeli, Palestinian, Lebanese, etc. If you know the MENA culture, you might be aware that I'm speaking of an elemental onion, cucumber, and tomato combination with different salinity levels and varying herbs preferred by distinct regions.

Context, context, context is part of the mental real estate here. Contested territory doesn't just refer to the land; it's the food as well. Falafel and pita and hummus and who makes them, why they make them, and when and where they make them are not trivial questions; they are essential. What these foods mean to Palestinians and Israeli Jews or Israeli Arabs or Druze or many other groups depends on the way narratives are shaped. To say "Jewish" can be tricky here as well. Ashkenazi Jews adopted these foods and others upon aliyah; Sephardi and Mizrahi Jews shared similar food cultures with their neighbors in the MENA region for centuries.

My friendships and bonds include Palestinian culinarians, and they have important stories to tell about what food means to someone from Gaza or East Jerusalem and beyond. There are also narratives of the Bedouin, whose food culture closely parallels many of the elements of food culture expressed in the Hebrew Bible. Sephardi and Mizrahi foods often have the same names but slightly different ingredients, or even precisely the same ingredients—but nobody knows when or where many of these dishes crossed the threshold in societies where

Jews had only *dhimmi* status. There is no ignoring any of these elements, no matter how dizzying, frustrating, or tedious to someone who would instead prioritize food's taste and comfort potential to its meaning and purpose. I seem to find myself in these spaces where disputed food—from the American South to the MENA world—is on the menu. I acknowledge it is because oppressed or marginalized people often shape those culturally critical regions.

MENA people who have been mixing and sharing cultures for centuries can also have their own grounded understandings of the dishes that are a part of their identity. Israeli food, however, isn't just part of this historical flow. Modern Israeli food does indeed draw heavily on Palestinian and Arab Levant traditions. Israeli food is also the mixture of people from across the Jewish Diaspora seeking refuge, each bringing ingredients and cooking styles mixed and enjoyed across populations on all spectrums of the conflict. At the same time, Palestinian and other Arab Levant food traditions are micro-regional and specific to places and histories of families who have been in those places for centuries. Simultaneously we must recognize Jewish communities as culinary creators across the MENA region as a Diaspora that has been in some countries since the days of the Persian Empire and beyond.

Yehudah Halevi, a medieval Spanish Jewish poet, once wrote, "My heart is in the east, but my body is in the west." This famous quotation, made bittersweet by the pain of recent memory, haunts me in my home kitchen. I try to gather all the stories I can. Marginalization is not quaint, so I bear the stories when I prepare food inspired by other people's cultures. No recipe comes without hurt in this world, or deep pleasure or even excess.

One night in Jerusalem I had the occasion to dine with famed culinary historian and culinarian Claudia Roden. We feasted on food made by chefs Jewish and Arab. Some of them were living under the Palestinian Authority at the time. Many of the foods offered that evening were *mahashi*, or stuffed vegetables. "Stuffing food was one of the hallmarks of Yerushalmi cuisine as part of the Levant or Ottoman Empire," Roden told me. "Jerusalem was the heart of this, but to make stuffed food means to love. It's a lot of work, so if you work hard in the kitchen, it means you love someone." There were many smiles and gestures of brotherhood and sisterhood that evening. It was beautiful. I had to remind myself that the food on the table required great responsibility and respect, but not as much as the human beings whom it represented.

Mayseh:
"SHALOM, BROTHER!"

I
f you forget Jerusalem, you won't be able to talk or sing or eat. The King James Bible, not the most Jewish of translations but certainly the only certified version in the traditional American South, poetically renders it as "If I forget thee, O Jerusalem . . . let my tongue cleave to the roof of my mouth." It's not a sentence passed from heaven to earth but from self to self. The mere amnesia of David's city is causing to bring down upon your head not only silence, but starvation. This curse is the power of the place Abraham's peoples posit as the navel of the earth.

Jerusalem is more than a footnote in the African American spiritual imagination. It became code for a Black Nirvana, a raptured Key and Peele–style "Negroland" where moral suasion and social and civil justice are vindicated. In this place, Black people obtain salvation from suffocating racial hierarchies. The danced anthem of Gullah-Geechee culture along the Carolina and Georgia Lowcountry was expressed in the "shout" or danced hymn of "New Jerusalem." At Fisk University, the Fisk Jubilee Singers made famous in choral form the spiritual "Walk in Jerusalem Just like John." The words are clear:

Ain't been there, but I've been told that the gates are pearl and the streets are gold.

I could not set foot in Jerusalem without my fantasies. I was running away from otherness and race. I was transcending being born somewhere powerless and secondhand. I would land in a neutral space, the Switzerland of spiritual authority. I could now walk up to G-d and declare my independence from the sneaking suspicion that the G-d of America was not the G-d of THIS place.

The G-d of this place was the Deity who declared an enslaved nation free after two-plus centuries in the Narrow Place. I had come to pray and submit. Here was a god who came before guns and bombs, who worked in miracles, dreams, signs, and a path with customs encrusted in meaning. Every food with its blessing, each holiday with its symbolic delicacies, each meal concluded with Thanksgiving and grace. The old god was Manifest Destiny; the new god was destiny co-created. We do our part; G-d does its part.

How far are we willing to go to come face to face with our fascinations, fears, faith, and problematic yearnings? And nostalgia? That word, which may have been born concerning Jerusalem, is a pilgrimage. Something inside or out is pushing you. Something wants you to go without any promise or prophecy about who or what might return. You just go, stripped down to your spirit bones, hoping your flesh is newer, shiny, hoping people notice you are renascent.

In 2004, I went to Israel courtesy of Taglit-Birthright Israel, which takes young Jews, eighteen to thirty-two years old, on their first adult trip to Israel. It was my first time out of the country. At age twenty-six, I acquired my first passport. I had the real sense my destiny was already changing. When you change your name, you change your fate, says the Talmud Rosh Hashanah, 16b. But also, when you change your place, you change your fate, and "place" is another name for G-d.

Everything felt monumental. I salivated over the thought of kosher McDonalds. I watched every tree the bus and train passed to get me to New York. I still don't remember how I got to JFK airport, but I do remember the heavy green leaves of the Eastern Seaboard wet with storm rains. If I was going to die in Israel, a grim thought occurred, I would remember the green, moist place I came from and the soil my Ancestors rested in. Or, would I go there and be overtaken by some kind of holy man psychosis and wander the desert in search of a message? Either way, I knew the trees and much more would not be the same. This fear of forgetting the oaks and hickories was what is meant by leaving home for the first time.

It is hard to see modern Jerusalem if you are a pilgrim, just as modern Africa has been hard for me to see. I wanted children's Bible stories, with their limited vocabulary of existence, their sci-fi elements of fantasy and innocence plastered over every adult narrative. It's the same way I wanted villages elsewhere, on the coast, in the rainforest, or on the plain, dialed back to about ten years before any European contacts showed any of their disastrous consequences. People have marital affairs in Jerusalem, cuss people out in traffic, eat *treif*, keep strictly kosher but still have marital affairs, and cuss people out in traffic while never dreaming of having an affair or eating *treif.*

But Jerusalem, and more specifically the Old City, does not wear its sins on its sleeve. It throbs with devotion—and constant, ceaseless devotion at that. There are moments when all the prayers merge and Judaism, Christianity, and Islam cry out together, and others when competing loudspeakers have the appearance of bickering. In between all of that, I moved, Black and American and different but not other. I was a pilgrim, but I was a Jew. No call to prayer or statement of faith could contain my emotions; no prayer book was sufficient for my thoughts.

Walking down to the Temple's remaining walls is a test of your senses and composure. The elders and yeshivah students are lined up for *tzedakah*. School groups and pilgrims, the latter mostly Christian, give most of the color to the scene, especially the West African ones, decked in their best. The different Jewish cultural factions—Ashkenazi, Sephardi, Mizrahi, Ethiopian, American, and progressive—make their presence known, and if you're lucky, they will cooperate and not cause a fracas. It is hard to walk this gantlet and keep your focus on your living rendezvous with the Creator.

I hurled myself at the Western Wall like I knew I would stick to it and have to be pried off. Nobody helped me put on *tefillin* or wrap myself in the *tallit*. It's possible to be singular and surrounded by a crowd.

Twenty-six-year-old me knew it was time to have a moment for the sake of the rest of my life. I was ashamed of my breakdown. I looked around and assessed who might try to interrupt the gut-wrenching explosion in my core. Then I shut my eyes. This moment was my date with G-d and nothing else mattered.

From my bag, I pulled dozens of notes from my students. I was a divine postman. On one note were prayers for a Hindu friend for recovery from cancer; on another, pleas to heal a marriage, for dogs and cats and love and everything else, including world peace. I didn't read them, my students had told me. They wanted me to know and pray with intent.

My note was last. Who was I to deliver my own note? Who was I to think I could stand before G-d, who stood up to the might of humanity time and again to free the enslaved and the captive? Why was I here? Did being here mean I was free?

I threw my note far into the cavity of the lower part of the wall. No knees, no groveling. I was in court, and I decided to leave my pain there and chose to walk away from whatever I was before that moment. No apologies for being someone others might not approve of, no fear of what would come next. I kept crying, but it was somewhere between delightful grief and the terror of freedom. I had something new and did not yet know how to love it.

A few Ethiopian Jewish teenagers sat hanging about on one of the areas just beyond the plaza. I composed myself long enough to smile and laugh. They fought over their Walkman. I asked them who it was playing, and they proudly said B2K, a popular Black R&B group at the time. They were cheerful and sweet to me, giving me high fives, and seemed thrilled I was a Black Jew from America. Three minutes passed, and my group had to move on.

"Shalom, *Achi*!" I didn't know the word *achi* yet. Someone told me it meant brother. Goodbye, Brother! I looked back. Every fist was raised. No translation needed. In no time, I was *mishpocheh*.

The walls of the Temple are covered in centuries of "I was here." On one of the other walls, there is a possibly deliberate mistranslation of a verse left by a pilgrim whose shell has long gone missing. It is from the book of Isaiah: "You shall see, and you shall stand, and your bones will shake like the grass." The goal, I think, is to never stop shaking.

Mayseh:
"YOU HAVE BEEN MISINFORMED"

All I have for you are fragments forming themselves into a narrative. These incidents are not essays; they come to us as attacks on our sense that the table is enough, that food is enough, and that we can weather those attacks on our calm.

—Author's note

I was presenting at the Smithsonian Folklife Festival, the Silk Road, 2002.

The world was still reeling from 9/11 as I stood onstage with a home cook, an Iranian woman, secular. We had been laughing and talking about my lack of more than ten words in Farsi and her much more functional but limited knowledge of English. I worked with Afghani, Turkish, Mongolian, Chinese, and Uzbek cooks for days; I felt joy being part of something of global healing and a lesson in understanding.

I said that sambusak, a dough-wrapped food like samosa and sambusa, egg rolls, and dumplings, was a family of foods common to the

Silk Road and that my new friend was making her version unique to her community.

I said we Jewish people with customs rooted in Mizrahi communities also had a food called sambusak that we fry and eat at Hanukkah time; I thought I was making a bond.

But then the guest curator of the foodways program, an Iranian American cookbook author, began making her way to the stage, and I knew I was in trouble. She climbed up onstage and grabbed the microphone from my hand; she was forceful and did not look happy.

I asked what was wrong but got no reply.

"You have been misinformed," she said. "This is a food of the Caspian Sea region; this food only contains . . ."

Her words melted away; I meekly corrected my stance to show we did not disagree as the microphone was placed on the counter and not back in my hand.

The woman I was cooking with, with whom I was initially very friendly, was mad at me; the curator was mad at me.

I had said one word that caused their ire: "Jewish."

And I didn't understand the problem, as the guest cook reluctantly made begrudging peace with me.

I didn't understand that, to her, I was starting a war with one word. I was trying to say that similar foods had different names but ultimately expressed different parts of different cultures and traditions.

I wasn't saying Jews owned sambusak or invented sambusak, but that the family of those foods played a role in something that I, as a Black American member of a Sephardi/Mizrahi congregation, understood and made myself. I was looking for cooking cousins, not enemies.

But none of that mattered because "Jewish" and things far beyond my understanding and reach started far away.

I sobbed later that day, but even then, I was just too naïve and too reluctant to say the other part—that being Black likely made my saying that word even worse. Nobody was "woke" then. Nobody was rooted. Nobody cared. I was humiliated. I wasn't wrong, I wasn't factually incorrect; I was just too much—once again, too much everything, and nobody wanted any part of it. I was culturally nonbinary, bringing America with its melting-pot-ness to a salad bar with partitions.

The word that rang in my head the most?

"Jewish."

The Armenian lady from Lebanon said, "You don't have to bring up that Jewish angle."

"Jewish."

She lied onstage about how some Armenians avoid pork in correlation with biblical dietary restrictions. After saying two or three times that I was right, the last time, she smiled at me as if to say "fuck you" and vehemently denied it. I had been well forewarned. I didn't have to bring up that Jewish angle. It felt so mean-spirited and unnecessary and highly tinged with anti-Blackness. I didn't understand why some of the women were more than happy to talk about this connection across religious and cultural boundaries, and some were not. It was a kind of culinary nationalism I had never experienced before. I felt like I had just walked into a millennia-old trap that nobody had warned me about.

Maybe we could not all just get along.

Maybe we would not be friends.

Maybe we could never be friends.

I felt such betrayal—I had spent months learning and researching and asking questions, going to different restaurants and cafes whenever and wherever, calling up friends, doing my homework, making connections, and trying to look the part. Jewish culinary learning taught me a lot about the foods of the silk routes and how everything connected. Still, some folks were not only hell-bent on not allowing me to make those connections but were rather insulted that I was at the table at all. Maybe if I had been Muslim, it wouldn't have been so glaring, but I was Black and Jewish and queer and seen as completely alien.

I never dreamed I would see the two converge—anti-Semitism and food—but why was I surprised? I had lived with racism and anti-Blackness and food my whole life. And yet, here it was—not some stale argument about who owned what in a region that sat at the crossroads of Europe, Africa, and Asia for thousands of years with dozens of ethnicities and languages migrating and crossing and interacting and making babies and eating; but it was that we should not address each other as family, as sharers and as humans who have exchanged words with different contexts. And all of this pushback was completely antithetical to the stated mission of that year's festival.

I tried to make nice with the Iranian lady who was doing the demo as she made lemonade for us. She begrudgingly passed me a cup; she looked disappointed in me, and I apologized if I made her uncomfortable. I think she half understood me and my feelings. As she gave me ice, it looked like we were getting somewhere.

And then.

"Why did you have to say that word?"

"What word?"

"Jewish."

I didn't say another word, and never saw that woman again.

7

TO SIR, WITH *AHAVAH*

I became a Hebrew school teacher, the toughest job you'll almost never love. A few Jewish studies classes, a trip to Israel, and hours upon hours of being in my personal one-person *cheder*/yeshivah led me to the job that saved my life. I can't tell you all my stories and secrets because, from that trademark chapter title, I must write a book one day on what that fifteen-year stretch of my life meant to me. But here we will graze on the amuse bouche, nosh but not fress. I'll give you a sketch.

I was deeply in love with being a Hebrew school teacher. "Hebrew school" is a relatively inaccurate coinage. Jewish supplementary school is not actually based around the Hebrew language as it once was in some communities, especially after 1948. Yes, some contemporary Hebrew is taught, but most of the Hebrew is that of the prayer book and the reading skills needed to recite one's bar or bat mitzvah Torah portion. For the sixth- and seventh-graders, I taught the *Amidah* or *Shemoneh Esrei*, the central prayer at the heart of weekday services; the *Shema*, our credo affirming the oneness of G-d; and the Friday night and Saturday morning services, essential to Shabbat. I also accompanied them to assemblies, where they practiced morning *tefillah* (prayer) and the Friday night service and trope (how you read the Torah). For older kids, post b'nai mitzvah special classes involved cooking, music, Black-Jewish relations, and classes on Jews and food and culinary justice, and even "Epithet University," where we looked at the ethics of language from a Jewish standpoint and confronted language that was considered offensive and the terms that people often use to demean one another according to their group.

For the most part, the kids loved me; I frequently got the moniker "favorite Hebrew school teacher." I was also known as a bureaucratic nightmare who often forgot to complete attendance (until they started sending someone to collect it) and was frequently late because I depended on a horrible county bus system to get around. What gave me job security was the results I got in my classroom; namely, having kids who wanted to come back. Being a teacher, a Jewish teacher, was a refuge to me, and bit by bit, I worked harder to clean up my rough edges. I was also the only Black teacher anywhere I found myself and often the only teacher of color. I taught with many lovely people, but inevitably some didn't like me, and some said or did things that I considered micro- and macro-aggressions.

What I keep from my days teaching Hebrew school is not so much the bad times, and there *were* bad times. It was the rides home in the dark, the invitations to share holiday dinners when otherwise I would have gone home alone, kids who brought me little presents at Hanukkah and the end of the school year. I treasure that I was exposed to a ton of love and openness that I had not experienced elsewhere. Phyllis, Elissa, Johanna, Judy, Adrian, my directors, never let me starve; my safety and dignity as a Black Jewish man were always respected and cultivated.

I love Judaism because I was allowed the opportunity to teach Judaism. I walked into the classroom devoted to teaching the truth, so I had to understand what that truth was. I had to think deeply about what I was teaching and why it was important to *me*. I told my students why teaching was dear to me or why I had problems with something and that it was okay to doubt and question and comprehend and debate because that is a deep part of being Jewish. I also affirmed my deep faith in things I could not explain or completely understand; I told them of times when I felt the Divine Presence and moments when I was vulnerable and afraid.

This is the job, I reasoned: to give the students all the pieces to survive everything, from the moments when life is at its worst to crises of faith to anti-Semitism and to how to embrace diversity and intersectionality (before I knew what the word meant). If it stopped there, it would be enough, but it never was. We talked about how to treat waitstaff with respect, the Jewish war between the sexes (apparently there was strong antipathy toward the thought of dating Jewish in sixth and seventh grade), and when things happened related to race, I was the go-to. Sometimes I left the job lighter in spirit; sometimes, more burdened than before.

Hebrew school also made me feel, in an isolated way, closer to being "American." Every day I had to go outside of my bubble, I was both a citizen and an immigrant, and that was humbling and challenging, giving me some limited perspective on how other people might feel in their journey. As a Jew, I was closer to the glories of this country that often get obscured as a Black person. No nation in the Diaspora had ever been so open and expansive for the Jews than this one. I never lost perspective on why and, more specifically, the boundaries I transgressed just by occupying the spaces I did when I went outside of my bubble.

Hebrew school was like my therapy for traumatic middle school years, so I came to the classroom with extra empathy. Sometimes I yelled, sometimes I let students get away with murder, but I always came back the next session adjusted and empowered, which led to my own personal growth. If you can teach a middle-schooler, you can teach anyone. If you can reach a jaded high school student, you can sell a salt mine vacation home to a slug family. It gives me great pleasure that my kids are all grown up, and soon they will all be in college.

On my last day at one synagogue, after ten years of teaching, I said goodbye. I decided to transition my work life to writing and doing presentations full time; making that break was emotionally exigent. On the one hand, I wasn't made to clock in all the time, and being a teacher requires wearing so many hats you never counted on wearing. On the other hand, I knew I would miss the minor moments of being a hero—of making Black and Jewish history every time I walked through the classroom doors. One of my best students brought her guitar to class, and I sat there with a room full of seventh-graders trying not to weep as she played and sang "To Sir, with Love."

Let me teach you some Hebrew: *ahavah* means love.

Mayseh:
KATIE–"I FEEL LIKE ME"

I remember Katie as a beautiful, happy young woman who especially hated Hebrew school. The main reason she showed up, much like most other students, was to be with her friends. It was my job to imbue the lessons with a reason for them to attend, and it wasn't easy. Elissa Kaplan originally brought me to the Conservative shul to do a special program based on my work at the Smithsonian Folklife Festival presenting traditional bearers. My job was using food and other material culture points and historical narrative to help the students create an exhibit on the Silk and Gold Routes and how Jews founded communities across the Eastern Hemisphere, especially in Asia and Africa.

Of the thirty-plus locations the students had to choose from, Katie chose Japan. It was an easy choice; her mother was Japanese American. Katie navigated her world as biracial, part Japanese, part white, all Jewish. In a class of mostly white, mostly Ashkenazi Jewish kids, she didn't always feel like she fit in. At least she could identify as a fellow tweenager, a suburban kid with plenty of after-school activities and tons of homework—all punctuated with the synagogue and nice dinners and trips. But there were other parts of fitting in that never seemed in the cards.

Katie's Ancestors on both sides had been in camps during World War II. Her Japanese American side knew the indignities and heartbreak of the internment camps in the West after Pearl Harbor, when Japanese families were robbed of their homes and resources and relocated under suspicion of being disloyal to the United States. Katie's Ashkenazi Jewish family were murdered in the concentration camps of Poland. For all the pleasantries of middle-class life in the Maryland suburbs, Katie came to school with old stings and traumas on top of the burden of having a complex personal story. This narrative stared her in the face in every mirror and in every glance at the classmates with whom she shared her Jewish world. It was subtle but real, and I understood it in my own way.

Katie is Jewish; I am Jewish. I had Indian-Caribbean students or part Bengali and African American students who were Jewish. To be Jewish and of color can be a land mine when so many people still define Jewishness by appearance. I never understood how emissaries from Chabad Jews were able to use the question "Are you Jewish?" with Mitzvah tanks (a kind of spiritual outreach food truck) if the basis for the question was "appearing Jewish." Brown and Jewish, that is.

"Looking Jewish" isn't an accurate or successful way of parsing who is or is not part of the family. If you're a Jew who looks different from the common perception of Ashkenazi Jewry, you have to be strong for a lifetime of double looks, side-eyes, doubt, disbelief, and assaults on your confidence. With Katie and other students, I realized I had to find quiet ways to teach them how to survive and how to demand respect. Being Jewish sometimes came with the pain of people assuming that you were not legitimate or, even worse, unequal because you looked different from the stereotype.

Elissa's innovation in the Silk Road Project was revolutionary. Through this exercise, she taught mainstream Jewish kids in middle school just how diverse and beautiful the Jewish people can be. Jews in Old Mali and Ethiopia, Iran, Iraq, Afghanistan, India, and Japan, among others, came together on cardstock and Power-Point presentations with maps showing journeys across rivers and seas and deserts. It made it easy to say "We weren't always white Americans" and "By the way, we still aren't in much of the world." Each time I taught the project, I waited for the jewel of a moment when a student said, "When *we* were in Ethiopia."

I'm sure Katie originally picked Japan because it seemed immediately familiar and promised to be easy. It wasn't. It led her down a rabbit hole. She wasn't just writing a report and reading it off index cards; she was doing what many of us do—constructing a history and a narrative where we are centered, where we are not abnormal, and where we do the storytelling rather than have stories told about us. For Katie, writing about Jews in Japan wasn't a report—it was a journey within.

The best of the Silk Road presentations took over the social hall winding through the corridors and parts of the old sanctuary. Parents of sixth-graders brought their kids in that morning, then waited for the exhibit, clustering together, drinking coffee, and trading notes on their common joys and miseries. Parents loaded their cars with poster boards and last-minute touches of glitter and highlighters. Kids brought in vegetarian and rabbi-approved food samples, and the more adventurous had freshly pressed ethnic costumes. Somewhere there was the smell of rosewater. New words—*Sephardi, Mizrahi, Edot Ha-Mizrach, Temani, Beta Israel, Bene Israel, Conversos*—described just the surface of Jewish ethno-diversity that appeared around the space.

My sixth-grader Henry did me proud. He made the black-eyed pea fritters from West Africa called akara for his report on Timbuktu and the Jews of Old Mali, Ghana, and Songhai. These three great empires linked North Africa and the Islamic world along the gold routes connected to the silk ones. He described them as African falafel, which made me laugh. Some sang the Four Questions in Ladino. Others spoke of the Jews in Herat, even if they were disappointed that it was Herat and not Heart, like the typo on the assignment sheet (not my fault).

There they were—the Jews of Calcutta, the Jews of Thessaloniki and Turkey, Syria and Morocco, Venice and Rome and Persia—almost forgotten, lumped into broad categories of erasure. Then there was Japan, the Jews of Japan, and Katie was in the most beautiful kimono I had ever seen and glowing so much I held back hot tears. She had made kosher sushi at home for everyone to sample. She spoke proudly of the Jewish history of Japan from stragglers to settlers to converts and showed how Jewish and Japanese cultures had intertwined. She made the presentation completely hers, and she hugged me.

"I feel like me," she said. "The whole me."

Mayseh:
ELLIOTT'S *TEFILLIN*

Elliott was the tallest kid at the Conservative synagogue where I taught. He was taller than most of the other teachers and me. He was bright-eyed and slightly goofy in a cool way, smart and athletic, and thoroughly steeped in hip-hop culture. He liked the fact that I cracked off-color jokes and made references from Black culture. From sixth to tenth grade, Elliott was a refuge when I felt like I was misunderstood or fellow teachers weren't so sympathetic to the struggles I faced walking in and out of a place where I didn't always feel wanted or appreciated for being myself.

Elliott and I loved to talk about food. He spoke about food the way most football-playing teenagers did—as a necessary good—making him my ally. Brisket, potato kugel, fried chicken, and kosher turducken—don't ask me where he got it from—he was a meat and potatoes kid who said "turducken" with closed eyes and a smile and a mock lick. Whenever possible, he asked me about Black culture—everything from Malcolm X to the politics of rap to stories from my family. He was one of the few students in that community who didn't see Black people as alien, silly, underachieving. Pop culture taught students that Black people were successful only in athletic, musical, kinesthetic, and sexual matters.

Elliott made me feel like an older brother, someone who fit well into his scope of what Judaism was supposed to be. Hebrew school wasn't really his favorite thing—nor was it for most of my boys—but his parents appreciated that I made it palatable and enjoyable. I knew that I was exotic to some degree, but more than that, I was a breath of fresh air. Hebrew school teachers were invariably deep insiders, distinctly part of a system born long before I was a thought. They were rabbis' wives, older Israeli ladies, and slightly uncomfortable college kids who needed a job. Most of them hated Hebrew school too, but there was also the occasional movement kid who was gung ho for the cause and would invariably end up in clergy or Jewish professional life.

I was none of those. When Elliott would bounce around between classes or activities, MP3 player blasting beats into his ear, making up crazy dances nobody else would ever perform and his-only rhymes, he vibrated to a different tone. When you feel the need for balance, you move; nothing is more classically African Atlantic: a problem is recast in music and resolved in dance. External motion and internal motion move together—philosophical resolution is piped into your ears with music as its vehicle. In the African Diaspora, the nature of music and dance is often misinterpreted by others as recreation when they have a healing element, a reparative function. I was born into that tone, and unbeknownst to him, Elliott kinda was too.

Elliott's Ancestors came from a settlement in Eastern Europe known as Belz, home of the Belzer Hasidim. Thanks to *Fiddler on the Roof* and many other cinematic depictions of Hasidic life, Hasidic music and dance are known for being colorful and fun. However, the almost meditative *niggunim*—wordless hymns that often intone the sound of *yud*, the first letter of the Creator's most sacred name, as in *ayayaiyaiyaiyai*—lead to hours of ecstatic worship expressed in dance and the singing of psalms, prayers, and folk songs that spin into a spark of *devekus*—the moment when prayer and celebration lead to a spiritual adhesion, a gluing of flesh and spirit. Elliott and I both had that vibe—born in West Africa and West Asia, channeled through different diasporas, one through the American South and another through Eastern Europe, paths that crossed inside of us, naturalized by our sincere commitment to the intangible nature of "soul."

Elliott was deeply committed to being a Jew and drew great pride from being Jewish even though, like most suburban Jews, it was wedged in his schedule between everything else in his week. There were, of course, parts of it he didn't understand or relate to and things that were completely unfamiliar because they had fallen out of practice. I thought that in some ways, Black culture filled for him some empty spots and indeterminate spaces where he, much like me, was working out the rigors of identity. Then, for three weeks, some family issues dampened Elliott's spirit. He didn't laugh, hardly smiled; he was sullen and inanimate, he was angry.

Because of the influence of the teachings of the Lubavitcher Rebbe, I believed in exposing my students to the wearing of *tefillin*. *Tefillin* are known in standard dictionary English as phylacteries, which is unfortunate because that word comes from a Greek word suggesting that *tefillin* are amulets, which they are not. *Tefillin* are small black boxes worn on the head and arm to honor the mitzvot or commandments expressed in the Torah to wear the word of the *Shema*, declaring the oneness of G-d, with one's body. Traditionally, males wear *tefillin* from the time of their bar mitzvah onward, and it marks a transition into a life of dedication to prayer and inward searching. I introduced my sixth-grade boys and girls to *tefillin*, determined that they know what they were and how to wear them.

Elliott never got that lesson because I wasn't his primary teacher in sixth grade, but the look on his face and the feeling he seemed to have made me want to make sure he knew it. *Tefillin* leave a mark on your skin from the pressure of the leather against it. The boxes feel like spiritual antennae; they feel and look ancient because they are. They are not that comfortable, but as much in Judaism, that isn't the point. *Tefillin* are a vehicle for focus and meditative prayerfulness that ultimately exist because, by wearing them, we are committing our thoughts and actions to the service of Hashem.

I brought Elliott my first set of *tefillin* and a page I had copied out of a Jewish cultural atlas. I asked him if he knew where his name came from and if he could point to a map and tell me where his Ancestors originated. After *Roots* but before genealogical reveal shows, a fifteen-minute conversation was all I needed to light a spark.

I pulled out the *tefillin* from the small deep blue velvet bag classically embossed with the word *tefillin* in Hebrew in golden yellow thread. I explained the *shel yad*, worn on the hand, and the *shel rosh*, worn on the head. I spoke of Belz and the Belzer Hasidim and traced the journey from ancient Israel to Belz to America in a rough fashion. He put out his arm, laid on the *shel yad*, wrapped the strap as tradition dictates, and then placed the *shel rosh* on his head and went back to the leather straps of the *shel yad* to tie in place the hand and fingers. His hands trembled a bit as he took possession of the blue velvet bag and held it, like a newborn, close to his heart.

Elliott's mom picked him up that night. She parked the car and came up and thanked me, hugged me, and for the first time in a few weeks, Elliott smiled the way he had when he thought about kosher turducken.

"You gonna be all right, Elliott?"

"Yeah, Mr. Twitty, I got this. I'm from Belz."

Mayseh:
SWEET POTATOES

When you want to talk to me to "be nice" as a Black
person, you mean:

Don't talk about race

Don't cause conflict

Don't say anything that might upset me or other
white people I care about

Don't be direct

Don't tell me what you really think

Tell me I'm a good person

Smile, be friendly

Don't cause me to feel anything

Don't pressure me to take action or own something
I did

Don't defend yourself against my racism lest you be
seen as a bitter angry person

Don't name my racism.

—Anika Nailah, quoted in "Nice Racism"

et over here and help me now!" The words were barked—a command directed at me, a man in his thirties. I was being told what to do by someone who did not have my five-year tenure in that school. He had been there less than a year, a teacher from the Philadelphia suburbs; but because he had the privilege, the platform, and the power, he was able to insinuate, in an email to my principal, that I was a thief for letting students use glitter for a class project he felt I was not authorized to allow them to use. His email suggested that by consequence of my identity and supposedly my values, I was an alien.

"We at [that Jewish school] do not teach our children to steal." That line froze in me. Whom was he talking to? Me, yes, but why express his concerns like that? Why was it me versus them? And what was worse, why was it "splained" to me that what he said was not racist? There is power in "our," so why was that word ignored in favor of "we"?

"Our" school was quirky and had unique flexibility and openness. It was nestled in a building owned by a Presbyterian church that welcomed the opportunity to not only help pay the bills but have a space where Christians, Jews, and others could come together; our students shared supplies—including the glitter and glue that led to my being accused by the Philadelphia man of theft. Bengali, Spanish, and Mandarin had been heard in the sanctuary during b'nai mitzvot. The food served at celebrations was kosher style but international, and challah and Chinese dumplings or other goodies sat side by side because the culture of the shul was driven by the relationships that made up the nexus of its community.

The shul was a refuge for interfaith couples and was a hotspot for diversity; it incorporated many of the values of the Jewish Renewal movement known for its forward-thinking and deep commitment to a reimagined Jewish future. One of the biggest issues that undergirded the shul's growth was the rejection that many couples and families faced over creating a community where interfaith people still sought to have a role in Jewish life. This congregation sold itself as progressive, welcoming, and understanding. With a bio like that, I would be part of "our." I would be safe there.

Adrian Durlester, Mr. D, had brought me in, and I loved him because he understood my worldview. I did not ignore his short stature, and he did not ignore my skin color and history, and because of that, we got along. He made me feel like I was a part of their experiment in the community, even when I did not share their points of practice or ritual. He was a composer and comedian at heart who nourished connections to all the legends of Jewish education, and we both had a passion for Jewish learning outside the box. This odd, small congregation with wildly smart kids was the place to be different and do different things.

"We" is an interesting pronoun. It's a beautiful word when done right. It confers belonging, security, bonds, and responsibility. "When we get home" is mellifluous when it means the dog is staying or the person you're with wants to make this a "we" thing or you're young and feeling a sense of belonging with a clique. It's when the bond with a friend and their kin gives you that German feeling—*Gemeinschaftkeit*—a feeling of genuine community and connection. When you are intersectional—as many of us are—the word is candy to the soul, and when it's not, "we" is weaponized, and no word is more brutal.

"We" in Judaism is also the predominant pronoun at Rosh Hashanah and Yom Kippur. We had a hardened heart. We had the inner thoughts of sinners, we sinned through our tongues, we desecrated G-d's holy name, and we sinned through food and drink. This "we" quietly shelters the guilty into a verbal communal hug so that they can find out together how to fess up and how to heal. The *Al Chet* prayer (the confession on Yom Kippur) is for the whole tribe, rather than singling out a few for embarrassment or ridicule.

This is not the "we" the man from Philadelphia used. His "we" was not inclusive or warm; his was an othering "we." He was not following the best Jewish tradition where we refrain from singling people out or politely asking a fellow Jew to amend their behavior or even asking questions without assuming guilt or blame minus evidence. This "we" was necessarily accusatory.

As long as Mr. D was at the shul, "we" were making community on the margins. "We" were not like the other shuls where stodgy conventions and purist attitudes based on ethno-religious particularism reigned.

"We" changed from synagogue to synagogue. Each was a different world with its own vibe. Because I have a buffet eater's hunger for experiential variety, I was grateful for the variety, yet it presented its own set of problems. I was a fledgling, problematic adult in a horrible relationship compounded by financial instability and dysfunctional family issues, and I was Black. The last bit bears repeating: I was Black. I was surrounded by people who said color and "race" were irrelevant to them, that it didn't mean a thing, but I found out that for all the diversity and openness they touted as strengths, they had not completely confronted what those words meant or how they were to be lived.

I had to become adept at reading between the lines. Don't get me wrong; I was still better off amidst "the tribe" than the rest of self-identified white America, and 75 percent of the time, all my troubles and struggles were made easier by people who genuinely cared for me as a human being. But there were moments when whiteness prevailed over Jewishness, and I was not in the in-crowd. I began to understand how the rope of race actually worked; it wasn't about merit or being different on the surface—it was about perception and assumption. My speech, my tone, my choice of clothing for the day, how I got to work (the bus), when I got to work (often late because of the bus) were all judged through a lens that was contextually clueless and had no sense of history and, if it did, would have little sympathy.

When kids were dishonest, their word was taken over mine—every time. When white teachers were angry with other white teachers for perceived slights, it manifested in cold, passive-aggressive gossip,

grumbles that lasted for twenty years. But if I was distracted or trying to quietly resolve behavioral issues with my students, I endured
screaming in my face. "Mr." was omitted in favor of using my first or
last name. A teacher at one school got in my face, positioned himself
chest to chest in front of our students, and used the term "buddy"
while scolding me for letting one of my students visit his class during
the last three minutes of the last day of school.

I wasn't perfect, but none of us were. I knew there were times when
I had to be twice as good to be just as good. But the screaming—in
Judaism, it is said that if you cause someone to blush in humiliation,
you are like a murderer who has shed blood. I suppose because my
blush could not be seen, no murder could be alleged. I felt helpless;
I was verbally abused at home by an abusive partner and then again
at work; at any moment, I could be on the wrong side of someone's
mood and treated like the help. Despite all the kindnesses and benefits
that being a Jewish religious school teacher afforded me in that part
of my life, the fact that some teachers chose to express themselves in
an impudent and fractious way with absolute moral blindness to how
that looked to our students—I cried at home without knowing what I
was crying about—made me know deep inside that I was being made
an example of.

The word is "performative"; that's it—they were performing a
very American act: putting Black people in their place. I was the only
Black man many of my students ever grew up calling "Mr." or saying
"Sir" to in regular school or Hebrew school, so the tone-deafness
was deep. In those moments when other teachers decided to express
themselves in a manner contrary to Jewish values, it was for me tied
into a braid with comments like:

"Obama is an Arab terrorist."

"So where in Africa do you come from?" (I had to explain four
hundred years in four minutes.)

"Why do we have Arabs teaching our children?" (A parent was
referring to me, an African American, as an "Arab.")

"My teacher at school said Black people don't want to leave the ghetto. Did you leave the ghetto yet?"

"You're, like, the whitest Black guy I know."

"I'm Blacker than you . . . Michael" (said to me by a high school student who had not received my permission to call me by my first name).

"So, are you going to serve chitlins at your bar mitzvah?"

"I know what it's like to be discriminated against; my brother [of Yemenite descent in Israel] is dark. It's the same as you, but he got over it . . . you just need tougher skin."

"You don't sound very intelligent sometimes" (if I used any speech patterns or idioms characteristic of African American Vernacular English).

"Why do you have to bring up race so much? That's not an issue here; this is synagogue."

"Why don't you have a car? Don't you want to grow up? You should work harder, get another job if that's what it takes."

"I'll give you a ride, but do you live in a safe neighborhood because . . ."

"Mr. Twitty, you don't understand; Trayvon Martin was a druggie . . ."

Yeah. The list could be significantly longer.

I was peeling sweet potatoes for a pie; that's how it started, and that's what you need to know. I needed every dime I could put together, and I had a big presentation after school for which the sweet potatoes were destined. I was trying to sell my little book about the foodways of enslaved Afro-Marylanders, and there was a recipe in the book for the pie. I didn't sleep; home was hell, my ex-partner was abusing me, and every day felt like I was on the verge of emotional collapse.

The man from Philadelphia had his elementary school class in with my confirmation students (tenth grade); they made cards for Jewish service members and other activities for *tzedakah* day. There was glitter, glue, and construction paper everywhere on his side of the shared room designated for the purpose, and on my side, a fairly orderly group of moody but fun tenth-graders and bowls with my sweet potatoes. My students were the oldest and most self-sustaining and incredibly well behaved, so dropping off the pieces to a fellow teacher and the shul's caterer in the kitchen upstairs didn't seem like a big deal. The man from Philadelphia had the fourth or fifth grade, and they were for him insufferable. He crept up on me in a skulking way. "What are you doing?"

"I'm peeling sweet potatoes for a pie while I work with my class."

"Oh, I see." He rolled his eyes and crept back to his side of the room—like Nosferatu's shadow on the wall. The look on his face grew tenser; he was angry because he felt that I should have been helping him do *his* job. We were sharing a room, not sharing instruction time. Fewer than five minutes later, he scowled at me and demanded I help him. "Get over here and help me now!"

I gave him the look that Sidney Poitier gave Mr. Endicott in *In the Heat of the Night*. My students looked embarrassed for him and angry for me. I gave him thirty seconds to change his face and his tone. "Mr. Twitty, would you please come over and help me?" I did, but I knew it was not the end of this situation.

His email was lengthy. He was going to write the authorities and document my apparent unprofessionalism. The man from Philadelphia wrote the letter as if he were naturally above me, as if I were derelict in my duty to him. I had been there more than five years, I was supposedly an adult equal to him in authority, and we did not share a class.

The response to my rebuttal—demanding that his racialized tone be checked—was pretty much ignored. I was told not "to burn any bridges." Despite his emphasis on my being a thief by allowing the students to use the glitter and glue from the closet and using "we" in a way that suggested a difference or even a chasm between us, the man from Philadelphia never heard it from the spiritual leader or the new principal that he could have done a better job expressing his concerns. I was beyond hurt. Why didn't the principal question his hubris and arrogance? Why did they not point out to him how unbelievably caustic his response was in a supposedly liberal, progressive, open, caring synagogue?

By the next fall, after I had been promised over the summer that my job would be secure, I was let go of my tutoring and teaching positions and told I could come back on an "ad hoc" basis. The principal lied to me. After being the "favorite" teacher once again, I felt unbelievably alone. I appealed to some of the parents for help, for guidance, but nobody responded. The spiritual leader sent me a couple of hundred dollars through a parent I was fond of. I needed money, but more than that, I needed respect and justice. I left, and I never looked back.

Mayseh:

TRUTH, RECONCILIATION, AND REPAIR

A Prayer for the Elimination of
the Sins of Racism (2020)

Al Chet *by Yavilah McCoy*
(reprinted with permission)

The following adaptation of the *Al Chet* prayer was created to support us in rooting our ongoing and developing
racial justice practice within the transformative High
Holiday practices of seeking atonement, valuing human
dignity, engaging in healing, and deepening interconnect-
edness. The confessional nature of the *Al Chet* prayer
is utilized to point our attention to the spoken and unspoken truths that we live out together each day as the
ongoing conditions of racism persist in our systems and
in our lives. It was composed to cause us to ask: What
leadership, humility, discernment, and reflection will we
need to engage this period of atonement by centering
the most targeted and most vulnerable among us as we
speak truth and seek forgiveness? What role will our
historical privilege and oppression play as we consider
the many among us who will arrive at this day wounded,
displaced, and in need of healing? How will our journey
to Yom Kippur 2020 strengthen us to give up playing
small in our fear and enable us to reach boldly for a
new year and a new future devoid of hate, unriddled by
shame, and filled with the audacity of our hope?

As we utilize this prayer, in this time, amidst a global pandemic and a national uprising for racial justice and equity, I am hoping that we can specifically use this prayer to deepen our own and others' commitments to fully dismantling racism in every space we navigate. In my personal observance of this ritual prayer, saying *Al Chet* in plural form welcomes my attention to the fact that in seeking truth, reconciliation, and repair in eliminating the sins of racism in Jewish spaces, I stand as one with my people, and my people, and my people, and my people— all of us commonly indicted and commonly responsible for doing what we must, across diverse entry points, to deepen racial equity, grow racial justice, and repair the brokenness of our world. Won't you join me in saying it together?

—*Yavilah McCoy*

The *Al Chet* confession of sins is traditionally said ten times in the course of the Yom Kippur services: following the *Amidah* of the afternoon prayers of the day before Yom Kippur, just before sunset on Yom Kippur eve, and twice during each of the following services: the evening service of Yom Kippur eve, and the morning service, the *musaf* service, and the afternoon service of Yom Kippur day. At each service it is said once at the end of the Silent *Amidah*, and once during the cantor's repetition of the *Amidah*.

In 2020, I'm saying Al Chet
For the sins of silence.
For the sins of using the "I" voice of individualism when a "We"
born of collective accountability was called for.

For the sins of using "We" toward erasure of others and the elevation of a single narrative.

For the sins of failing to acknowledge our own and others' Power.

For the sins of acknowledging Power that is misused and misplaced.

For the sins of judging others favorably and unfavorably without gaining proximity to their lived experience.

I am saying Al Chet

For the sins we have committed through conscious and unconscious racial bias.

For the sins we have committed through hardening our hearts to the need for change.

For the sins of colluding with racism both openly and secretly. For the sins we have committed through uttering racist words.

For the sins we have committed through acts of racial microaggression.

For the sins we have committed through insisting on urgency and perfectionism as a measure of human value.

I am saying Al Chet

For the sins we have committed through the denial of the tzelem elokim *(the divine spark) within Black bodies.*

For the sins we have committed through segregating Black bodies from participation and leadership within our institutions.

For the sins we have committed in deceiving others by not teaching our children the worth, value, and contributions of Black people.

For the sins we have committed in not honoring and protecting the journeys of Black elders and Black children.

For the sins we have committed in commoditizing Black people and Black bodies in our business dealings.

For the sins we have committed in not caring for the ways that race and class intersect in our efforts to deepen community with Black people in Jewish spaces.

For the sins we have committed through turning Black bodies into objects of lust and sexual gratification.

For the sins we have committed through confessing our commitments to ending racism insincerely.

For the sins we have committed that desecrate the divine name by allowing White Supremacy habits to shape/determine our practice of Judaism.

For all these, we seek pardon, forgiveness, and atonement.

For the sins of racism that we have committed knowingly and unknowingly that continue to do damage to our siblings, children, families, and community.

For the sins of racism we have committed through creating hierarchies of value between our siblings from Europe and those from the Middle East, Asia, and Africa.

For the sins of racism we have committed through engaging in foolish racial talk and gossip in our places of worship.

For the sins of racism we have committed through haughty demeanor and proud looks.

For the sins of racism we have committed through the glances of our eyes.

For the sins of racism we have committed through passing judgment.

For the sins of racism that we have committed through baseless hatred.

For the sins of racism that we have committed through turning a blind eye to pain and suffering around us.

For the sins of racism that we have committed by not seeing racism as an evil among us.

For the sins of racism that we have committed by not committing to end it.

For all these, we seek pardon, forgiveness, and atonement.

May all of us be written and inscribed in the Book of Life. May joy and blessing follow our reflection, our atonement, and our commitments to living truth, reconciliation, and repair in our time.

8

KIPPA'ED WHILE BLACK: BEING A BLACK JEWISH MAN

A t the beginning of my book *The Cooking Gene*, I describe what it's like to put on eighteenth- and nineteenth-century clothes and enter the twenty-first century to bring out elements of my African American Ancestors' past. At first, the shock of just barely putting yourself in their shoes—and I mean the sensation of barely letting your toes touch the sole—gives way to routine, the clothes fade, and the power of letting the dead inhabit your body but remain alive in spirit through you becomes routine. The clothes are not me but a lens, and just like taking off glasses that belong to someone else, the lenses change your perspective. I'm not the Ancestors, but I am of them, and they are certainly in me. When I interpret in the third person (speaking as my twenty-first-century self), the wardrobe change is not so much time travel but wearing garb that imbues me with a sense of responsibility. I will confess that this is in some ways immediately traceable to my relationship to Judaism.

Before the day in the kitchen comes the routine of making myself spiritually ready for the day. The double-handled laver by the bed is there to wash my fingers off before I say the *Modeh Ani: Modeh ani lefaneicha, melech chai v'kayam shechezartah bi nishmati b'chemlah, raba emunatecha*. "I thank You, living and enduring Ruler, for You have returned my soul to my body in grace. Great is Your faith in me."

Wow. G-d says I have something to do, a destiny to fulfill, food to cook and people to feed, and things to teach. I wash, I dry, I dress. On goes the *kippa*, and, I hope, I am crowned with splendor. Next, the *tallit katan*—if only I had money for the number of times people on the train or bus thought my clothes were coming apart. Then come the *tefillin*, black boxes tied with leather straps—arm, then head, then back to arm. They are called phylacteries in English—a bad New Testament term because they are not amulets; they are literally a commandment from Devarim, or Deuteronomy, to bind the words on my body and affirm the *Shema*—Hear, O Israel, the Lord your G-d, the Lord is One.

Deuteronomy 11:18 (KJV)—*Therefore shall ye lay up these my words in your heart and in your soul, and bind them for a sign upon your hand, and they shall be as frontlets between your eyes.*

My favorite part is the *tallit*, the prayer shawl. I missed out on the Ghanaian kente cloth *tallitot*. It's okay; I have a Ghanaian one with Adinkra symbols, another from Sierra Leone made from country cloth, and an Ethiopian Jewish *tallit*, a rainbow *tallit*—B'nai Or, but let's also call it a Pride *tallit*. And then there are the old favorites—blue and white, the colors of mystical splendor, and black and white—the type you see in Hasidic shuls.

From Bamidbar (Numbers) 15:37–41:

G-d spoke to Moses, telling him to speak to the Children of Israel, and have them make tzitzit *on the corners of their garments for all generations. They should include a twist of sky-blue wool in the corner* tzitzit. *These shall be your* tzitzit, *and when you see them, you shall remember all of G-d's commandments so as to keep them. You will then not stray after your heart and eyes, which [in the past] have led you to immorality. You will thus remember and keep all my commandments, and be holy to your G-d. I am*

*G-d your Lord, who brought you out of Egypt to be your G-d. I
am G-d your Lord.*

You spread it over yourself like a hawk or cloud that protects you
and clothes you and keeps you warm and safe, and then you wrap
yourself in it, and the hug you've always wanted from G-d is real
and present and ready for you, and then you pray. Prayer in Judaism is not *precare*, the root of our English word "pray," Latin for
begging. Prayer is called *avodah*, which means "service" or "labor."
Prayer is also called *tefillah*, from the root *lehitpalel*, which means to
judge (oneself). Some of the rabbis of old suggested that if you have
the time, you should spend an hour deep in thought before you even
begin this very serious process of self-reflection.

*Who am I today? I miss my mother. I'm getting old, even if I'm not
that old yet. Twenty-plus years have gone by. The dog is snoring, but
that's peaceful. I've made so many mistakes; I keep making mistakes. I
hope I get this right before I leave this plane. I've never needed you more,
G-d, than this morning. Please need me back. You got me up; I guess
that's the hard part; the rest is up to me.*

I want to remind you that the sense of the holy here is not about
piety. It's not about perfection or being a *tzaddik* (the closest thing we
get to sainthood or holy person status in Jewish thought). It's about
the attempt to be grounded, and its execution; to be real in your conviction that you are special and your life is special and set apart for a
purpose. *Did I really come here to do this, to be a wonky foodie, to talk
and to cook a few things? Does this thing I do really matter? Food is so
fleeting; I'm not that important.*

The holiest of holy is to do good in the world, to live a life centered in justice, to work at having integrity. I struggle, but in grace,
my soul was given back to my body since the rabbis say that sleep
is one-sixtieth of death; and so here I am standing before the sun-
rise imagining my Creator somewhere behind it but also in the soft
whisper of my blind dog's snore.

In one pocket—the world, the universe, was created for me. I have access to it all. Waking up is like a quick-fire challenge in a reality TV show: you have all of this stuff and resources to do something impressive and amazing in a very short amount of time—just like the brief human life. In the other pocket—I am but dust and ashes.

But I'm also Black. I might be profiled when I'm in public. I might have an uncomfortable run-in with the cops. I may be policed by people—of any group—just for being a young-ish Black man. This hasn't changed in twenty-plus years of widening social circles, a little more money here and there, a growing profile. I am still Black in a society that has lowered expectations for Black males.

In one pocket, the world is a marketplace—*Ayé l jà run nile*—but the other world is home, say the Yoruba, one of my many Ancestral ethnic groups, the keepers of ancient spiritual knowledge and royal splendor. *Uwa bu afia!* The Igbo (another part of my DNA, also known as the "Jews of Africa") say the same thing—the world is a marketplace—and it's not just about commerce or human interaction; it's about what we make of life and our life journey, the idea that more things are possible than we can dream.

In the other pocket: "You are Black, proceed with caution in the market."

The Familiar Stranger

Every now and then, I would allow myself the fantasy of social amnesia and pretend I wasn't seen as different as I bounced from situation to situation in the Jewish community. Of course, those Jewish communities were never the same people or in the same "place." Sometimes I thought, "Well, you're not as different as you thought you were," or "This time was a little special, but that's to be expected, look where you were." There were those moments—being picked to be part of a minyan on the way to Israel for the first time by Haredi

Jews (Breslovers and Black Hats who looked nothing like me) and parents saying, "He's Jewish like us"—that saved me from complete alienation. Those moments made up for the times I'd walk into a shul and people would return "Shabbat Shalom" with a thanks that was flatter than matzoh. The worst to me was always "same to you," something *mishpocheh* doesn't say to *mishpocheh*.

The advice was: *You are a Black man in a yarmulke. People don't know what to do with you. They don't know if you're actually Jewish. You're not an off-the-shelf type. There just aren't that many of you. Don't take it so personally. People in Israel called my cousin* kushi [dark or phenotypically Black] *and discriminated against him; you'll get over it too.*

It was a parking lot dispute; I wasn't even the driver. I remember the older white woman leering at me and throwing words at me like, "You know, in this country, WE don't do that." I immediately called her a racist and an anti-Semite. The two cops, both Black men, rushed to defend her even though her assumption that I was a stupid Black foreigner who might be extra upset that a woman was yelling at him was completely wrong. I was told I would be detained for escalating a situation that I didn't start—or have any role in—until the white woman brought me in screaming and kicking. I was wearing an Abayudaya Ugandan knit full green-and-white *kippa* that covered my whole head; this was not that long after 9-11, and it set her off.

"First of all, I'm not a Muslim, I'm a Jew, and if I were a Muslim, that would be perfectly all right. Second of all, I'm not the driver, so I don't know why you're talking to me. Third of all, my friend didn't do anything wrong, so you really need to leave me and us out of it."

"Fuck off, kike, pass away!"

"What did you call me?"

As she walked past me, she repeated herself and pushed me—hard—even though I knew better than to touch her or anyone else in the situation.

The cop not only hushed me, but he physically threw out his arm as she walked away with a smirk. The privilege and power were extremely serious. If I were her, I'd be filing a police report right now. Instead, I was left to sulk in my feelings of being a legal adult who had no standing as a man and furthermore had been called a kike, and nobody but my friend seemed to care or want to do anything about it. He, a white man, the subject of the dispute, was not cursed at by the woman or had any of his behaviors circumscribed by the cops.

You know what else you bring into the kitchen? Being KWB— *Kippa'*ed While Black—the reaction to the fact that you are not just like the others, that you are Black and Jewish and many times but not always cis-gender and male. The suspicion is real and deep. I have certainly had moments when I felt that an insistence on saying and self-identifying as "Jewish"—rather than "Hebrew," a contentious term often used by other Black folk involved in Judaism or Jewish-adjacent practices—marked me as someone who could be trusted only so far.

My late mother once relayed a message from a relative who, upon seeing me with a *kippa*, said something to me for the first time in years: "Tell Michael there is only one way to the Father, and that is through the Son." I don't remember my answer, but it was sharp and pithy, I assure you. I never said my path was better than anyone else's. I didn't want to convert anyone; I was just trying to be myself. At a family reunion, my father pulled me aside and suggested that I take off my Obama *kippa*. Nobody cared, nobody asked, nobody struck up a conversation; only my father seemed embarrassed and confused.

The polarizing nature of a piece of cloth followed me to one of my first serious jobs, where I was given the name "little Amish boy" by one of my fellow Black employees. When somebody joneses on you, the appropriate reaction is not to flip out or go to HR but to take it in stride, play it up, and be only as defensive as you need to be. You don't run from it; you run to it. The range of opinions about me went from cute bemusement to resentment. People thought I thought I was better than them just because of a little piece of cloth on my head.

Projecting. I had been there before. "I bet you're Republican too," said the lady helping me get my ID card for the Library of Congress. She looked dismayed, pissed off that the race had lost another one to the bullshit. "Jewish and Republican," her lips were as pursed as my mother's when I broke something, and she shook her head from side to side, immediately deciding I was a waste of space and time. I assured her that I was not a Republican and asserted, "I'm Black just like you; I was born in Chocolate City, and so was my dad, and we have been here since my grandparents migrated in the 1930s." As quick as I had a response, so did she, "I ain't never seen no Black Jewish people in DC."

It wasn't always that messy. Most of the time, the call-outs were pleasant. The Nation of Islam brothers were the least likely to be offensive. I would return their "Shalom Aleichem" with "Alaikum Salaam," and the nods and smiles would commence. There was something about the head covering, something about the sense of difference and distinction, about choosing a path that engendered spiritual discipline, personal pride, collectivity that went beyond our respective understandings of prophecy and law. Black Christians would often ask, very loudly, in public, "Are you Jewish?!" I replied in just as enthusiastic a voice in the affirmative, and they would say "Shalom!" or "That's so cool!"

Honestly, it's exhausting. It's something on the other side of peace. I crave acceptance even as I worry that around the next corner is rejection. The marketplace has its consequences for those of us kippa'ed while Black, and I'm not the only one.

Gregg: Z'hug

Part of knowing your journey is having someone to journey with. First, there was Gregg; he showed me I could be Black and wear a kippa and a tallit katan in public and not be anything but normal.

Knowing Gregg brought me to being Jewish. We were about the same age, both Black and searching. "My attitude now is, 'I'm not your guest, and you're not my host,'" he tells me. That's always been Gregg, spicy as his favorite condiment, Yemeni z'hug, the "hot sauce" of Jewish food. "I'm a Black nerd—a blerd—I cut my eyeteeth on Sailor Moon," he says. "I was a Black Metalhead, spent time as a Goth, and people assume that you're always the minority if you're not in a group that they expect you to be in, but there's always more of us than anyone knows."

He continues: "I knew I was Jewish when I was at Howard University in Drew Hall. We were talking about Israelis and Palestinians, and instead of saying 'Jews,' I said 'we.' My late uncle had Malachi Z. York's Black Hebrew writings. I have his old copy of *Hebrewisms of West Africa*. At some point, with that influencing me, when I was growing up I came to a place of loving religion. I love learning about what makes people tick—consciousness and thought and emotions—those things are fascinating. I considered Islam for a while, but at some point, I considered Judaism. I worked at Borders bookstore, and my section was religion, and I saw a book called *Black Zion*."

That's where Gregg and I first met. I was there to buy books on Judaism, and *bashert*, he was the one to sell them to me. He was wearing a *kippa* and *tzitzit*, and in an instant, I knew that part of me was possible. I knew I was not alone or would be alone, *kippa*'ed while Black. We became fast friends after my first trip to shul as an adult. He was the first person to greet me at the door—and only G-d could have planned that. We bonded very quickly over matters of Jewish intellect and found out together just how that path caused both blessing and confusion.

"If you throw me a breadcrumb, I'm going to see where it leads," Gregg says. "I thrive on connections—how are these things related to one another? I've always loved the idea of finding your higher self, a part of you repressed, finding your higher self and unifying it. When you're Black in this society, part of the structural oppression is keeping that higher self repressed. The idea that a human is inherently flawed and incapable of fixing themselves doesn't work for me. My mom was born in Jim Crow–era North Carolina—lots of trauma. We dealt with a lot, and I'm a lot harder on my son than I guess I should be, but it comes from what my mother went through, and also what I know is waiting for him as a Jew of color in America."

Gregg is very traditional in his observance, and because of that, he has found himself in spaces where things have been said that all of us Jews of color have heard many times—things that remind us that our difference may get ignored but not in a good way. One rabbi gave a *shiur*, or talk, where he said that Black people get killed by the police because they insist on being minorities that don't educate themselves. "This guy knew me," Gregg says. "I would often talk about the parts of Black community life and culture that they had never been exposed to. My mother was a teacher; I was more than insulted. My wife and I left. He ran after me—but my wife turned around, and the New York came out of her."

"You guys are the whitest Black guys I know," I say. "Remember when A— said that to us?"

"Yeah, I remember the look we gave each other. It wasn't easy to push back then, but things have changed; we grew up, we got grown. Somebody accused me of being an undercover Muslim. I was walking to services, like, Shabbat services. Not exactly a Muslim thing to do. At one shul we visited, they gave me an *Aliyah* [a blessing over the Torah scroll during the reading at Shabbat services], but someone came up with me to say the *brachot* on the presumption I wasn't really Jewish."

We sigh. I don't want this to be our common experience, but it is.

Gregg says, "'I'm not your guest,' that's what I've centered. And they aren't my host. I'm a citizen here; my soul was at Sinai; there's nothing more to discuss. We are not white. We're Jews. Y'all also have to accept the Spanish-Portuguese gave rise to the largest group of Black Jews outside of Ethiopia, and then to separate themselves from Black people, they began to pass laws to prevent emancipation. One-third of the Portuguese Jews in Suriname were Black. They had their own synagogue for a year. Beth Elohim in Charleston changed their laws to exclude Jews of color. This isn't Black Hebrew stuff; this is actual record."

Part of the key is cultivating our own histories. I wanted to write a whole chapter piecing together these footnotes and endnotes that pass as a history of Black Jews, but that's not good enough. Our story isn't footnotes and endnotes. It's whole burned chapters that have been left out of the Jewish, African, Middle Eastern, Western, American, and Atlantic history books, a history that dares anyone to imagine us as an exotic novelty.

Gregg is a bit younger than I am, but I've always seen him as my elder; he was doing the work long before me. "We're Ethiopian, but we're also Lemba," he says, "and we're in West Africa all over the place, and now in Uganda and beyond. But we're also tucked away in places people never dreamed of. The records of the Inquisition in Mexico talk about Black Jews. Judaism is as much a part of the Afro-diasporic fabric as Christianity and Islam.

"Honestly, I think that a diasporic community, if you take the time to understand the similarities and differences, really sheds light on the transatlantic nature of the Sephardim after the expulsion from Spain. I find it easier to understand and parse the Atlantic nature of Blackness. We didn't have the luxury to rebuild in the same ways as others did, but we did rebuild some things and create new responses.

"For me, I have this cohesive Atlantic consciousness. My biological family is from Jamaica; my adopted family is from North Carolina. That's where I am; I have this transatlantic identity, and that's the heritage I want to pass on to my children. My middle name is Du Bois, for G-d's sake, I grew up with Carter G. Woodson, Anansi the Spider stories, and African proverbs; my Mom and Dad argued about taking me to the South African embassy to protest. I grew up with the consciousness that my late uncle imparted to me—we're Moors, we're Hebrews, we are not slaves."

As Gregg talks, I feel peace. This is one of the hardest parts for people to comprehend. We are happy with our complexity. Sorting ourselves out gives pleasure because everything begins with knowledge of self as the esoteric approach to wisdom. As impossible as that seemed in our increasingly distant youth, it's real, and it's ours.

"My spiritual upbringing is exile, reconciliation, reconstruction," Gregg says. "Sephardic, Yemenite, Ethiopian, Caribbean, African American. Black consciousness is an Atlantic consciousness. Both of those groups were forced to pretend to be Catholic."

"*Iparada*—'masquerading' in Yoruba," I say, "the practice of concealing power, what Baba John Mason says is the real 'syncretism.' Hiding your Shabbat prayers and hiding Shango" (a Yoruba deity).

"Exactly. And now we can be on the other side of that," Gregg says. "For me, making a Black *minhag* looks like the next chapter, the future. I have begun looking at the Commandment Keepers and other groups looking for parallels in other Jewish communities from the Sephardic communities. Where does what they do match up with these paths back to some sort of commonality? Where do these two diasporas overlap? Commandment Keepers had Spanish Portuguese prayer books, Ashkenazi scrolls and *mezuzot*, and *tefillin*; they're Hebrew Mizrahi-Yemenite, but they were Black in Harlem.

"I want a *tallit* with Adinkra symbols. If I can get a custom-made *atara* [band on the *tallit*], it will be black, red, and green. At Pesach, before we read the Haggadah, we sing 'Go Down Moses'; on the seventh day of Pesach, I sing 'Wade in the Water' with my wife and children. What better song can you sing to commemorate crossing the Yam Suf [also known as the Red, or Reed, Sea]?"

"Why is it important to do that?" I ask.

"Because it's jazz. It's something old; it's something new; it's

African, Middle Eastern, it's all of us. Everything about us is mixed and has been for quite some time. Black life in America is jazz, our language, our food, our music, our way. The critical thing about our food—Black and Jewish food together, separate, mixed—is that the most important elements are meaning and feeling. Z'hug is soul."

Tony Westbrook: "Israeli Salad Is Everything!"

My friend, educator Tony Westbrook, was born and raised in St. Louis. He is a self-described product of the desegregation program, where they bused students from the city of St. Louis to St. Louis County. "The Voluntary Transfer Student program—p.c. name for integration," he laughs. His dad's family is from Ripley, Tennessee, while his mother's family is from St. Louis and Milwaukee. His great-grandmother was from Syria and passed down her recipe for the traditional upside-down stew called maqluba. Many of his Ancestors ultimately came from West Africa by way of Virginia. "I believe those survival techniques have been passed down through the generations," he says.

Tony continues: "I grew up as a religious evangelical Christian. My mom is a minister. Church could sometimes be from 8 a.m. to 7 p.m.: Sunday school, announcements, worship services, and repeat.

"I always felt there was something higher than me. I always viewed Jesus as the middle man. It was clear that in Judaism, the middle man was cut out. Emphasis on education and family resonated with me. One of the big things was the emphasis on ritual and how things revolved around food. I just felt like Judaism was chock-full of these rituals and so many things around food and was respected and elevated. As a kid growing up, I knew of Jews through the Old Testament, 'the god of the Hebrews,' as I remember in Sunday school. In fourth grade, we had a reading unit about the Holocaust. I couldn't figure out who Jews were, but the fact that other people didn't like them just because they were Jews resonated with me.

"Most of my experiences were never entirely Black. My parents wanted better for me than what they had, but it came with consequences. We were the sprinkling of color in a white bowl of rice. Our neighbors would call the cops on us—and claim we did things we weren't doing. It didn't endear me to people who were different.

"When I was in college, I was in a program called Cultural Leadership—I was a sophomore or junior—and I first got to experience actual living Judaism. A big part was experiencing the other cultures in our community. Black and Jewish families traded places. I didn't know what Shabbat was, but there was food, singing, and weird little chanting before and after, and I was there for it. The thing that stood out was every Friday night, the entire family got together for this meal. It was like going over to my grandmother's, but what made it different was that the entire family unit was together and did the same thing week after week. [Judaism wasn't this ancient, ritualistic people sacrificing to G-d, and the angry, vengeful G-d we were often taught represented the Old Testament.]

"I decided I wanted to convert to Judaism; I recognized my soul as being a Jewish soul. I went off to undergrad, went to both synagogue and church; these were free meals I didn't have to eat in a cafeteria, which was great. I found myself more at home in Judaism, mainly because of the emphasis on education—one of the most prominent features. I've always been a lifelong learner; if I don't understand how something works, I learn it until I can teach it.

"I met up with my friend Mayan; I had a coming-out moment as a Jewish convert. Rabbi Susan Taube said, think of your faith as a garment, and now you want to try on another. I would end up reading every book I could find. That was a two-year process that culminated in my conversion.

"I came out of the *mikveh* with a fire inside me. That Saturday, they called me up to the Torah for the first time. I felt, after two years of intensive learning, that there were still many things I didn't know. I felt like it certainly wasn't Black church, but the music was how I connected to G-d. I was too old to go to camp, so I studied for another two years, learning how to chant Torah, how to chant *haftorah*, learning Hebrew and the prayers; I became bar mitzvah of the entire Jewish community of St. Louis. There were many different people there, including many older white Jewish folks whose children and grandchildren had no interest, but here is this young Black Jewish man.

"I invited most of them because I made so many connections on my journey. It was like everything I was moving toward came together. The party was fantastic. It was like blending my Black and Jewish identities: fried chicken, falafel, all of the great things from Black and Jewish foods; it just all worked. Immediately people asked me about the next step; I decided to learn more about trope—how to chant the Torah reading. And then came the Mishnah and Talmud; a friend's girlfriend introduced me to Pardes—a learning program in Israel. I knew I needed to be in Israel and wanted to study there—I was twenty-eight. Was I crazy, was I worthy? The voice of self-doubt was there. Three years of Pardes followed.

"When I first moved to Israel, it was going to be for only a year, but immediately I was, like, this feels different—no one is asking me to share my story. They saw I was Jewish—a *kippa*, *tzitzit*. But it's funny; the Ethiopians told me I wasn't Ethiopian—of course not—my name is Tony, and I'm from St. Louis. I felt at home and fell in love with Israel, but I felt very guilty, not the burden of being Black in America."

I stop our conversation for a moment because I had a very serious and very similar reaction. There were times when being Jewish felt like being on the other side of the looking glass, of dodging the curveballs and pains of being Black—not all of them, but some of the more substantial ones.

"I made aliyah in December 2016," Tony says. "Didn't tell anyone.

I am now both an American and an Israeli citizen. It was the resolution I needed and wanted, and it also made it easier to keep learning and growing in Judaism.

"All of my American friends were asking me how I was experiencing racism, but it wasn't the same as in America. One of the Blackest experiences I had in Israel was going to the barbershop. We made small talk in English and Hebrew. 'I'm going to run out and get something to eat. Do you want something?' He started to grill some meat. If someone was chatting with their kinfolk, they would put me on speaker and go, 'Here, talk to my mom on the phone.' In Ashkelon, everyone knew everyone, and there were more Black and brown people. I didn't know how to exist in a system where I actually could just be a person. When my dad talks about growing up in Tennessee—everyone looking out for each other—that's what it felt like."

Tony loves to cook, and he often posts beautiful pictures on social media from his preparations for Shabbat. It's magical to know someone mixes everything up as I do. Our conversation turns to food.

Tony says: "My favorite Black kosher foods—hmmm . . . greens, macaroni and cheese, and I have an incredible sweet tooth—sweet potatoes and 7-Up cake, you name it. I hate okra, but I make black-eyed peas for News Year's Day—saw them on the table for Rosh Hashanah—I didn't know non-Black people ate this. I was like, oh my G-d!"

"What impressed you about food in Israel?" I ask.

"Israeli food—*salatim*—salads were a big influence. I always have liked vegetables—granted, they weren't a huge part of my diet. But when I got to Israel, the vegetables actually tasted like something. I make a lot of my own hummus or falafel im basar—with the cooked meat and chopped vegetable salad on top. Kurdish hot cheese pastry with sweet and savory cheese is one of my favorite dishes and, of course, Israeli pickles. And I love olives. Israeli salad—cucumbers, onions, tomatoes—is something I make every day in the summer now. Tabbouleh is fantastic, and I am an expert dolma maker."

"Your Syrian roots are showing!" I say.

"Trust me, I know!" he says. "I introduced Israelis to real macaroni and cheese, the Black way! I gave the recipe to a friend from a village in the north of Israel, and he loved it and gave the recipe to his mother, and now the whole family loves it. And at the same time, I was introduced to Yerushalmi Kugel [a sweet and savory noodle pudding with black pepper], taddig [Persian crunchy rice], and lentils; you can do so many things with lentils.

"Za'atar, sumaq, cardamom, a lot of cinnamon—almost exclusively in a savory way—became part of my spice cabinet in St. Louis and Jerusalem. I consume way more fresh parsley than I ever did before, mostly because I eat Israeli salad for breakfast. I buy five or six bunches. I love amba [hot pickled mango from Indian-Iraqi Jews] and silan—date syrup."

"What do you want people to know about being Black and Jewish?" I ask.

"That our identities are as diverse, multifaceted, and complex as any other group. In my experience, I am constantly juggling different aspects of myself—which hat can I wear at any given moment. More than anything, we just want to exist and walk through the world without having to explain or justify who we are. There is so much richness in our cultures. It's not a monolith on either side, especially at my table."

Shais Rishon: Orthodox Black Rabbi

Full transparency: Shais Rishon, who goes by the name MaNishtana on social media, is my distant cousin, something we found out in the aftermath of my book *The Cooking Gene*. He is part of a nexus of related families from the Orthodox community of Brooklyn, Black families that trace their roots back generations and who have most recently been part of the Hasidic world. Shais is the author of some very good books, including *Thoughts from a Unicorn: 100% Black. 100% Jewish. 0% Safe.* (2012) and *Ariel Samson: Freelance Rabbi* (2018), which was nominated for the National Jewish Book Award. Both books go deep on Black Orthodox Jewish identity and the ways in which other Jews of color navigate their identity Maginot lines. Are you an Uncle Tevye or Menachem X or somewhere in between? Do you go Black-shenazi, MENA and use q's for k's, or are you an Afrocentric Black Jew? Using a blend of real-world observation and satire, Shais tells it as he sees it.

Shais does not soften his words. He self-identifies as "*minhag fluid*," but much of his practice is a mix of Ashkenazi and Nusach Sephard—the customs associated with most Hasidic groups, including Chabad. His Black and Jewish wife has mixed origins, partly German Jewish, and he jokes, "She's a Yekki!" He walks a fine line between being a translator and a firebrand:

"Look, the most important thing about us Black Jews is not how we got here or why we're here. It's that we ask Jewish questions and make Jewish decisions, and live Jewish lives. Those are the things that people don't want to address because it forces them to think of us as Jews—not Black Jews, Jews. We can show up in full Jewniform— *kippa, tallis,* beard—and people don't get that we're not cosplaying. I mean, Ron Jeremy riding a pig and eating a ham sandwich on matzoh on Yom Kippur gets a pass, but here you are—checking our papers like its 1860."

He continues: "Growing up in a Black Jewish Orthodox Chabad family in Crown Heights, Brooklyn, in the late '80s and '90s was, to quote one of my many least favorite Dickens novels, the best of times and the worst of times. A constant tsunami that washed over us in ebbs and flows of waves of presumed conflicted identity that drowned even some of the best of us in its floodwaters.

"Though those storms were frequently just as often tumultuous as calm, what navigated my siblings and me through many of them was my mother's cooking, with a specific warm spot for me being her Shabbat spaghetti and meatballs recipe. It was almost always the go-to meal for Friday nights. This staple was quick and easy enough to make in time for those early winter sunsets, filling enough to satiate a family of seven and somehow *still* having leftovers sufficient for a light lunch the following Sunday afternoon and maybe even later. And no cheese on that spaghetti, because the Torah prohibits the eating of dairy and meat in the same meal, so much so that after eating a meat meal, one has to wait a whopping six hours before eating a dairy one! Or three hours for German Jews. Or an hour for Dutch Jews. Of course, Judaism is full of all kinds of rules and minutiae around food."

He continues, "Kosher isn't just some magical thing that means a rabbi blessed something, and it has nothing to do with health benefits. Kosher means if you're eating a land animal, it has to have split hooves and chew its cud. (Sorry bacon, but pigs don't chew their cud!) It means seafood has to have both fins and scales. (Sorry shrimp, but you're the cockroaches of the sea! Also, you don't have fins or scales.) It means knowing that fruits, vegetables, nuts, and seeds are all inherently kosher in their natural, unprocessed forms. And if you're Yemenite, it means you still remember how to identify which types of locusts are considered kosher by checking the underside of their thorax for a marking that suspiciously resembles the Hebrew letter *chet* (ח).

Shais continues: "And *then* there's the juggernaut known as Passover that kicks regular kosher rules into overdrive and for eight days Jews don't eat *chametz*—anything with grain that has risen or fermented or contains any other leavening agent. I know! It's a lot, right? I mean there's people out there whose diets are composed solely of organic dew-fed unicorn tears and charcoal-activated motes of light, so no, not really."

If that didn't wake you up, this will. Shais famously compiled an image in the aftermath of the summer of protests surrounding the murders of Brianna Taylor, Ahmad Aubrey, and most vibrantly,

George Floyd. The image was challenging—a figure of a Klansman in a black-and-white *tallit* surrounded by brutally racist comments, all of which came from major organizations and social media posts.

"Nothing was interpolated," Shais says. "Most of them were around George Floyd. I wanted to have more than the comments about George Floyd, but I didn't have the patience. I'm pretty sure the same number of people who say they are being targeted for anti-Semitism would say that police aren't targeting Blacks and there's no structural racism or that Black people were permanently disadvantaged by *choice*. But putting a mirror to people who think their truth is the only truth is what our Ancestors did, every year, every generation; *l'dor v'dor*, it's just that it's our turn now."

The image had no face, just a hood—the anonymity and lack of empathy made it more sinister. Some people cheered; others were appalled. How dare he? People wrongly claimed that there was no discussion of phenotype or ethnicity in Jewish texts. Others pushed further, claiming that Shais had to prove that he was really Jewish and not just a *ger*, or stranger. Some people were only tangentially Jewishly literate and demanded to see the papers of a Black man raised in Judaism who had a *smicha* (rabbinic ordination) and was the product of Orthodox schools. Shais has memories of the 1991 riots in Crown Heights, so this pushback didn't faze him. "Now, I'm not sure if I mentioned yet the fact that I am an African American Orthodox Jew," he says, "and thus a veritable cornucopia of racial, social, religious, and generational trauma, so I'm good."

I ask him, "What do we make of our history? Our story is fragmented; it's all over the place."

Shais begins with a clearing of his throat and a laugh. "The history is and isn't important to us. We are who we are—we know where we come from—and things are what they are. That's it. Some of us can attach ourselves to lineages and stories within mainstream Ashkenormative or Sephardi or Mizrahi communities, others are outside of those. Some of us need to have that line to show to the rest of Judaism that we are as valid as they are. But, we are here now, and we are who we are now. We don't have to obsess over it and prove it to others.

"Look, the Maggid of Mezeritch—his mother was upset, his *yichus* [family tree or pedigree] was destroyed. He said, 'Don't worry, I'm going to start a new line, a new thing.' We need to establish this new line; we are going to write our own story. We know where we come from and what we were told in our families; now it's time for us to do our thing. We never had a chance to make a stand and say this is what we are, and we've been MacGyvering. We didn't have a place of strength to define ourselves; now we do.

"Speaking of George Floyd, speaking of law enforcement over-reach and Black Lives Matter, Black American Jewish history starts something like this. The 'Mulata Jue,' *J-U-E*—they couldn't even spell it right—'Solomon,' is detained by the constable in around 1668 for traveling and profaning the Christian Sabbath. Of course, he's not traveling on HIS Sabbath. Solomon Franco, the 'Mulatto Jew,' and his first record on these shores is a police report."

Solomon Franco was, in many ways, our Kunta Kinte. Shais continues: "There's this constant thing, right?—being tested to prove our authenticity and validity. What brings you here? There's the assumption you're the stranger. And it's like no, *chaver*, welcome to MY shul, what brings YOU here? I've been here for fifteen years; you're the stranger, not me. I'm the *frum* from birth; you're the newbie, don't ask me what brings ME here."

Shais is not angry; he's just intolerant of bullshit. It's exhausting not being able to feel any sort of respect from our coreligionists because of agendas that compete with the observance of basic Torah-based ethics about how to treat others. At the same time, there is a less vibrant but disturbing prejudice and suspicion about Black Jews among Black folks. Shais's irreverence, using humor as a shield, comes in handy. "I was at a bus station in Brooklyn," he says, "and a sister had a twelve-piece and offered me some; I couldn't eat it, and

I politely declined, and she looked me up and down as if to say, 'It's only chicken, motherfucker!'"

I ask: "Speaking of chicken, please explain kosher jerk chicken in Crown Heights."

Shais answers: "I mean, the one thing about Chabad is that it's an international movement. You have people coming in from all over the world, and because of *kiruv* [outreach], you have a culture that absorbs people who have a taste for something beyond the usual. It's people who haven't spent their whole lives in Chassidus and those who are in other places who are bringing *kashrut* to another part of the globe. It's great because before, it was, like, 'Jewish.' It was Diaspora food with no pork, twice the salt, and half the flavor. I can take my daughter out for a barbecue now, which is great because we're nowhere near North Carolina."

I chime in, "It's also just because you have West Indian, Caribbean culture side by side with Hasidic Jewish culture. I mean, I've seen it and heard it. Kids sing songs about Moshiach [the Messiah] that kind of sound like Rastafarian."

"To be fair, we did take 'If I Were a Rich Man.'"

"Gwen Stefani is we, Shais?"

"Naw, Negro, the better question is who is we?"

And like every good Jewish conversation the circle was complete.

Mayseh:
"GET IN!"

I was standing in the rain on a corner in Rockville, Maryland. The eve of Pesach was approaching, and I was rushing to get everything done. My umbrella had holes in it. Every dime was going toward Pesach with its prohibitions against *chametz*. I was going to cash a check, and the bus was late.

The longer I stood, the wetter I and the check got. I was wearing my *tzitzit* and a *kippa*. Three metro buses should have shown up, but none arrived. My *kippa* started dripping. I was pity made person.

Then a car pulled up: four young North African Israelis. "*Chaver*! Get in!" After a lifetime of being told not to get into a car full of strangers, I totally did. They greeted me in halting English, and I paid my respects back in halting Hebrew. They were not religious and said as much. They asked me where I needed to go, and I replied, "The bank." Smiles were exchanged, and seven minutes later, I was at the door of the bank.

"Do you need to go anywhere else?" they asked. I told them, "No, I'll be okay."

Every single one shook my hand and warmly wished me *Chag Sameach*, a happy holiday.

For roughly eight minutes of my life, for the first time ever, I did not feel suspicious or scary or dangerous or bizarre or exotic by association . . . I was just someone that was a part of something bigger, holier, sweet.

I suppose this would seem like nothing to most people except for the fact that I live in a society that has always made me feel just on the other side of unwanted and contagious. Contagiously Black, contagiously fat, contagiously gay, and, if I am honest about my experiences over the past twenty years, many times contagiously Jewish. Whatever the rejected thing is, it has its own lore of being unacceptable and disease-like. The rejection of the things I carry is the rejection of me. People resist my praises for including me, but there is deep pain in being left out and rejected just for being.

For me, that means a lifetime of clutched purses, people crossing the street to walk the same direction, assumptions of ignorance and poverty, false accusations of crudeness, rejected hellos and smiles, unacknowledged door openings, and heavy suspicion.

The Jews—we don't always stick together, but when we do, it is a marvel to the other tribes we share this planet with. Why do we care about each other so much? Being a family, a people, a tribe, or part of a "covenant" doesn't quite explain it. It's the Apple store employee who helped me get a new iPod to play in Hebrew school when my own was damaged. It's the older lady volunteering to help manage the vaccination line who talked to me using our code words and a smile. These people tell stories of gratitude through tears when something I've said in a speech reminds them about their relationship with Judaism or G-d. The answer isn't something that words can resolve. The answer is a look I can't explain, a sigh that endures across time.

I am never alone if I have my people.

Mayseh:

THE WORLD'S NICEST WHITE LADY

The most crowded metro line in the DC area is always the Red Line, which goes through the heart of Washington and bonds the two sides of the Maryland suburbs. You get your seat as early as possible, and you cling to it lest anything go awry. It's a contested urban transportation space. People go into their shells; they don't talk. Work is bad enough, so nobody smiles or makes small talk outside of their bubble.

That day I was on the train reading the book of Psalms—Tehillim—*kippa* on my head, *tzitzit* overflowing on the seat. One man got up and left after Dupont Circle, and a woman sat down in his place. She glanced over and saw the big, bold Hebrew print, a version of the square Assyrian font. Unlike most conversations where people are surprised I read Hebrew, she leaned over and said, "I love to read Tehillim too!"

I wasn't asked to qualify anything, and that alone made me smile. I smiled even wider because not only did she know that I knew what I was doing, but she was prepared to have a conversation with me as an equal. "What shul do you go to? I go to B'nai Israel. My name is . . ."

This was the dream—she presented her Jewish journey first before prying me open as someone to be vetted or tested. When we arrived at White Flint station, I politely suggested that I should excuse myself, but she was going there herself.

"Do you need a ride?"

"I wouldn't mind one!"

The world's nicest white lady, a fellow Jew, gave me a ride to the shul. I saw her maybe twice after that, once at my main Hebrew school job. I never had the opportunity to tell her just how profound this was for me after a lifetime of people walking faster, avoiding me on elevators, dismissing my "Shabbat Shalom" at services with a "Same to you" or "Thanks" (read Thx). It was an entire lifetime of distrust not completely abated but slightly curtailed in favor of the moment or occasion when someone not like me might take a chance on me just being human.

But this is the thing: she didn't have to read me as Jewish; she didn't read me as someone she might have a friendly conversation with or as someone she shared her immediate community with. Yet there was the feeling that I didn't and still don't get to have regularly—we share the world with people, we hope we will keep a certain social contract that allows us to be vulnerable, available, and possible. Because she gave me that opportunity, I have faith that I can give that opportunity to others. It is a privilege to show up in that quiet little space fully, safely me: Black, gay, Jewish, Southern, American, human.

Part III

NESHAMAH:
A SOUL SUITE

9

LEARNING

Everybody asks, "Why Judaism?"

I needed a place where learning and relearning were compulsory parts of spiritual and everyday practice. I adored the obsession with getting it right; and a love of books, interpretation, and reinterpretation of scripture and texts that took the role of scripture was a habit that would live with me until I was no longer alive. For years I was teased for always being accompanied by an armful or two of books and questioned about my real intentions, as if reading were still illegal for a Black person. Having spent most of my lifetime defending my love of words and books and ideas, I found a home with a people with whom I didn't have to spend so much energy explaining why an idea occupied so much space in my mind that I had to go over it again and again until it had nothing else to say. I just wanted to be a passionate learner and be respected as the messy and overstimulated autodidact I grew up to be.

I still had to fight to prove my legitimacy—as an outsider, a Black person, and a young man with roots but no Jewish foundations—but the challenge was irresistible. It changed my life. I found myself in spaces where I saw a different me respected for my curiosity, not condemned because of my mistakes; where I was encouraged to climb, not disparaged when I fell. Jewish learning emphasized character refinement and straightening one's path, not living sainthood or piety for piety's sake. I discovered for myself everything from Jewish mysticism to *mussar*—the effort of character and ethical improvement; the goal was not being perfect but perfecting, and I had to do my best to do the least possible harm to others and reflect and judge myself each day.

The sages say that if you change your place, you change your fate. One of the many names of G-d is the nickname Ha-Makom, "The Place." My Hebrew name became Akiba Ben Avraham v'Sara. Akiba, the son of converts, was a man who began to study in middle age and became a rabbi of such great spiritual and intellectual stature that the rabbis imagined Moses the Lawgiver himself wishing to have Akiba take his place in Jewish history. I liked the stories of Akiba, an illiterate shepherd and devoted family man who witnessed water wearing down rock in the river, the way he conceived Torah wearing down hardness in his soul.

Yom Kippur

On my first Yom Kippur after the *mikveh*, I bought white sneakers for the first time, my first white shoes. On Yom Kippur, you don't eat, wear leather, bathe for pleasure, drink, or engage in work. It is a day of prayer and reflection and reading the Torah passages about the festival and ethical laws. The Torah is traditionally walked around the shul while people at worship kiss and honor the source of their connection with G-d. While Ashkenazim tradition-ally keep the Torah scrolls in cloth wrapping, the Sephardic way uses the *tik*—the heavy metal or wooden containers that take great strength to carry in the procession.

When it came time to divide up the honors for the carrying of the Torah scroll, I watched as the silver *tik* was brought out, gleaming, the *rimmonim*, or bells, atop it making a sound sweeter than wind chimes. I pulled up the corner of my *tallit* to kiss the scrolls as they passed by me. And then, one gentleman gave the silver *tik*, an honor given to him, to me. It was extremely heavy, but I didn't feel a pound. As we made the *hakafah*, or procession, the truth began to melt down my face—as they say among the Dagara in West Africa—and I carried the Torah with a face covered in tears. The entire synagogue, from women to men, was bawling too, and every child I taught gathered around me and held up my *tallit* until I reached the Ark.

The *mikveh* felt like a formality, but this was the moment I was transformed. This was me making my peace with G-d, and all of my sins and mistakes vanished with every step. There I was in front of the Ark, facing the holy city of Yerushalayim, and I had my own private audience with G-d. I became something anew—not something perfect.

My favorite name of G-d is the "Healer of the Broken Hearted," and here I was broken but now made whole. I felt all of the pieces of myself coming together, and things that hurt really bad—like being told I was the oddball of my family or the moment my uncle cursed me and told me that I wasn't going to make it—those things didn't matter anymore. I belonged to the Lord G-d of Israel, and on the day when no food or drink crossed my lips, I became at one on the Day of Atonement.

Shabbat

"The Jews don't just keep Shabbat; Shabbat keeps the Jews . . ."

In the past twenty years, I have striven to make my material culture align with the intersections I represent. The *kippa* can be round and knit from Uganda, kente-aesthetic style from Ghana, or a special one made by an artist friend, on which the likenesses of James Baldwin, Zora Neale Hurston, Audre Lorde, Jackie Robinson, and other Ancestors accompany me into the day of rest. The challah covers are from Sefwi Wiawso, a Jewish community in Ghana—the land of many of my Ancestors. The *kiddush* cup, also by a Ghanaian artist, is emblazoned with *sankofa*—the symbol of returning to one's culture and history to move forward into the future. The concept of *hiddur mitzvah*—or beautifying how one practices and honors the laws and customs through curating one's surroundings—is at once Jewish and Afrocentric in my home.

Preparing for Shabbat was self-care to me before I knew what self-care was. I had never had an excuse to push myself to be punctual or organize things or practice the combination of time management and planning that accomplished anything practical or meaningful. Shabbat changed that. I had to begin to think days in advance and even organize my diet and menu planning around the key meal of the week—Shabbat dinner and the meals meant for Shabbat lunch and the third meal, *Seudah Shl'shit*.

The menu always varies, but I try to mix things up Afro-Ashkefardi style by making sure my kitchen smells somewhere between the diasporas, and the dining room table becomes the place where people meet everything that I am and have to confront it through taste.

Shabbat is a reminder to have respect for the people of the past for whom no respite might be given. It is a reminder never to return to those days of constant grind, of forever labor. It is to have in mind at once the enslaved and the serf and the peasant. I swear there is a newfound excitement in getting ready to meet G-d, the kind my grandmother had getting ready for a Sunday or a celebration where even the mundane tasks leading up to the gleam were part of the pomp and circumstance. I never understood what she felt as she pressed those rags into my hand; I wanted only the good part—the party, the meal, the chance to show off the new clothes. The sweetness was in the mind, acknowledging that time set apart was more important than things.

If I Were a Seder Plate

Passover is known in Hebrew as Pesach. It refers to an event thirty-five hundred years ago when Jews believe G-d sent Moses and his brother Aaron to liberate their Ancestors, the Israelites, from several hundred years of bondage to the Egyptian Empire. The presence of the Lord and his angel "passed over" the homes of the Israelites as they brought plagues and slayed the firstborn of Egypt. Then Pharaoh heard the cry of Moses, "Let my people go." Pesach literally means open mouth. When you see injustice, you have to open your mouth and scream—how fitting, given some of our recent politics.

Passover is a spring holiday and always falls after the spring equinox, but it does not occur at the same time every year. In ancient Israel, new grain crops, the steady maturing of the lambs, and the appearance of spring greenery and herbage symbolized the renewal of nature. Once liberated from Egypt and settled in the land of Canaan, the Israelites were instructed to teach their children from generation to generation about the miracles the Lord performed for their Ancestors in Egypt through a ritual that is now known as the "seder" (the order). When the Temple stood in Jerusalem (where the Western Wall still stands), thousands of people would journey there each spring and offer a lamb in sacrifice to G-d, and the lamb would be roasted and eaten with bitter spring herbs, called *merorim*, and matzoh—the hardtack of slavery—the flat, unleavened bread of the poor and downtrodden. After the Temple was destroyed, the ritual fully morphed into its rabbinic form; in a ritual based on biblical passages and oral tradition as well as aspects of Greco-Roman culture, the modern seder was born with its seder plate, four cups of wine, and symbolic reminders of the Temple sacrifices and biblical references.

Five to six symbols are found on every seder plate. Parsley, onion, potato, or celery usually represent the *karpas*—the spring vegetable and appetizer dipped in saltwater reminiscent of the tears of the enslaved. Suppose you are from a Sephardic or Mizrahi homecoming from those countries around the Middle East and Mediterranean basin. In that case, you might use lemon juice or balsamic vinegar to represent the bitterness of slavery. The *beitzah*, or egg, represents cycles—human and natural—and the hard-boiled nature of the Jewish people. It also is a symbol to remind us of the Temple sacrifices. The *zeroa* is the lamb shank bone, another symbol of the sacrifices. The *maror* is the bitter herb—usually horseradish or romaine lettuce. For some people, there is a second bitter/sharper herb called *chazeret*—which may be horseradish as well. Finally, the *charoset* is a combination of fruit, wine, and nuts that symbolizes the mortar made by the Israelite slaves.

The seder is a fifteen-step ritual, including a meal that leads participants through the Haggadah, a retelling of the story of the exodus from Egypt from the perspective of the rabbis living about eighteen hundred years ago. This ritual, which incorporates different elements of all the cultures Jews have encountered since the enslavement by the Egyptians, involves the fulfilling of specific biblical and rabbinic commandments passed down for thousands of years. The *Shulchan Orech*—the prepared table—is the step in the seder that many Jews look forward to the most. It's a special holiday meal made of dishes that do not have any *chametz*—which is flour, yeast, or any prepared product thereof. You are allowed only matzoh—the flat, unleavened bread made of wheat, spelt, oats, rye, or barley. Some Jews do not eat what is called *kitniyot*, or legumes, rice, corn, soy, sesame, and the like (I do eat them because I follow Sephardic customs). Why not eat *kitniyot?* Because in the old days, these things could be made into wheat flour look-alikes or might contain fragments of wheat or barley grains. Other Jews take this a step farther and do not ingest *gebrokhts*, which are foods made from matzoh, such as matzoh ball soup. These dietary restrictions last from the first seder to the close of the holiday about seven or eight days later. Most Jews outside of Israel have two seders, the first two nights. Jews in Israel usually observe only one.

Most Jews, religious and secular, observe some aspect of Passover or go to a seder. Passover, because it's a ritual oriented toward family/framily/friends and the congregation, tends to attract to the table 95 to 99 percent of all Jews to celebrate with others during this time. The seder has many cultural forms: Ethiopian, Yemenite, Indian, Afghani, Persian, Turkish, Greek, Italian, Eastern European, Spanish-Portuguese, Latin American, Southern, etc. To these, I add my own take on African American Jewish custom, including the following on my African American seder plate:

Chicken Bone: In place of the lamb shank bone, this represents traditional sacrifices and migration from oppression to opportunity during the Great Migration. This was also called "the preacher's bird."

Charoset: Traditionally made of fruit, nuts, and wine, this one is made of molasses and pecans, representing the sugarcane that fueled the beginnings of slavery and the duality of our culture in exile. Though we were in bondage, we found things in America to help us cope and overcome.

Sweet Potato: In place of the spring vegetable, traditionally parsley or potato, the sweet potato is symbolic of using the American environment to perpetuate West and Central African tradition.

Egg: The egg is a symbol of overcoming oppression and of the Supreme Being, spring, and the cycles of nature.

Collards: Bitter herbs symbolize both the bitterness of enslavement and how we survived it.

Hot Pepper: In place of horseradish, this sharper variety of *maror* is meant to give a sense of the sting of the lash. Also, it is a spice central to West and Central African foodways, proverbially associated with speaking the truth. Pepper symbolizes the hot times, and for the spice of life, we added it despite dangers and snares to represent the Wolof proverb from Senegal that "the truth is a hot pepper."

Hoecake or Ashcake: Made of corn, these cakes are the closest analog to matzoh, the flatbread of slavery, and yet the first food in freedom. This corn cake simply prepared was the hardtack of enslavement in colonial and antebellum America. (*Kitniyot* is forbidden for strict Ashkenazi Jews; matzoh may be substituted.)

Orange: This is a modern symbol for those who are often excluded from the forefront of religious communities or spiritual practice, from women in leadership to sexual minorities to the poor or differently abled. The orange symbolizes the flavor and sweetness inclusion brings us all.

Okra: These seed pods represent the African heritage and cultural intellect carried over on the Middle Passage and sustained in the Americas across the centuries.

Saltwater: This represents the tears of the enslaved and the waters of the trans-Atlantic passage.

Part IV

ERUVIM

Eruv—Mixtures and Boundaries

Eruv: *An* eruv *is a boundary, usually meant to unify a space so that objects may be carried from one place to the next, like a bag or a stroller, on Shabbat. The word has connotations of both boundary and containment and mixture and blending. Food in certain circumstances can be used to mark an* eruv *in space or in the case of an* eruv tavshilin—*marking the continued preparation of food on a holiday. The word can also mean other kinds of blending, as in* "erev rav," *the expression in the Torah for a mixed multitude leaving Egypt during the Exodus, or even the term* "erev," *for evening, meaning a mixture of night and day.*

10

PEOPLE OF THE LAND

When I met Shani Mink, cofounder and executive director of the Jewish Farmer Network, in 2019, some things became pretty clear to me about how our identities related to farming and the land were defined. African American young people are following in the footsteps of some of the pioneers of Black homesteaders and land-based civil rights and working hard to connect with a piece of our heritage that we lost connection with during the Great Migration. It wasn't just about leaving the land but being forced off of it. We became an urban people after millennia of being on the land in Africa, the Caribbean, South America, and the American South. We struggled with going back to a place that, for many, could very well be associated with oppressive times or with a time in our culture when we weren't seen as cultured or in a place where we could advance. Shani and I had a conversation, and I asked her first to talk about the parallel in a Jewish context.

SHANI: The Jewish Farmer Network was born out of an express need of the community of Jewish farmers. I grew up with a robust Jewish education and found myself in a community of agrarians. Most people who are Jewish think being Jewish and being a farmer are two opposing identities. Much like your work, our work is about combating external tropes about Jewish identity. To be Jewish is to be some sort of urban professional—a doctor, lawyer, accountant—that's the stereotype, but the Jewish tradition at its core is an agrarian tradition. The cycles of the Jewish calendar are mapped onto the cycles of agriculture. Our calendar is anchored in three harvest festivals that instruct us to rest and celebrate our work.

ME: I feel like in that reconnection in our combined and respective communities, there's a great opportunity to have an encounter with Ancestral wisdom. For me, I think there's this awesome place where intergenerational learning, a respect for nature and the forces of nature, and for some, like the fantastic Leah Penniman of Soul Fire Farm, there's an opportunity to connect this to the wisdom and traditions of African spiritual paths and Indigenous spiritual knowledge. The kids learn delayed gratification, ownership, and the importance of sharing resources with others in the community. What do you think Jewish agrarian traditions have to share with the wider community?

SHANI: The Jewish wisdom tradition conducts agriculture in such a way that it is both just and regenerative. The Jewish agricultural ethic prioritizes care for the earth, for the community, and for ourselves and the soil through sacred cycles of work and rest. It is incumbent on every Jewish farmer—it was required of ancient Jewish farmers—to set aside portions to support those in need, which includes the orphan, the widow, and the stranger, as well as institutions.

ME: So both traditions have the space for the border-crosser, the oppressed, forgotten, and marginalized. It's like the trauma is tempered by resourcefulness, but people tend to forget about that—taking care of one another—since people tend to be self-reliant. I know that many of the generations of Blacks who came north looked down on farming and a relationship with the land, not least because sharecropping was in living memory. But with that came other concerns and values and folklore and folk knowledge that was a part of our culture. What does the Jewish community have to lose in not repairing this relationship with earth-based traditions?

SHANI: Unfortunately, I feel we have a lot of Jews who have forgotten a piece of the Jewish story. They weren't taught this in a real-life context. We grew up with no Jewish farming role models; I had never seen someone doing work like this. We have these young people who are turning to this work, and the response is something like a Jewish farmer—isn't that an oxymoron? If you don't know why we practice these things, it's because they look like fables from a storybook—because they aren't being lived in context, instead of being meaningful guides for shaping your life drawn from your people's sacred literature. These traditions are foundational, like *ma'aser/eser*—which means ten, *ma'aser ani*— giving 10 percent to those who don't have. We were at Pearlstone in Maryland, at their you-pick strawberry operation, and we encouraged people to donate 10 percent of what they picked. This very religious family from Park Heights, their little boy, said, "Why are they talking about *ma'aser*?" Here we are, not the same kind of Jew, in this strange place, and I'm a woman, and he's seen this only in texts, never in a lived context.

ME: So the land helps us tell stories not only about our Ancestors but also about ourselves? I believe that's why our relationship with the land and earth is so critical for healing. I also feel like the narrative of us as Black people—not having agency and ownership and contributions and being a hardworking people who wanted all the trappings of the American dream—is born out of our extraction from the homesteads and farms we once made for our own communities. What are you doing to promote that reversal of narrative and create healing and hope?

SHANI: We are a people of the land. I see our work at the Jewish Farmer Network as a story of repair. We are reweaving, restitching the story of the Jewish people. We are undermining the anti-Semitism—particularly true of the Ashkenazi Jewish narrative. The story of Jewish weakness—that we can't do physical labor and we are weak—is part of Nazi-era anti-Jewish propaganda that we have internalized and that we then tell to our children. It becomes a self-fulfilling prophecy.

This new generation and those who came before us undermine the story of Jewish separation from the land that Ashkenazi Jews were not allowed to own. They were forced into the money-lending business because it was seen as dirty or unseemly. We were not allowed to own land, so now we have this story about who the Jewish people are that is infected by persecution and propaganda. The work of story repair is to tell the story of a people whose lives revolved around the natural cycle in intentional and deeply spiritual ways to take care of the land they stewarded, along with the people and animals and plants. We are connecting the story of the land with the Jewish people. We are letting them know they are the living legacy of Jewish people as people of the land.

ME: But even as we transitioned into the cities in ancient times, during the Greco-Roman times, we were called *am-ha-aretz*—the people of the land—which meant someone who was illiterate. This is sort of an ancient problem for us—divorced from the dignity of being farmers and pastoralists. Even for African Americans, I think there is that gaze on the people of Africa—the

Ancestors of our Ancestors—the idea that somehow they were primitive or simple or unsophisticated and the cultural genocide of slavery cut us off from what made our root culture so valuable.

SHANI: We used to enact our spirituality through our relationship with the land—physical sacrifices and offerings of crops to the table. It was only after that, when we moved en masse toward books and commentary and text, that we became detached from the specific land where those customs and laws and traditions were granted. Then because of *galut*, exile from Eretz Israel, we were not in the land that defined our seasons and traditions. So we ended up in this weird, splintered existence.

How do we do this when the seasons, when the flora and fauna, aren't there anymore? Everything in our traditions grew up in response to and in conversation with that ecosystem. We cycle through time on a schedule that was built in response to that ecosystem. Our ritual system is built on that—our shofarim from the rams of the field or antelope in the desert, our Four Species-the date palm, the myrtle, the etrog or citron and the willows that lined the Jordan—we aren't detached from the land altogether but from those practices.

ME: I think that's why the sorrow songs from Babylon were so damn pertinent to Black folks who were enslaved and their descendants. As it says in Psalm 137, "How do I sing the Lord's song in a foreign land?" Especially when our tormentors require of us mirth.

SHANI: Yeah, you carry that stuff with you, and things can fall away. And then, in conversation with Native Land folks, we have to acknowledge other deep truths. The central question of our work: to be a Jewish farmer embracing our agricultural heritage on land that isn't ours—land that was stolen from other people and on which other people were forced to work. The two original sins of America are Jewish problems in that we have to navigate those spaces and that history.

ME: How does that navigation work for you?

SHANI: G-d wrestlers. We are a G-d wrestling people. Our job is not to have all the answers to these hard questions but to hold space to wrestle with them. We are cultivating a community of question-askers who are willing to embrace the complex questions and do the work of *tzedakah*—not charity but justice; and *tikkun olam*—repairing the world. It's in our Ancestral memory, and it's in our DNA deep within us. Connecting that embodied way is so refreshing and helps us see the world in a new way.

Mayseh:
GARDENS—LANDSCAPES OF
THE THRIVING SURVIVORS

For lack of an alternative history, we have this consistent theme in Black-Jewish engagement that centers around trauma, the victimizers, cruelty, trophies, and scary dominance and shadow over our lived realities. These are not to be fully avoided. For the discussion of these to be absent is to be dishonest. And yet, purely being trauma centered and death centered often sends people the other way. For me, teaching and learning about our people's glories and joys and vibrancy is where we need to be to have balance.

Cultural gardens have been for me and my work a way and means toward healing. Gardens say a culture was not completely destroyed; many lives were taken or diminished in the Maafa, the Inquisition, pogroms, or the Shoah, but many strong elements of the cultures that suffered so much are here and present. Each plant tells a story about the peoples or individuals who shepherded the foods, medicines, or fragrances into our contemporary lives. Whether they are ornamental, medicinal, or culinary, the plants in our gardens are living mnemonic devices for ancient narratives, proverbs, riddles, and wisdom.

This is also about severed ties with lands where we originated or sojourned. For enslaved Africans and other Africans in exile, any touch or semblance of Africa could spark passionate resistance and reconnection. For Jews, the state of being in *galut*, or diasporic exile, was exacerbated by a frequent denial of access to land or title. How long a place could be home depended on how long the hosting country or kingdom allowed us to sojourn in peace. Simultaneously, the land and nature are an important part of Jewish spirituality and religious practice. Even when outside Eretz ha-Kodesh, the Holy Land, Jewish practice retained legal binds to help the people remember and pray for the well-being of their homeland's natural cycles as well as being strongly drawn into the worlds and ecosystems in which they found themselves.

Walking into a garden maintained by a specific people or collective community is like walking into someone's house and seeing their book or music collection. It's a living library belonging to someone who very long ago made choices that endured. Often, across human families, the flora that we make part of our civilizations and their products achieve the level of the sacred. People cannot imagine what their culture would be like before these seeds, barks, leaves, roots, shoots, and grains showed up. Then there's that incredible smile that rolls over someone's face when something coming out of the ground resonates and tells a story they've known all their lives in a very different way.

African traditions from across the continent (where more than two thousand indigenous species of food plants can be found) are replete with acres of knowledge about plants and their significance, and that knowledge and those traditions extended in exile to the Middle East and India, Brazil, the Caribbean, mainland Latin America, and the American South and Eastern Seaboard where much of it was transformed to fit the landscape around them. Many plants brought over from Africa were planted as food crops or as exotics by Europeans and, rarely, were smuggled in power objects or other forms. These associations and survivals were life-saving elements to Africans' interior lives and culture in the Atlantic world. Botanical cognates like persimmon trees and palms, alongside introduced crops like rice, okra, and Angola gherkin, told a different story than the narrative of a people stripped of their culture. My grandmother's cures and wild-crafting and foraging knowledge came down to me from those first Africans brought to American soil so long ago.

Much to some people's surprise, the Talmud and other rabbinic literature is full of cures, botanical references, and lists of foods grown in gardens at the time. In fact, the rabbis insist that you make sure you live in a community that has a garden. At their time, living in both the land of Israel and the Diaspora, the need to communicate the biblical dictates, such as the Four Species of Sukkot and newer glosses formed in life under Greco-Roman and Persian rule also lived alongside accrued layers of tradition from other groups with which they shared their world. The oral Torah's job, to elucidate the fine print of observance, meant having a textured and acute sense of what a "bitter herb" was or what the "goodly trees" were. The rabbinic "garden" was rich and full of onions, garlic, turnips, colocasia, dates, citrons, pomegranates, edible gourds, and black-eyed peas—the result of being at the crossroads of three continents.

For me, the culinary world sings with its own unique lessons in ethnobotany from seed to plate. Beyond the power of nature's cycles are the words, the colors, the symbolism, and the textures, scents, and taste each plant brings to the everyday and the holidays and seasons that make up our traditions. It's the taste of sage dried and blended into fresh homemade country sausage in the fall (I make mine with kosher ground turkey) or the jewel tones of compotes, sherbets, and other soft sweets in the summertime. I am not a fan of shakshuka, but I still cannot deny that it's probably fantastic with fresh tomatoes that have that fecund grassy musk from the field. The range of heirloom peppers from across the African Atlantic speaks to all the distinct languages and looks of satisfaction that tell a different story from person to person across the centuries.

There are so many human stories to tell through the gardens of the oppressed and marginalized. Here's the powerful part: pirates, rabbis, doctors, explorers, enslaved people, missionaries, scholars, soldiers, mothers, and traders moved plants across the waters and the face of the earth from place to place for a variety of reasons. Some plants even accompanied people or animals on their clothes or their fur. An eggplant that showed up in a limited area of Lithuania or a peach tree that grew and survived in the Kongo Kingdom—both can provide us windows of insight into how our global world wasn't born with us but took centuries to evolve.

In this context, we're still trying to resolve some issues in food history that put Africans and Jews at the heart of culinary and botanical dispersal. For example, the inclusion of black-eyed peas at New Year's in the American South and at the Sephardic Rosh Hashanah service—based on a text in the Babylonian Talmud, or *Bavli*—is intriguing but inconclusive. Did John de Sequeyra, a Jewish British doctor in eighteenth-century Williamsburg, introduce the tomato and break the prohibition against them long before other examples in the nineteenth century, or was it enslaved Africans living in Virginia and other parts of the American South? We know that tomatoes came to Italy partly through the immigration of Sephardic Jews and that fish and chips have a Jewish provenance as well. There is a whole culinary history to be written about the impact of the marginalized, dispossessed, and oppressed on the cuisine of the Western world and, with it, global eating.

That's why I wanted to share these thoughts about the resurrected gardens of our Ancestors. I hope that you will go further and use in your cooking some of these favorite regional heirlooms listed below. Doing so is more than just searching for authenticity or something close to it. It's about keeping the traditions inherent in making those matches alive. A big part of both cultures is knowing that someone in the past harvested the same crop, walked the produce to their humble kitchen, and had a similar need for satisfaction from the table to give some respite from the outside world and the penalties it exacted for being Black or Jewish or both.

I love to put ingredients you have to grow into the recipes I share or encourage my readers to try them using historically and culturally significant plants. Sometimes it's not about the rush to the grocery store to dig in. What if you have to think about the season you're in or the season that's coming, acknowledging prime availability or the need to practice delayed gratification or the satisfaction or disappointment that comes from working up to making something that may or not be what you wanted? That's the past—not the taste or even the ingredients list, but the wisdom behind each food or dish that endures and the lived experience around making it.

In so many ways, it's the power of both African and Jewish wisdom guiding me in that practice. Your Ancestors and their merits and their knowledge and faith are supposed to drive you in both traditions. In West and Central African spiritual wisdom, your Ancestors even eat with you—your food is more than supplication; it helps maintain the bonds of community across spiritual space. In Judaism, the foods we eat or don't recall are the narratives of historical figures past from the TaNaKh—the Torah, Prophets, and Writings. From the injured sciatic nerve of the patriarch Yaa'kov (Jacob) to the smell of fresh bread from the tent of our mother Sarah to lamb eaten with unleavened bread and bitter herbs with the gloss of rabbinic charoset, spring vegetables, and other elements of their world—history, Ancestors, and having just a small sensory impression of their world is a big part of being Jewish.

Gardens tend to bring people together. Everybody wants to help or be engaged. If nothing else, somebody somewhere wants a gorgeous, flavorful bite when things are ready to be harvested. The big key words are community, tradition, peoplehood, sharing, hospitality, generosity, and stewardship. And, if we are honest and not afraid of being vulnerable, love.

We were created to be aware of cycles. We have in us a temporal sense of the sacred and the urge to engage with nature at large. This is just a guide to get you started. I hope you will plant all of these gardens and expand on the plant lists and write down the significance of each plant, take oral histories, and ask people what they know about the relevance behind them. I hope you will discover for yourself how your own familial legacy ties in—and if you are not Black or Jewish or both, chances are that you can relate to something on this list.

If you don't have a garden or access to one, you can also be a conscious buyer at farmers' markets or international stores and shops. You can even try growing a few things on your windowsill or in pots if the seed-saving bug gets you. The most important thing is being aware of how you build up your pantry if you choose to explore heritage cooking. This is a process, so one should be patient and try a little at a time while remembering that for the people whose blessed memory fuels this work, it took millennia, but for us, we have the internet.

Another piece of advice is to refrain as much as you can from doing this work alone. Creating and maintaining a garden is meant to happen in community, to give us the opportunity to get to know one another within and outside of our various tribes. I want these gardens and the recipes I share to bring together people who might not have otherwise had the opportunity to grow food or eat with one another. Whether we know it or not, we share a lot of our food culture right now and should treat the matter as such. We are a Venn diagram of personal and individual and tribal and global. We can and should preserve the memory and conversations of our relationships with certain foods and plants because it is a sacred part of who we are as ethnicities, peoples, and seekers. At the same time, we must remember this planet has always been for us a shared space; a remarkable amount of mixing in love and war and peaceful trade means there are cross-cultural stories to be told.

You can use the following list of plants to create a garden to make the traditional foods of the cultures discussed in this book. I want you to provision your kitchen literally from the ground up. Each one of these plants carries narratives that link us with our Ancestors. Keeping them alive keeps the links to our past alive and provides nourishment for future generations.

As you create your garden, keep a notebook and write down things you learn along the way. Investigate each plant—where it comes from and how it relates to the people discussed here and beyond. Think about its sojourn with your family and have an ongoing conversation about the people you share it all with. Whatever else you do, have reverence for this journey and, even more so, for the earth from which we bring forth bread.

Ashkenazi Garden

Feher Ozon Paprika Pepper (Hungary)

Ha Ogen Melon (Hungary)

Red Kalibos Cabbage (Eastern Europe)

Russian Pickling Cucumber

Russian Banana Fingerling Potato

Hungarian Blue Breadseed Poppy

Turga Parsnip (Hungary)

Crosby Egyptian Beet (Germany)

Round Tropea Onions

Taiwan Flat Cabbage or KY Cross Cabbage

White Wing Onion

German Extra Hardy Garlic

Large Smooth Prague Celeriac

Purple Top White Globe Turnip

Amber Globe Turnip

Horseradish

White Icicle Radish
Yukon Gold Potato
Scarlet Nantes Carrots
Dill, Parsley, Thyme, Tarragon, Chervil, Savory, Marjoram, Caraway

Sephardi Garden

Lebanese Za'atar
Maloukhia
Tomatoes: Homs II, Turkish Ayla, Crnkovic Yugoslavian
Spotted Aleppo Lettuce
Peppers: Aci Kil (Turkey; for salads), Kandil (Turkey; for stuffing),
   Haskorea (Syria), Bulgarian Carrot Pepper
Ayse Kadin String Bean (Turkey)
Homs Kousa Summer Squash (Syria)
Kandahar Pendi Okra
Homs Landrace Watermelon
Eggplant: Badenjan Sesame, Rosa Bianca, Topak Adana (Turkey)
Ali Baba Watermelon (Iraq)
Yellow Onion of Parma (Italy)
Swiss Chard
Meram Cucumber
Chesnok Red Garlic (Georgia)
Muscade Carrot (North Africa)
Italian Flat-Leaf Parsley
Cilantro and Coriander Seeds from Cilantro
Sesame
Basil, Dill, Oregano, Chives, Mint

African American Garden

Fish Pepper
Long Red Cayenne Pepper

Sesame (Benne)

Cowhorn and Chopee Okra

Mirliton or Chayote

Sea Island Red Field Pea

Grey Crowder Cowpea

Kentucky Wonder Pole Bean

Green Glaze and Georgia Collard Greens

Early Flat Dutch Cabbage

Tomatoes: Large Red, Aunt Lou's Underground, Plate de Haiti

Carolina African Runner Peanut

Virginia Gourdseed Corn

Pearl Millet

Coral Sorghum

Sugar Drip Sorghum

Louisiana Long Green and White Beauty Eggplant

Seven Top Turnip Greens

Elephant Ear

Squash: Cushaw, White Pattypan, Yellow Crookneck, Upper Ground Sweet Potato Squash

West India Burr Gherkin

Rice

Sweet Potatoes: White Hayman, Georgia Jet, Beauregard, Japanese

Georgia Rattlesnake and Nancy Watermelon

Anne Arundel Muskmelon

Callaloo Greens

Scotch Bonnet Pepper

Basil, Thyme, Sage, Rosemary, Mustard, Horseradish, Chervil, Coriander, Parsley, Mint

11

KESHET

*K*eshet means "rainbow" in Hebrew.

Being Jewish and queer means my Ancestors include Harvey Milk and Larry Kramer and Leslie Feinberg. They join Audre Lorde, James Baldwin, Sylvester, Bayard Rustin, and Marsha Johnson.

I am fortunate to have so much to draw on to create myself as a queer Jewish man of color. I know some people may not stomach that or comprehend it, but it's me. I've resisted writing this sliver of this book because I'm still terrified of what people may say about me or do to me even though I've been openly gay since I was sixteen. Sometimes it doesn't come up, but when it does, the words "I'm gay" come out just as I did many years ago. I won't lie to you; this is also who I am.

American Jewish culture is, for the most part, a very accepting place for queer people. Still, I'm not sure I have the space here to break down the comparable energies of African American/African Atlantic queerness and American Jewish queerness. I need to work on that. It's not the accuracy of what I say that concerns me as the need to ask the right questions. I'm just beginning to understand that journey. I want to be led down the most helpful paths that illuminate the pathways and brighten the blueprint for others in any part of the Venn diagram, especially in the kitchen.

I'm still trying to understand this. Until then, I'll keep looking at the rainbow and others for inspiration.

Mayseh:

PURPLE VELVET

Being a non-Hasidic Jew in Chabad territory in Crown Heights, Brooklyn, on Shabb(os) is quite the experience, especially if you are Black. I sat with the old gents in the back, including my host, an affable and seemingly open guy. A part of me felt honored to sit around their table. In many ways, the whole experience had an anthropological feel; there was a constant grumble and disorder. Someone praying loudly half a line ahead and someone praying softly two lines back shared the same airspace and then came spitting on the floor during the prayer, *Aleinu*—a custom I had never seen before or since. The women could barely be seen from their *mechitzah* on the second floor, and the two factions in Chabad life— those who see the Rebbe as the Moshiach, the Messiah, and those who do not—seemed to vie for attention and authority.

There is a pot of the traditional stew cholent at the front entrance of the main sanctuary of the Chabad synagogue at 770 Eastern Parkway in Crown Heights. Since ancient times, Shabbat has been honored by followers of the oral tradition, that is, rabbinic Judaism, by "making a delight" of Shabbat by having a hot stew ready for the

Saturday midday meal. Cooking is forbidden on Shabbat, so having a hot meal ready signified making Shabbat a delight, especially to followers of other forms of Judaism who adhered only to the written tradition and assumed that no hot food was to be consumed on Saturday until the conclusion of Shabbat. During the second half of the service, a steady stream of yeshivah *bochers* (unmarried young men studying in the community) streamed in to enjoy a bowl and continue their wanderings. The cholent pot was not open just to the community but to Black folks who needed food as well. As the Haggadah says, "Let all who are hungry come and eat," including the stranger.

All of this ritual Sturm und Drang stopped when a visiting cantor arrived at 770 to sing the *musaf*, the additional service on Shabbat mornings. Everyone shut up. The man's voice was operatic and full of Ashkenazi *s*'s instead of *t*'s, and *o*'s instead of *ah*'s. It was like the croonings of Yossele Rosenblatt, one of the first recorded masters of traditional cantorial art brought from Europe. This was equivalent to famous Sister So-and-So's solo at a Black church.

Twenty minutes earlier, I had been inundated with statements made to make me feel welcome. Such as: "You know, the Rebbe had a colored maid, and he was very, very kind to her." Even better: "It doesn't matter if you're white or colored like you; being a Jew is what is important."

Oh, boy. I was caught between laughing and screaming, but logos got the better of pathos, and I kept my mouth as shut as a locked *tzedakah* box. They were trying to be nice, and if not that, they were reminding themselves to make room for me as their guest. It was better than the alternative.

I felt every bit the stranger and yet at home. My host referred to me only by my Hebrew name, something that rarely happens, and with very little prompting, handshakes were given with a *shkoyach* (congrats) for a davening well done. Apparently, they were impressed by my attention to the mitzvot and *minhagim* (the laws and customs) of prayer, including *kavvanah*—a value deeply held by

Hasidim. *Kavvanah* is praying with the utmost concentration and intention, entering a state known as *devekus*—in which one is so enraptured that one is seen as being literally glued (the root of *devekus* is *devek*, Hebrew for glue) to the presence of Almighty G-d. Given the seeming lack of *kavvanah* around me, I was a bit chuffed that I was the role model for the day.

Occasionally, little boys and girls would glare at me until they were shoved away. I was not shocked by that. They are surrounded by Black people most of the time. Blackness was not the surprise, but being a non-Hasidic Jewish Black was. For quite some time, there has been a trickle, not a flood, of Black and Brown Hasidim. Despite racism within the community, nobody can deny that in the more open movements of Hasidic Judaism, which would most certainly be Chabad, with its penchant for outreach, people of color can be Hasidim as well.

Although I was never able to meet or talk to him, I tried to track down Rabbi Yisroel Francis for many years. I remember the night—September 10, 2001—I spoke to his lovely wife, Rebbetzin Francis, and her oldest son. Rabbi Francis and his family are one of a minority of Black families with a multigenerational history within Chabad. His wife is Jamaican, and his family was from Curaçao. Both were born and raised Jewish with Sephardic and Ashkenazi roots going back generations and the blood of exiled, enslaved Africans. Rabbi Francis's son told me his father was not likely to call me back because "these calls are a dime a dozen," and, trying not to be dismissive, he told me I was better off seeking information somewhere else.

That chat might have changed my life. I had been talking to Black rabbis from across the country, including Chaim Frazer, who was able to give me about an hour of his time. Rabbi Frazer famously said during one dialogue that he was Black but no longer African American.

"When I said that," he explained, "I meant I was no longer a clear and visible member of the African American culture." In the world of Rabbi Frazer, the Litvakish (non-Hasidic) Orthodox community's piety and practice manifest in strict but less visible ways than in the Hasidic and other Haredi or religious communities. There isn't much room for fusion.

Despite my devotion to being Tevye with a Tan, keeping my balance like a fiddler on the roof, I had respect for Rabbi Frazer, who told me, "You can't have a conversion without a conversion." For him, it was about leaving one life path and embracing another, but from the perspective of a life shaped by the Torah.

"My children once had a report due in Jewish Day School about the Trail of Tears and slavery," he said, "and because their grandmother was of both Black and Native extraction, they were able to include that in their report." Outside of that and a few more anecdotes, the Frazers were not a Black Jewish family in the sense of being a different, sovereign identity.

Rabbi Francis's conversation with me might have been a "dime a dozen" to his son, but to me it represented an affirmation of not being so strange, so outside, so foreign. Apart from a drift from Shearith Israel (the oldest Sephardic [and Jewish] congregation in Manhattan) to 770 Eastern Parkway, the Francis family had an important story to tell. I could discern that the fantastic creolizations that may have become layered over the centuries were part of their story that was buried under some of the corporate spiritual culture of Chabad. And despite all of this—and a prominent role in discussing matters of color in Chabad media—many in the community were still confused about Rabbi Francis's origins. Several people in the community referred to his family as *geirim*, converts/strangers, even though they had a *yichus*, or pedigree, going back to the colonization of the Caribbean and the Middle Ages.

Stranger. I wondered whether the real stranger was the Blackness that Rabbi Francis despaired of speaking about, and that Rabbi Frazer exchanged for a life of Black Hat school Torah. I lost no respect for either man, but those conversations and my visit to the village did form me and my perspective for life. No matter how devoted I was to

Judaism, my aesthetic, my food, my style, I had to confess Blackness, deep African roots. These figures were demonstrating not shame, but rather a resolved commitment to the community around them that otherwise might not agree with or understand the blending of selves and cultures even though, quiet as it is kept, that has been the life-blood of the survival of Judaism for centuries.

Stranger. As all of the thoughts in my head came together, in walked another kind of stranger, very different from me and yet quite the same. In my own way, I had tucked away parts of my identity from this crowd. This was not the place to be gay or to talk gay liberation. Nobody says that I was the only gay in the village, but if they are there, they are not a vocal plurality. The Hasidic way is the joy of sex and love in cis-heterosexual marriage, modestly practiced with children serving G-d as proof of a blessing responsibly enjoyed.

The stranger appeared out of nowhere. He was in his early twenties and quaintly beautiful. He was wearing a deep purple velvet coat, black breeches and white opaque tights, old-style shoes, and a head covering called a *streimel*, a circular hat rimmed in foxtails, typically worn by married men, but clearly, he was not married. His fingers were ringless, his face looked powdery, his lips looked redder than they should be, his sidelocks were long and not only curly but bouncy and shaped by curlers like Shirley Temple's curls. The stranger's hands were manicured.

My, my, my, I found a sister . . . I thought.

"The *faygeleh* is here," one of the *alter kakers* whispered, nudging another. Frowns spread. Of all the *bochurs* in Crown Heights, he had to come to my table. I'm sure this was way too much for the old gents, me and this one, and had they known my T, I'm sure it would have been explosive, two hundred steps beyond mind-blowing. The stranger paid me no attention. Like the Black Chabadniks, a part of me was desperate to talk to him about how—he—survived—here.

The queerest thing about him was not the fact he had on makeup or wore tights. It was that his chosen otherness was going deep inside the Hasidic ideal—to preserve the distinctive dress and to live within the realm of the Ancestors—by dressing like a Hasid of, say, eighteenth-century Poland with a healthy dose of dandy. He was not in the standard uniform of Chabad or any other Hasidic sect, solidly black and white. He was not, as they say in Israel of the Haredim, "a penguin." He was completely, sartorially subversive, and he spent what little ostentation he could muster to be seen in the drag of his choosing. The anti-gay slurs around the table seemed to fall on deaf ears, and whatever his business, the table seemed much happier when he went away.

"Who was that?" I asked.

"Just some fairy," one of the men replied.

I understood them; I understood *him*. Like any number of cloistered religious communities, they used reproduction and idealized marriage to perpetuate a way of life. He was the outlier, the stranger born in every generation and in every community, who personally had to see his way out of the *mitzrayim*, the narrow place into which he had been born. He was not ready to leave it all behind, and because I never saw him again, I don't know whether he stayed or left. Many have left; a few have stayed and married and hidden themselves to tragic consequences; others have made quiet spaces within the Hasidic underground for networks of lovers and friends.

And off he went, each step incurring another side-eye as he went to the cholent pot to spoon out some potatoes and beans and a chunk of fatty flanken, hungrily wolfing it down with drops of reddish-brown gravy dribbling into his beard and one staining his shirt. He probably did not have a stable home or source of food, like many of the young men who come to study or sojourn here. He was gay, committed to Orthodox Judaism and Hasidic culture, but still different and unwilling to sacrifice camp and queer flair for anyone. The (Black) rabbis made more sense now; I could see there was a price to pay to be in this world and show all your true colors.

Mayseh:
THE LETTER I ALWAYS
WANTED TO WRITE

Dear Former Students Who Are LGBTQ,

It wasn't until I pretty much tapered off any teaching that I realized that I was not just shaping young Jewish lives, but young Jewish queer lives too. Inasmuch as I am proud that I made Black history and Jewish history as your teacher, I hope I made LGBTQ history as well. For those of you who did not see me come out to my seventh-grade class on the last day of my employment at the Reform temple or teach as an openly gay man after coming back to the Conservative synagogue, I am sorry I didn't have the chance to really effect change as my full self, but those are the cards we were dealt. Our community was revealed to have at least one clergy member who was unsavory and unlawful in his intentions. That made it unsafe for me, someone who does not share his behaviors, to be fully open about who I was, especially being African American. You've found out by now that sometimes it's not safe to be your full self everywhere, even in a place that promises to give you room to be expansive.

I came out when I was sixteen years old in my high school newspaper. I thought that was it, but coming out as LGBTQ is often not a one-time event, but many events across your lifetime. Think of it as breaking down a brick wall with a huge beaming light on the other side. The first brick is the hardest, and the other bricks are tough to destroy, but it gets easier brick by brick. Some people take down the whole wall, others have big beams of light coming through, and others have nothing more than that one solitary brick.

I learned the hard way that not everybody wants you to live your truth or is ready to hear about it. I also learned that you could be stronger in your youth than you are as a full adult, and that strength of character and promise is something you might have to fight to regain as you push toward reclaiming who you are and being true to your destiny. Not everybody is ready to come out at the age I did, and unfortunately, some circumstances can push us back into the closet, arms and feet getting wedged in as we feel the pain of being squished back into a form we rejected. Being a teacher, a gay teacher, is not easy—especially when your students are at the age when becoming an adult, let alone realizing they might be LGBTQ, produces floods of anxiety, fear, and doubt.

Apologies aside, let me tell you about being Jewish and gay. You are twice blessed. You are both candles and both challahs and all of that; you are a double portion of everything good about both. I never said it was easy, but it is a sacred journey. I believe we choose our paths in the other world to teach the world something we never knew before.

Judaism is a family-based tradition. Don't let anyone fool you; family is not exclusively mother, father, sister, brother. Family is not strictly heteronormative, although we as humans need those families too. Family is a code word in the gay community for other gays, and mishpocheh *is our code word in Yahaduth for other Jews. Family is an important concept to both communities regardless of what some bigot here or there says.*

Judaism also wants you to love yourself as you love your neighbor. We often talk about loving your neighbor as yourself but forget how reflexive that mitzvah actually is. In LGBTQ life, it is all too easy to adopt the fears, doubts, and denials that society presents to us even though we live in one of the most queer-friendly eras on the planet. Despite our progress as a people, prejudices still run rampant, and self-hatred and self-hurt are still possibilities that many of us struggle with. These can be mitigated if you remember that the mitzvot are yours too.

Loving yourself means you remember you are betzelem Elokim—*made in G-d's image—as much as any other person. It means that G-d has love for you as an LGBTQ person and that your struggles and strengths matter to our Creator. In the LGBTQ community, we have conflicts between one another as men and women, cis and trans, white-identified and people of color, disabled and not, wealthy and financially challenged. Your duty is to apply the best of Jewish values—mainly a concern for the stranger and those in need, and the urge to support the oppressed—because we were all of those in the time of our enslavement and captivity, and we are duty-bound to be compassionate and loving and empathetic. Be grateful and thankful for your difference in this world and for the opportunity to feel for others what you feel for yourself.*

I have often said that Judaism is one of the best gifts I ever received. So many LGBTQ Jews are engaged in the act of making that light known to the world. Rabbi Sandra Lawson, Rabbi Joshua Lesser, Rabbi Michael Lash, Rabbi Denise Eger, and Koach Baruch Frazier come to mind as queer leaders in American Jewish spirituality and social justice. And there are thousands of gay, lesbian, bisexual, trans, and other queer Jews who see pur-

pose and meaning in different parts of Jewish life and create spaces where being both Jewish and queer is not an exercise in polar opposites. My friend Liz Alpern and others use food to bring us as a people within a people together, to be nourished by food and spirit.

Still, there are thousands of Jews who are LGBTQ who don't feel at home in any part of Jewish life. Although I am pleased to know there are more and more opportunities to be Jewish and queer, some of you may have left organized Jewish life or abandoned our quest for tikkun olam altogether. There is always space for you, and if you find none, create it. The solution to being lonely and feeling isolated and dealing with conflict is to align with those whom you can help and those who can help you. Be love and light to each other, and don't forget our allies and family and friends who can add their power and soul to our journeys—have a seder, a Hanukkah candle lighting, a Shabbat dinner, hold High Holiday services in a park together, go to a creek or the ocean and perform tashlich, have women-only Rosh Chodesh celebrations, or just get together and sing and dance—bring it to the runway or be drag kings on Purim—you can create the observance and engagement you want or need if it isn't right there already.

Jewish food is a powerful way to engage with our tradition. It has become a huge part of my life to make a part of Black Jewish culture by remixing and remaking food traditions and pushing forward the ways of the past while making the next waves of the future. Make that rainbow challah. Have Shabbat or Sukkot or simchah meals where every color of every pride flag is represented. Encourage diversity within diversity, and make your tables or circles beam with all of humanity and the lessons that being different and yet being cohesive have to offer.

There's a story based on the midrash I want to tell you. When all the creatures were made, the birds were the most disturbed and cantankerous. They complained about their feathers, about their beaks; they were envious of the lions, the giraffes, the fish, the *butterflies and elephants, the bears, and beyond. They didn't feel majestic or beautiful or important, and some of the other wildlife laughed at them.*

But then softly, the Holy One, blessed be, said, "But of all my creation you are the ones who can fly to the heavens, and you can sing, and you can dive or dance about or prance on top of fences and wake the Adam-creatures up!" The birds began to flex their wings; some could fly, and others could swim, and others opened up each dawn to humankind. And from then on, the birds are the ones who wake us up, davening in the increasing morning light, singing their praises for being different, for being strong and unique and as beautiful as they were made to be.

I love you, your teacher,

MR. TWITTY

Mayseh:
QUADRUPLE QUEERNESS

A black gay person who is a sexual conundrum to society is already, long before the question of sexuality comes into it, menaced and marked because he's black or she's black. The sexual question comes after the question of color; it's simply one more aspect of the danger in which all black people live. I think white gay people feel cheated because they were born, in principle, into a society in which they were supposed to be safe. The anomaly of their sexuality puts them in danger unexpectedly. Their reaction seems to me in direct proportion to the sense of feeling cheated of the advantages which accrue to white people in a white society. There's an element, it has always seemed to me, of bewilderment and complaint. Now that may sound very harsh, but the gay world as such is no more prepared to accept black people than anywhere else in society. It's a very hermetically sealed world with very unattractive features, including racism.

—*James Baldwin, interview with Richard Goldstein, 1984*

Going into the kitchen, you sometimes carry the weight of the world—and yourself—with you. I'm unable to function with one lens, one dimension, one part of me to the distraction of others. The minute I wish for some sort of personal simplicity, a one-note personality, I wish it away because I know I'd be bored. I'd be a life made of three awful ingredients: bland inane ennui. Who the hell wants to be bland in the kitchen or anywhere else?

I'm different—I know, so is everybody, but I'm *very* different. I know what people expect me to be and want me to be, but something in me just doesn't want to be that. The frustration is palpable; it beams through people's eyes: "Why can't you just be what I expect?" "If you were only an off-the-shelf type." I don't want to be on a shelf.

I was born different because I chose this on the other side; the Yoruba of Nigeria and Benin and other West African peoples say you choose who you are in heaven. The Yoruba say, "The earth is a marketplace, and heaven is home." This can be read as a metaphor for cooking; the open West African marketplace is primarily a spot to acquire things to consume, to make a tasty stew, to spice, to flavor. We cycle through this reality, gathering the ingredients necessary to add fire, neutrality, or coolness, to push along a satisfying meal called life.

But what if my ingredients aren't good enough? What if I have too many ingredients to work with? What if I add too much to this dish? What if I'm confused? What if you're supposed to be in your bubble, segregated, particularistic, a good boy or girl—never in between—stuck as it were in old perceptions, moments, and frozen in life.

"You're Black, you're gay, you're Jewish, you're fat."

"You're queer as fuck."

"This is why you feel so alone."

"Why do you always have to be the fucking oddball?"

"Am I just cooking for me? Table for one?"

I need to see a doctor; I'm just too queer for my own good.

My friend Dr. T. J. Tallie is a professor of African history, gender, colonialism, and sexuality at the University of San Diego. He is the author of *Queering Colonial Natal*. I go to him wanting to understand what it means to be "queer."

"One of the things I think is really important," he tells me, "we live in a world where queer is just an adjective applied to sexual identity, a term that was formerly an epithet, inverted, and reclaimed. Queerness is also a relation. It is a relationship between normativity and power. In other words, you and I are off the line of what normative is supposed to be. Queerness is a broader relationship to norms."

T.J. continues: "Blackness, in a white supremacist world, is already queer. It is a relationship to a norm that does not make room for you or denies you're normal and makes you other. Black bodies challenge this by simply existing and challenging what is normal and appropriate in a world that imagines them inferior, odd, or at worst, vanished. Blackness is a revolutionary act. It already bucks the norm. Queerness is an identity that you can have in terms of your sexuality, but it is also a relationship that you can have to the normative structures of your wider world. This is not saying that every Black person is queer in the sense of sexuality—certainly not. It is saying that according to the norms of our dominant white supremacist society, black bodies are queered."

I chime in: "So, by extension, Black culture or Jewishness can be marked as a 'queer' existence. There's a larger norm, and our bodies, behaviors, and background aren't it, even if that larger world chooses when and where it will take, borrow, or appropriate. I mean, when I've gone to West Africa, all these little things seem so normal and natural to me—gestures, tones, words—that I've been made to feel awkward or alien about in America around people who don't share root elements of the same culture. I've said that in Africa, I've felt some things that I couldn't explain to white people in America were perfectly okay there."

"Well, Michael," he says, "you're not queer in an African deep cultural context in the way you are outside the norm here in the United States."

"How do we explain issues between groups?" I ask. "So, I'm Black, Jewish, and gay, and fat—I'm four times queer. But each of these groups seems to take turns in the circular firing squad of the oppressed."

T.J. continues: "These are bodies that are already marked as queer. Part of the reason homophobia exists among Black communities, for example, isn't ignorance, but it is a way to prove that they are normal and acceptable. It's the 'It's already hard to be . . . why you gotta be that?' formula. Hating, in a way, is proving that you belong. It's a group looking at the system and saying, 'I was supposed to be part of an insulated set.' They grew up in a world where they were supposed to be normal but can't beat back the mark of queerness."

"In other words," I say, "when people say Jewish racism or anti-Blackness or Black anti-Jewishness, and homophobia or gay anti-Blackness anti-Jewishness, as practiced by both groups, it really comes down to wanting not to be queer. Nobody wants to be marginalized. So that's a forever cycle. Where's the solution?"

T.J. clears his throat and gives one of his intense stares imbued with humor and the passion of scripture. "Embracing the queerness means looking inside that queerness as a relation to power. I'm not going to win in this system; I can't hate myself enough to be like them. I can't kill myself enough to be desirable, to be acceptable. So you reject those norms. You say, okay, well, I'm going to live."

José Muñoz, the late queer theorist, described this as "cruising Utopia." Utopia may not be where we are, but it doesn't mean I want to live there. Choose the "not there." You might as well aim for something positive and outlandish. It's scary because it is technically impossible. It feels like you're leaping into the unknown, and you're doing it knowingly. But you must. Muñoz describes the alternative as "the very unimaginative and boring straight time."

In a way, I get it. This is what marginalized people do all the time.

Very Black, very Jewish, very LGBTQ, very fat. We find heaven. We worship, we dance, we argue passionately and soak up learning, we club, we cruise, we play, we eat, we celebrate the nowness, and we celebrate each other. We seek out little glimpses of heaven, between days of purgatory and moments in hell.

"Can food be queer?" I ask T.J.

"Practices around food can be queer," he says, "the way we eat it and the way we think about it. You have to ask what the relationships between normative food and power are. You know, Black food is constantly queered—it's the backward, the nothing, the gross, the disgusting."

Jewish food was similarly queered from myths like the blood in the matzoh narrative and many of these same accusations against Jewish food throughout time—we were smelly garlic eaters and silly for clinging to the Law in the pursuit of *kashrut*. These aspersions fed into Jewish food, particularly that of Ashkenazi Jews, as having gross or boring or impoverished ghetto and shtetl origins. Celebrating and owning your queer food is in its own way a means to unqueer your food as marginalized people.

T.J. tells me: "You queer food by reminding people about Southern food and its origins with cooks in slavery and roots in Africa. You're queering that table by saying you don't want the erasure, the mitigation. Nina Simone said, 'You've got to learn to leave the table when love is no longer being served.' That's a queer act of refusal. Or you just slam your fist down and say 'This is our food—and I don't remember asking you if you found it attractive at the table or not, even as you occasionally appropriate it or try to change it to fit your arrogance and self-centering.'"

My favorite midrash is about a rabbi in ancient times who is interrupted while planting olive trees—symbols of peace and long duration, progress and ubiquity of purpose. Olive trees can achieve remarkable antiquity. They were the food, the soap, the lotion, the grease, the light of the ancient Eretz Israel, and beyond. The other rabbis rush to him, proclaiming that the Messiah, the Moshiach, is on his way and that the rabbi must abandon his task. He refuses and encourages them to run along to meet the Messiah. "When the Moshiach comes," he says, "I will greet him, and we will plant these olive trees together."

At that moment, the rabbi is both acknowledging the fervor of a moment that never was and making his own version of paradise or utopia manifest. It's what Black people contributed to society in the expression "I'm going to do me." It is a sense of being personally charged, of being invested in the generations to come; it's a way to march your way through to a different world. It's about planting seeds or saplings for harvests that you may not get to see.

I spoke with Jessica Price, a vocal personality I follow on Twitter. One of her tweets caught my eye: "The closest identity to Jewishness in terms of marginalization is queerness."

"The signature event for both Blacks and Jews is a coming-out moment," she says, "the exodus narrative in the Torah. It's not even the grand Cecil B. DeMille moment either; it's putting the blood on the doorpost. I'm here; I'm marking myself; you didn't mark me this time. I'm different from you, and my survival is at stake."

I interrupt, "And I've got somewhere to be!"

"Yes, I have to leave the narrow place [Egypt, or the *mitzrayim*, narrow place] that you put me in and go somewhere else where I have wide-open spaces to be myself. Jewish and Black women are queered by society at various points—'Jewess' and 'Negress' signify them and their sexuality and their bodies and as queer and other."

I respond: "Right, you can be stereotyped as any number of tropes—the power-seeking Jewish princess, like Monica or Shandra, or the welfare queen or baby mama—but you're not; you're Michelle Obama, but they can't let that old shit go. I often feel doubly queer as a Jewish man alone."

"That's because the Jewish man in the West is a learner," Jessica says, "not someone who is trying to achieve physical dominance.

That's its own queer, and it comes with plenty of overtones and assumptions about sexuality, masculinity, and strength. The wimpy boy, the nerd, the weakling, all come from stereotypes of the poor yeshivah boys of Eastern Europe. But part of that tradition in a secular context, as you know, led into a certain type of immigrant eager to learn other things in an intense way adjacent to the sacred tradition."

Jewish smarts are a queer thing themselves. Unfortunately, it's something read as devious or genetics gone wild. The written and Oral Torah, when interpreted, argued, debated, and reinterpreted, require a lot of skills. Debate and study are whittled down to sharp words like *pilpul*—literally "pepper." My mind flashes back to when I went to Mike's house as a tweenager. I was arguing and debating with him and his parents, especially his mom, a veteran of Squirrel Hill, Pittsburgh.

Martin Luther, the sixteenth-century Protestant reformer, famously answered Jewish resistance to conversion by demanding the destruction of European synagogues, targeting not so much the Jewish version of "holy" but the Jewish mind. He wanted to annihilate the *cheder*, the traditional Jewish school, and burn the volumes of the Talmud and destroy yeshivot, our traditional academies of learning. Jewish thinking in the mind of anti-Semitism has been core identified with Jewish difference and independent thought. What would it mean to have a world not without Jews per se, but free of Jewish uniqueness and cultural, spiritual, and personal agendas? The question began before Luther, and unfortunately, it did not end with the Shoah.

Jewish learning and its American aftermath are not the same things, but many authors have tried to draw a direct parallel. The skill set is similar. You have to read the manual over and over until there's nothing left—but wait, there's more . . . You have to apply it and, if necessary, add your own wisdom when absolutely tested and experienced. You have to translate and teach and question and ask more questions, and if you're a true learner, you get to write the next manual on the manual yourself.

The Black experience with learning is not the opposite of this. Let's be clear. Traditional African cultures have parallels to Torah or qur'anic learning: for example, Ifa among the Yoruba and their neighboring civilizations and many other oracular or proverbial traditions. However, enslavement sought to strip Black people of their traditional wisdom paths; and later, an enslaved African who could think, use his or her mind and against the law in most places, read and write, was a catastrophe, a failure to guard white supremacy by subduing the Black mind. Antebellum enslavers created crazy diseases like drapetomania (a mental illness that was thought to cause enslaved Africans to run away) and labeled and condemned other forms of resistance to suggest that Black intelligence was psychotic, a weapon in the wrong body.

James Baldwin, among many others, experienced the updated version of this kind of racism. It didn't matter that he came by his manner and intelligence just as naturally as the Jewish and Italian and Irish boys he went to school with in New York, but he was Black, and he was not supposed to be "like them." His shyness, his bookishness, was taken as a problem rather than a phase of youth. What makes this so appalling is that it is not uncommon for Black parents to hear the message "your child is special-needs" when their kids are smart and have trouble adjusting socially to surroundings that aren't normative to them or they are just smart in a world where Black brains are used but not tolerated.

So there I was, a queer Black boy performing a queer act—not only a boy who cooked but a boy who read incessantly, a socially awkward bibliophile. Teachers tried to persuade my mother that I was a special-needs student because of my lack of social skills in a new place and because I was terrible at math and got beat up or harassed nearly every day. They said I should be put in special education, and that would be my lot in life—institutionalization. My mother told them to fuck right off in the nicest, most passive-aggressive way. I always had a book in my hands or backpack—several. Growing up and into young adulthood I got the "queer look" every time I was not performing Black maleness the way people wanted me to.

It was not normative for me to sit there and study Judaism and take endless notes and go over and over my favorite books—*Beloved* and *Roots* and *The Color Purple* and *The Piano Lesson*—looking for the keys to an art unique to me, tailor-made for my journey. I was often met with annoyance by people of all types; I was the butt of the joke, a queer little bookish pre-fat kid. One of my uncles—arguably my most accomplished and degreed relative—smirked in derision, shook his head, and said to me, "You're not gonna make it." But there were also people who would aid and abet my one-man yeshivah, and because they believed in me, I am a proud autodidact and not a victim of suicide.

But that's just it. Part of the reason I transplanted into Judaism was because I really liked that I could be that part of myself, the learned blerd, and have it be both a sacred and a secular experience. People who could see past queering me as a Black man (who wasn't supposed to be into learning or education) gave me the validation and feedback I had wanted my whole life. The best part was when I needed to correct myself and grow, which is also a very deep part of Jewish tradition. When you have confidence in the journey, you don't feel like you've failed; you feel like the challenge is to conquer your failings.

There was once a rabbi, a real, living, breathing person, who was told he might be sightless after an eye operation. The rabbi made a vow and set to learning an entire tractate of the Gemara—the partner to the Mishnah in the Talmud. He examined his life, his sins, his shortcomings; and all the while, he committed the tractate to memory. If he could never see to study again, he would become the book he loved the most. He was like a character from Ray Bradbury's *Fahrenheit 451*, becoming a living embodiment of the text. As the story goes, he became the text, and he awoke from surgery, healed, and he could see.

After thinking through it all and talking with friends, I feel different about my location. I am absolutely queer, and the pressures I feel are from pushing back and existing. All of these things that I obtain as I work my way through the marketplace of life on earth are for my good. My difference doesn't just make my life or my food interesting; it gives me a toolbox to navigate a world that can and often does seek to eradicate part of me or render me exotic or odd or negligible. The tools are not just for me but for all those in the future who choose in one fraught moment in heaven to be different just before they descend.

Part V

THE PREPARED TABLE

Mayseh:

CHAVA'S QUERY

How does something become seen as authentically Jewish?

Because people see food or music or other cultural artifacts, those things as coming from people they perceive to be authentically Jewish, they are perceived in a different way.

We are sometimes seen as foreign to as opposed to inside of the culture, and the solution to that starts with just being recognized and seen.

I don't think that there has to be a tradition per se. But maybe we can ask the question, "What is Black Jewish *mesorah* [tradition]?" What does it look like? What does it mean to have a Black Jewish *mesorah* in food?

—*Chava, Black Jewish culinarian*

Chava is an African American Jewish woman with roots in south Louisiana, from the capital city of Baton Rouge to Pointe Coupée, the port city for much of Louisiana's late colonial trade in enslaved West Africans. She has spent time in Brooklyn's Hasidic hub of

Crown Heights and now lives in Los Angeles. Her husband's family is Jamaican. She is koshersoul personified. "Where my family is from," she says, "the staple dishes are jambalaya and étouffée, and gumbo and dirty rice and boudin, red beans and rice, white beans and rice—everything with rice. Rice was a very important entrée; rice and a meat and a vegetable—that was our family dinner. When it's Pesach, we do basmati rice, three times on a tablecloth just to check for *chametz*.

"Our key seasonings are things I have in my pantry: seasoned salt, garlic salt, oregano, onion powder, garlic powder, black pepper, paprika, filé powder, cayenne. And, of course, you have to use tomatoes, onions, bell pepper, celery. If you have all of that, you can make a meal out of anything. I make my own fish fry; none of the commercial stuff is *hechshered* [rabbinically approved], so I just make my own. You have to keep the integrity of the taste—for coating chicken, or something similar—but I dip the pieces in egg and almond milk, which is pareve."

Kitchen traditions are too crucial to Chava; the goal is *l'dor v'dor*—to pass her culinary heritage in a Jewish way on to her daughters and son, the next generation. "Blackness and whiteness—it's still something my daughters are integrating and trying to understand," she says, "especially as we are introducing conversations about race and racism. Someone gave them a book about Ruby Bridges, the first African American student to integrate an elementary school in the South. We talk to them about pride in themselves, affirming their beauty and confidence. We have just begun to talk to them about geography and their origins and culture. Figuring out their place in the world is an ongoing process."

In an instant, our conversation is a very koshersoul conversation about where we come from, where we fit in, and where we see the future going for those we educate and pass the baton to. Our community is a loosely defined confederacy of voices and visions that in any other guise might not be as in communication with each other because of our differences; but it is our shared identity as Black people who are Jewish—whether we are lesbian or Reconstructionist, trans men or straight cis men, Orthodox, Conservative, kosher compliant or kosher style, *frum* from birth, raised Jewish, mixed ethnicity, or converted—that bonds us, and with it is an awareness of a shared cultural experience that is layered on top of our membership in the Jewish people. Koshersoul is my self-coined term for our vantage point, not a group affinity, trend, or even tradition. It's another word for kinfolk.

If that weren't a bond, Chava and I are both passionate food people who began to try more diverse foods and tastes as we broadened our cooking knowledge. "When I went to law school, I learned about different foods—like avocados!" she says. "I had a friend from California, and there it was, something new. When we used to live in Crown Heights, you have to understand there are Habadniks from all over the world and people in that community who have been all over the world; so there are a lot of hip kosher restaurants in the area where you can have a nice meal with your friends. Synergies, there are synergies everywhere. Whatever food tradition is in the secular world these days will soon have a way into the kosher world. Food becomes a point of access into other cultures in a way that, as *frum* Jews, we don't always have. Hibachi, ramen, barbecue—people want to engage with the outside world, but they want a kosher way to do it."

Her comment reminds me about the impact of constant interaction between the African American and Afro-Caribbean culture of Brooklyn and the Lubavitch Hasidic scene. Although insiders in both camps are not comfortable claiming cross-pollination, music, dance, food culture, and cultural expression have all had touches of the other. There is a desire to access Black culture, so musicians like Matisyahu and Nissim Black have been very popular. It's everywhere around you. There's a lingering antagonism, but people want an entrance to it. The question many ask themselves is, "What are kosher ways to access that world?"

For example, there is the annual West Indian Day Parade in Crown Heights. The Lubavitch community sees and smells the jerk chicken; foodie culture is all around them, they are exposed to a lot of different types of food, they are exposed to different cuisines, so they will want to try the recipes, especially if it's a culture or cuisine that's right in their midst. Food is a great access point to relationships. One of the realities is that one purpose of *kashrut* is to keep distance between people based on belief and practice. For you to even create these recipes means some separation from points of connections and empathy that help you see how the food has similar stories or traditions.

Chava continues: "*Kashrut* is divorced from the cultural aspect. You're not going to the Japanese restaurant to try hibachi, so you're not getting that lesson. I would like to see a greater connection between the two elements—exploration and education—because I think it would do a lot of good for people to understand each other. What would it take for consumers of the kosher market to see the creators of these food traditions as authentic members of our community, to see carriers of these food traditions as members of our community and not as outsiders?" When Chava says "authentic members of our community," she's also talking about us—the Chocolate Chosen, our people within a people, Jews of African descent.

This is the heart of it. We don't leave our issues or interests or identities at the kitchen door; we take them in with us. Most importantly, we work out our Jewish identities partly through the enthusiasm and vibrance that food plays in the cultures of both diasporas. Understanding where our journeys have taken us and where we fit—or don't—is side by side with hearing the stories of others and applying their wisdom to our lives.

Black Jewish stories are Jewish stories, they are Black stories, they are stories of the African Atlantic and stories of the Jewish world and people. Because they are all these things, the culinary repartee in Chava's household between her Jamaican husband and his love of oxtail, rice and peas, curried chicken, and other classic Jamaican delicacies and her deep Southern Black love of potato salad and okra is just another chapter in the stories of Black and Jewish food. "Kosher goat does amazing things for my *shalom bayis*—the peace of my home!" she says. This entire conversation is another part of American Jewish life that is just as valid and just as authentic as anyone else's, and it's not always about the food and technique and ingredients—it's also about the difficulties and navigations we are forced to contend with as we cook and eat and share our experiences with each other or the wider world.

It's all a part of our Torah.

Like every good Louisianian, Chava has a gumbo pot that comes out during Sukkot. "For me, gumbo and Sukkot go together; that's the start of my gumbo season. It's filé gumbo with chicken and kosher sausage." I see so much of her in myself and my journey that as we speak, I nod in enthusiastic kinship. Our Sephardi affiliation means that a good portion of our kitchen material culture is decidedly Middle Eastern and North African (MENA), which has strong connections to the continental side of our West African Atlantic heritage.

Our culinary spaces are a mélange of all the different parts of our heritage, travels, and experiences in Jewish life. "Basmati rice, cumin, coriander, ginger, turmeric—have all appeared in my pantry," she says, "and allspice and Jamaican curry powder from the Caribbean side. I use tahini; I use it as a condiment or an ingredient." Then, "rosewater," she begins; and I finish: "A little bit goes a long way." We laugh because we've both made the same mistake, given its water-clear appearance. "Seasoned salt and smoked turkey leg—in cholent, sure," she says, "but I find that there are different cravings and food moments. When I want étouffée, I want étouffée. It doesn't mean that hummus and z'hug and other things can't share the table with it—*salatim*, I just don't mix them in the same dish.

Chava makes another point: "I love to mix things on the table, but I feel like when I want something, it's also because it's familiar or 'authentic.' I get intimidated by things because I don't know what they are supposed to taste like—like beef patties. My question isn't 'Does it taste good?' but 'Does it taste right?'" I know what she means, but I am different. I like to mix flavors and see if they can tell me a story about me or others that hasn't been experienced before. And other times, I'm just like Chava—each food and meal must have its own space depending on my guests or family preferences. We also understand a fine line between experimentation and adjustment for a more comforting palate. "Some people want the authentic food," she says. "Otherwise, it's like Israeli food—lol, you know you could be eating Mexican food, but it tastes Israeli. Similar ingredients in different proportions prepared slightly different ways changes everything."

Los Angeles has exposed Chava to Persian Jewish foodways, and she loves it. Things she didn't eat growing up are now a regular part of her family's rotation. There is sabzi, a green herbed rice, and sabzi gormeh, a meat and herb stew; kabob, again with rice; and not to be outdone, she is a culinary ambassador. She once took Southern cornbread dressing to a *kiddush*, and people raved. "A friend from the shul, Moroccan, said she wanted that recipe! I was, like, 'Recipe, hmmm, that's a good question!'"

Chava continues: "In the long run, I don't like the way people juxtapose Southern food or Jamaican food versus Sephardi food. When we do that, we are furthering this idea that, oh, you brought this from somewhere else or it has questionable authenticity. Jewish food is much more expansive and inclusive than that. We're not separate things. It's all negotiation and navigation. I don't love how people will say x, y, and z isn't a Jewish food. They don't care enough about our version of Jewish life to get it right. You have three thousand opinions about matzoh balls, but if I'm telling you what jambalaya is not, and you're, like, this isn't a Jewish conversation, the disrespect is palpable! People should try things and learn more about others."

And through all of that, Chava has a solid koshersoul kitchen. "I'm still working at the perfect challah bread pudding—with raisins! And I still need to figure out how to make pareve pralines because I have a dairy allergy in the house!" She binges on dates until the next Tishrei rolls around and makes sweet potato pie in the fall and sfinj—Moroccan donuts—at Hanukkah. Her neo-traditional Sephardi Rosh Hashanah seder is not just for plump ripe dates; it includes her Southern-style black-eyed peas and plantain; roasted lamb's head with wine, rosemary, and garlic; salad with apples; keftes de prassa (leek patties); pomegranate honey chicken; candied butternut squash; and not to be outdone, apple crisp. Her only real problems are a daughter who loves gefilte fish and a husband who doesn't love grits. "It boggles my mind," she says.

"Everything I do has a source; I curate my table. I sometimes wonder if people really think about it and try to make room for the history that locates me and my table in the multiple spaces that the food I put on it shares. Where is the space for us and what we bring to the table?"

Mayseh:

MY AFRO-ASHKEFARDI KITCHEN

If by now you imagine my kitchen to be fully stocked with a crew of enslaved cooks and shtetl women, pickle makers, and ancient African women pounding grain in standing mortars and pestles going back to the Niger River valley, you're almost right. But they are my teachers, not my servants. The Ancestors are powerhouses of a different source in my little culinary ecosystem. Women from the *mellah* and the ghetto imitating the Levitical priests of old and Mende women making red rice alongside their South Carolina great-great-great-great-granddaughters are not there for symbolics; they are part of my system. It is these people—Philadelphia butchers and Williamsburg pastry chefs, Persian sabzi experts, and Ethiopian masters of tibs, dabo bread, and berbere spice—who give my kitchen *meaning*.

One fine day after some reconsideration, I decided to "organize" because, as you can probably tell by now, that word is relative and not firm in my life or my kitchen. To date, my kitchen has become something of a temple to attainment and display, even though not many of the people I catalogued above had a fancy kitchen, and I just got one two multi-nanoseconds ago. Drudgery lived there, not poetry; necessity ruled rather than documentation; survival had its place over self-awareness. To that extent, I am already a dandy, a person of luxury; my showroom is that I have the conceit to not worry myself like the people of the past.

But their kitchens had rituals, key ingredients, spells and songs, and prayers and magic. In Yiddishe kitchens, there were little prayer cookbooks containing personal petitions called *t'khines*, and mothers would pray over the challah and cholent and entrées with wishes of deliciousness and perfection—not out of a burning concern for flavor but for the spiritual sustenance and blessing of their kin. These little medieval "chicken soup" books were in no small way literature of yearning, devotion, and dedication for a segment of Jewish society left out of public learning and worship—the women. But to their credit, the mamas made their *t'khines*, and the *Tzene Urena*, the Yiddish gloss of the *Chumash*, some of the highest-selling published books after moveable type became a mover of ideas. These treasured prayers still guide my cooking—I've never really written them down, but I spontaneously start speaking over my food, asking G-d to bring people together, to bring down peace, and to help the food make people talk to one another. They are my secret spice.

There is more than one way to set the welcome table. The African side bids me pray over the seeds I plant to put my emotions into fiery peppers and into cool, peaceful curls of lettuce pushing out into the springtime. Traditional African spirituality is no less philosophical and potent than that of biblical agrarians; it comes from the same place of dependence on nature and appeals to its forces. The land, our mother, is a gift. The rain is a gift, and the life forces that move from Creator to Earth to air, water, space, and time include a long list of blessings that require acknowledgment and ceaseless and seamless appreciation. There are blessings in both traditions for all of these as the food moves from the garden to the table.

I have been to eight countries in West Africa and have found that the spirituality of processing food into meals has many parallels but does not necessarily equal the investment of "holiness" in *kashrut*. In other words, they don't have the same meaning, but the import and respect are the same. Kosher, I repeat, does not mean that something has been blessed by a rabbi. It means that a food or utensil or fabric or practice is inherently or by ritual practice able to fulfill a proper execution of Jewish law, or *halakhah*. In West Africa, tools and utensils often go through quiet rituals of spiritual perfection so that by the time the ceramic pot, the bowls from which the family draws their meals, the wooden mortar and pestle, grinding stone, farming cutlass, or any number of tools made by the blacksmith from the field hoe to the knives that cut the yams reach the user, they are invested with spiritual power and purpose so strong that one does not dare to use the tools of another cook without permission. The long flat sticks and specially carved spoons for women who are masters at the craft of making the family fufu or rice for mass gatherings are not interchangeable. They are there because the family is the most important institution; the community assures a link between the Creator, the Ancestors, the Earth, the sky, and those waiting to be born.

How the hell do I even draw breath with all this saturating spirituality and meaning? It gets worse, skeptics, believe me. Don't forget about time and space. If Shabbat did not exist with a stop-clock or the holidays, the seasons would still be real and monumental and essential to me as a culinary person. Even if nature weren't a constant dance of rainfall and leaf change and distinct gusts of air, people have seasons of life, making societies, cultures, and civilizations; festivals and food mark the seasons of the history of a people. New Year's Day will always mean black-eyed peas and collard greens as sure as Juneteenth will mean red sauced barbecue, red drink, melon, and other foods and drinks celebrating emancipation or clear, sweet, sour, bitter, and other flavors will mark a Yoruba naming ceremony or wedding.

Time having a vote and a veto means that hamantaschen will always be at Purim time and matzoh means Pesach. Meals are mnemonics; they help us tell time and keep track of ourselves. The delayed gratification of putting things away for our somewhat arbitrary making of meaning is an important value; it teaches patience, encourages an eagerness for tradition, and establishes a reason to form and build community. Gone are the days of childhood impatience. I now understand the need for the wait, the deliciousness of the buildup and preparation, from cleaning the kitchen to making it free of leaven to waiting for the first late fall frost to make the collards sweet. Time—its river flow, the way it makes our mouths water, the way it makes us eager and full of desire—is, along with meaning and space, indispensable.

SPACE—ah yes, back to space. Space can be holy, meaningful, and important. In contemporary American culture, kitchens can be dirty, and kitchens can be cluttered. But how often do you see people ask the question, "Is your kitchen sacred?" I will leave "holy" the whole alone because that is a far more subjective question than whether your kitchen is sacred. I guess I feel the need to say this because "sacred" does not need to have a specific religious or spiritual context, even though, in my case, they absolutely do and beyond.

Old treasured cookbooks can indeed make a kitchen space sacred. Or pictures of the family—from the Ancestors to a family vacation. Drawings magnet bound to your icebox from an irreplaceable childhood, jaunty and unfettered, are sacred, as is an entire fossil dig of *Elbowsaurus rex*, slowly flaking over time, with one piece of macaroni after the other falling from the glue and construction paper. Every kitchen table where spouses commit to recommitting despite illness or loss is sacred. Each kitchen table where a child comes out and is immediately hugged, kissed, and reassured of unconditional love is sacred. The promises of the generations in lessons on heirloom techniques and the meals that say goodbye make our kitchens sacred.

And there is the sacred that comes not because we inherited it or were born into it or were given it, but because we create it—within ourselves, with each other. The unfortunate presumption that all tradition is a gift rather than a welcome responsibility and presence comes out of a general slump toward letting go of the weight of everything we were and are in favor of letting others tramp along with the leavings and scraps of whole worlds. I don't find community with those who let it all go as we run into the future. Simultaneously, those who pick up the parts left behind don't have to be purists; we can repurpose, but with respect.

My kitchen space is not *meant* to be a museum. Many people's kitchens are unwilling and unwitting junkyards of culinary technology's forward march toward peak cleverness and ingenuity. Chances are, if you walk into your kitchen, just as if you walk into mine, you will see greeting you a waffle iron or four and skillets from cast iron to copper bottoms and stainless steel to whatever is being sold for $19.95 at this moment. We can't help it. On the one hand, the scriptures of our cultures and their layers of meaning and power have been abandoned; but apparently, someday, our descendants will see how hard we had it when we fired up the Belgian waffle maker—and they will appreciate their ungrateful ease.

Because I am really no different from many other people in my society, it would be hypocritical for me to be a snob in anyone else's culinary ecosystem. My prevailing ethic is "As for me and my house," as it goes in the elevated poetry of the Hebrew Bible. I assure you this isn't about what we all *should* do but how we could and might give thought to how we curate our food spaces. My kitchen is slowly becoming a space where not only the rules but the values and cultures from which I come and that I have adopted meld into a system that works an aesthetic that prioritizes the survival of old recipes, the process of creating new ones, the beauty of fusion and the absolute, and the unrestrained celebration of joy in seeing peoples meant for destruction being able to say, "They tried to kill us, we won, let's eat."

The Senses

"It smells Jewish in here" and "Lord have mercy, what you got cooking?" are equal in my heart. I know what they mean. They mean that someone somewhere wished that they had created an air freshener that smelled like maqluba or brisket or albondigas chicken soup heavy with parsley and celery roots, carrots and shiny little golden water coins of poultry fat or the smell of when the opposite smokiness of barbecue and earthy stewing greens meets plump vegetables on a plate at a family reunion with the promise of oozing peach cobbler with spices as pungent as incense in the Temple.

Both are a compliment. Both are a blessing. Both mean I've done something right by bringing you into my Afro-Ashkefardi kitchen, and I won't let you go. Those smells are me hanging on for dear life to your nose—which I want to be your first "mouth."

Afro: Means smoked turkey and onions plus water and vegetables means potlikker, the sauce du jour of Blackness going back to the colonial and antebellum South. It also means the tang of hot pepper in the air and the promise of spices—a spice cabinet crowded with savory and sweet spices that, much like the flavor profiles of our Ancestors, put Africa at the center of a flavor crossroads where the points of the compass met and sped up the spread of genius combinations and flavor pairings that now can be found all over the African Atlantic. I cannot live without ginger, garlic, fish and cayenne peppers, scallions, paprika, cinnamon, lemons, basil, alligator pepper, guinea pepper—the list goes on. The things I need have expanded to turmeric and adobo, bird chilies, suya spice, berbere, and beyond.

The grocery list of ingredients doesn't stop there, but how do you describe the way cane syrup feels on your tongue and fills your nostrils? Not just any cane syrup but one from Louisiana, one from Florida, and another from Georgia? The terroir of the Southern Black Belt is in a renaissance stage. People are rediscovering things discarded during exiles and forced migrations and coerced movements that meant something to the people of our past. We are no longer bound by the narrative that ten things or so make up our food tradition or that it means the same thing to others as it does to us by virtue of having similar ingredients. The smell of things frying, barbecuing, steaming, stewing, and pots bubbling on a stove are the source of our perfume.

Asheke: Here a smokiness-free chicken broth or vegetable broth replaces or dances along with the smell of potlikker. Everything builds. Root vegetables join leafy vegetables. The smell of pickled things plunges everything into a brine. Growing up I never had white or red horseradish or celeriac or kohlrabi, but there they are—markers of centuries in Central and Eastern Europe along with dill and caraway and rhubarb—friends I rarely knew until Judaism. There is so much onion and garlic, but I love it—they are the soul of both Black and Jewish food, making things animate and full of motion that would otherwise be still or flat.

Fardi: From the Iberian Peninsula to southwest Asia and South Asia, another crossroads comes into view. Yemen, Iraq, the Horn of Africa, India over to North Africa mean that several times a year, I am sniffling and sneezing over fresh spice mixes. I pound my own spices in my hand-operated spice grinder. There is so much pleasure in smashing cloves against a raw stone surface. A brilliant yellow and oranges and more complex browns and burgundies come into the palette. Olive oil smooths everything out. Here comes the garlic again, but much more subtle than before. Dips and rubs come to vegetable and meat surfaces. The Western brain registers much or all of this as "curry," but not only is that not true, it's not generous enough. These are spice mixtures—hawaij, baharat, berbere versions two, three, and four, among others—that also know seasonality and place. They are also healing, soothing, and remind us of how much gratitude we should have for the flow of history that now brings us the same ingredients that we enjoy *sans souci.*

The Things

My trips to West Africa changed me. I began to look at the massive pots, grinding stones, table mortar and pestles and the standing ones for fufu or rice not just as endemic to the countries I was visiting but as a long lost part of my own culinary past ripped away from me by the forced enculturation of slavery and its aftermath with all of its unknowns. The culinary implements are accompaniments to a song, to dance, to ritual. They work your muscles and move with your body.

Each trip, I brought back a new tool, one at a time. I love the banku stick the most—you can easily taste a sauce with it without breaking the taboo against dipping a used spoon back into the pot. In Ghana, they praised me for tasting on the back of my hand. I hadn't realized how profound that was until I understood that they knew that something had been passed down from generations of mothers to other generations. The man who made the banku sticks from soft palm ribs eagerly sold me three—two short and one long. I was part of a story that I had been denied access to for several hundred years.

Jewish implements have similar kinesthetics—like the chopper used for gefilte fish that I never intend to use for said purpose because I don't like gefilte fish. Mezzaluna-like, the rocking knife is good for onions and garlic and other such foods—to make a salad and break down bread crumbs. It is the Far East cleaver of the Jewish kitchen. It joins the other tools as noisemakers, creators of a conversation across time and space, migrations and exiles, diasporas, villages, cities, towns, households.

I have only two hands, so I opt to cook with others. Other people jam; I rock culinary implements that tell stories. Their phantom smells and real music force me to think about the things held in common, about the feelings behind the veins and blood vessels that led to the people who used them originally. They include an antique plantation waffle iron, a discarded raidel—the spikey tool used to put holes in matzoh, which I make only for fun since I cannot make kosher matzoh—handleless rolling pins, and old spice boxes. The people who join me in cooking have often never held these things in their hands—touched things that touched the people of the past.

The bigger blessing isn't so much in our encounter with the past but the fact that as we pass these smells and flavors and tastes and textures on, we pass the conversation on. It did not begin with us, and it will not end with us. The recipes will change even if followed to the letter. Mistakes will lead to innovations; the absence will extend flavor palettes. The key ingredients of others will change as mine have evolved and grown. We are not done with the gifts of exchange. We are ever in a cycle—we old people—we are all human tribes, but here in me, Blacks and Jews—the momentary bite turned into an eternal revelation of the food, the land, the gratitude for another day alive, to savor and to be happy.

Our kitchen ecosystems are crowded little places. Mine is packed to the rafters with spices and a pot rack we thankfully nailed solidly to the wall. As much as the past of the foods I cook intrigues me, and with them, the human stories they embody, the new stories around my kitchen table help me increase my idea of sacred. It is not enough to be a museum of what has gone by; it is equally important to cook up the memories and visions of the people around us today, each adding to the spirit of our pots and the stories they tell. Our spices, our key ingredients, and our utensils, along with the smells of our cooking, are more tangible than time, space, meaning, and spirit, but they are the ways our kitchens—like my humble Afro-Ashkefardi one— may have a chance at being eternal.

12

ADON OLAM TO THE TUNE OF DIXIE: SOUTHERN JEWISH FOOD

Southern Jews created regional cuisines that were shaped by local animals and plants in the area, as well as by access to seafood, kosher butchers, bakeries, and imported goods. In the colonial South, Jews interacted with enslaved African Americans, Native Americans, and newly arrived immigrants from France, England, and Germany. In the nineteenth and twentieth centuries, Jews encountered immigrants from Italy, Greece, Latin America, and Asia. Food traditions passed back and forth between these new Southerners as they assimilated into their communities. Together they learned the rules and rituals of a place sharply divided by race, class, and gender, and much of this learning was shaped in the kitchen and at the dining table.

—Marcie Cohen Ferris, *Matzoh Ball Gumbo: Culinary Tales of the Jewish South*

You can't talk about Koshersoul without talking about Kosher-Southern. It's a thing, very much a thing, and it's one of the defining features of Southern Jewish culture. Yes, Virginia, there are Southern Jews, and although the small-town Southern Jewish communities are not as vibrant as they once were, Southern Jewish life pushes on with the ever-familiar "Shalom y'all" signs and "Yiddishe Mama" aprons sharing space in kitchens from Charleston to Memphis to New Orleans to Atlanta and Birmingham. Southern Jewish food—part immigrant carryover, part Black Southern, part homegrown innovation—is not, as some might perceive, a novelty of American Jewish or Southern culture, but is in fact a confirmation of the vibrant power of both experiences and strength that each culture has given food in creating and sustaining identities. Southern Jewish food isn't always necessarily "kosher," but it is very much Jewish Diaspora, and it's no secret to those in the know that it's also very much African Diaspora.

"We became Americans and Southerners through the Black ladies and gentlemen we associated with down on Dryades Street," said Mildred L. Covert, the coauthor, with Sylvia P. Gerson, of the *Kosher Southern-Style Cookbook*, the *Kosher Cajun Cookbook*, and the *Kosher Creole Cookbook*. It was a fateful meeting, our only meeting, one afternoon during my Southern Discomfort Tour in 2012. At first, her statement was just a matter of fact, her history, until I realized that many other white-identified Southerners—non-Jews mostly—would never be so honest about their own cultural genesis. Yes, because *Jewish*: her mother was an immigrant from Galicia, that is, Austrian Poland. She thought bananas could be eaten whole and didn't trust tomatoes because they seemed to be full of blood. Even with such culinary ignorance and fears, this was a new start, and it was exciting.

Yes, because *Jewish*: there were elements of their lives and identity that didn't quite fit into anyone's schema of how the world worked or was divided. In the words of one of my former principals and mentors, "I wasn't Black, but I wasn't the blond, fair-skinned Valdosta, Georgia, beauty queen at all the football games and parades either." Yes, because *Jewish*: Mildred Covert's family lived in an area historically absorbent of not only multicultural influences but especially Black ones deriving from a strong center in West and Central African cultural influence, and because of that, the culture thrived in it, and so did the Jews who were able to create new versions of their religious and secular culture in relatively open human ecosystems. And also, because: white-identified Jews of said identity were able to cross lines and do things white and Black gentiles could not; it was an old dynamic in a new and brutal setting, all of which contributed to a food culture unlike any other.

Miss Mildred has since passed; may her memory be a blessing. I dreamed of sitting down with her and the great chef Leah Chase of New Orleans, of beloved Dooky Chase fame, over chicory coffee and beignets at Café Du Monde—talking history and food and life with two ladies who represented parts of me, but it was not meant to happen. A little but significant exposure (I was obliged to stop in each time I was in New Orleans to see Ms. Leah) to both was all I was to receive outside of their books and other credits (Ms. Leah passed in 2019). Some people are unforgettable—and legendary—and you absorb everything they can give you when the opportunity arrives.

This is part of the frustrating nature of my work. Research, reconnecting, and re-creation; the alliteration is not just for fun or wordplay. These food cultures, koshersoul and kosher-Southern, are not fun little trivial glitches on the way to something far grander. They are opportunities to divine something deeper about the American experience divorced from empty tropes of cultural, let alone political, exceptionalism. This extraordinary window into overlapping histories and diasporas and individual lives and group experiences deserves a history, but that history has to be gathered from not just luminaries but from the people who "wore the shoe" from day to day.

This is a very long-winded way to say I wish I had more time and more resources to have more moments with the amazing people who have given life to the world I enjoy. The roadmaps of the intersections between Black and Jewish food identities were made by many. There were colonial dames and enslaved Black cooks who for a generation or two had to master the ways of a kosher kitchen and foods that were relatively different from the usual fare of other citizens of Norfolk, Savannah, or Charleston; they were Black people of

Jewish descent, Jews who fought for the Confederacy, abolitionists, Black domestics, and Ashkenazi and Sephardi immigrants at the turn of the twentieth century in the world of Jim Crow, not to mention those who actively fought against it and Black people without whom many modern Southern shuls could not function. That's not niche; that's a microcosm of the American experience that cuts across many different parts of who we are, and whether we see it or not, it's part of the longer story of the movement of the Jewish and African Diasporas across time. Perhaps more important than any of this is that it's largely a story crafted, like much of human existence, by the interactions and confrontations of women.

Southern and Global

Throughout Southern history, the politics of power and place has established a complex regional cuisine of both privilege and deprivation that continues to impact the daily food patterns of southerners today. . . . In food lies the harsh dynamics of racism, sexism, class struggle, and ecological exploitation that have long defined the South, yet there too resides family, a strong connection to place, conviviality, creativity, and flavor. A constant tension underlies southern history, and that same tension resides in southern foodways, a cuisine largely shaped by the divisive history of the region. Contradiction is a central theme in the history of southern food, where the grim reality of slavery, Jim Crow segregation, extreme hunger, and disenfranchisement contrast with the pleasure and inventiveness of the region's cuisine. . . . The DNA of our region—its mix of racial and ethnic populations, its politics of colonization, and its abundant food resources—created an extraordinarily rich and dynamic cuisine. Examining the historical arc of food in the American South uncovers the tangled in-

teractions of its people over time, a world of relationships
fraught with conflict yet bound by blood and land.

—Marcie Cohen Ferris, *The Edible South: The Power
of Food and the Making of an American Region*

Being Southern is often read as being parochial or particular. The lines drawn around Southern identity are often made geographically or by some cultural trait or by using a word or phrase or even cooking style. In the popular imagination, "Southern" means white gentile (Christian) first, and everything else falls into place after that assumption, as if only Southern white gentiles could have come up with the unique mix of various traits that makes Southern identity authentic, viable, and valid. This is despite the tremendous impact of Native American, African, and non-British cultures on the origins and deep culture of the region.

That's why Southern Jewish food and its origin story are so important. From that history comes the conversation about other Jewish food cultures in America that are not typically discussed, like the long-standing food traditions of American Jews of African descent. Africans and non-African Jews didn't just show up in the early American South. As Western Europe was expanding into the rest of the world, the expulsed and exiled went with it—that meant that the refugees of the Spanish Reconquista and Inquisition and the fledgling transatlantic slave trade rubbed elbows more often than we know. Although Jews were a minority, the South was a cultural hearth area for American Jews until the mid-nineteenth century, with eighteenth-century Charleston, South Carolina, having the largest and most prominent Jewish communities.

Western Sephardic Jewish families moved from Spain and Portugal into the British and Dutch worlds—in both continental Europe and their colonies in the Americas. For the brief period that the Dutch ruled part of Brazil, Jews lived there, and when Portugal and the Inquisition had control, Jews moved. Some lived in the free republic of Palmares—a maroon polity under Zumbi, an African king who made no rules about the free practice of religion. Others went north to found the Jewish community in New Netherland, which became New York City, now one of the largest concentrations of Jewish life on the planet.

Jews further settled across the Caribbean basin—Jamaica, Barbados, the Virgin Islands, Curaçao, and Suriname, just to name a few places. In each of them, Western Sephardic Jews also found themselves a glaring minority in formerly Native American lands with Black majorities. The need to get goods and services to these isolated outposts of great agricultural and mineral wealth successfully recruited the connections of Western European Jews. Yes, that included the world of the slave trade, but it was not limited to it. The sugar islands and beyond were so driven by monoculture and curtailed by limited resources that the constant flow of ships and goods was crucial; landless people like the Jews came in handy.

As Charleston and later Savannah and the port cities of New York, Boston, and Providence became more prominent and important, Jews from Western Europe and those in the Caribbean began to migrate to colonial mainland North America. To be clear, the triangular trade between Europe, Africa, and the Americas made these networks possible and quite fluid. However, any attempt to suggest that Jews were the majority of this operation or were absent at all is an absurdity. Jews were there—they were merchants, settlers, pirates, and traders living on the outskirts of a society that was still trying to decide what to do with a people they felt were rooted in blasphemous denial of Christian theology and had a sinister devotion to a calculating chauvinism that no white gentile could trust.

Among all of these extremes, the families who were now spread out across this new transatlantic map lived new realities. Quiet as the fact is kept, Jews of this new scene practiced both piety and permissiveness. Some kept their relationship with enslaved Africans separate from their religious and cultural lives. Many others would have children with enslaved African women, some of them going on to be emancipated and participate in mainstream Jewish life. Some held in bondage enslaved people who practiced Judaism.

We don't talk about this because the assumption—and it's a completely bogus one—is that Jews have been this cliff-hanging minority that only interacted with their own kind. Obviously, cultural, social, and sexual congress across lines of race, power, gender, and class existed. In that context, we have a lot to answer for over centuries of stereotype-busting truths and evidence that have been ignored in favor of simplistic narratives that live in their respective bubbles. It is not all complete bullshit, but many of our assumptions are. People were trying to survive and exist in a world where lives were often short and brutal. It goes without saying that Africans and non-Black Jews lived in different and precarious realities in that nexus.

Beyond that, Jewish life demanded that experts in Jewish ritual be dispersed across the new Diaspora. Rabbis, mohels, kosher slaughterers and butchers, and wives of the individuals knowledgeable in the laws regulating ritual purity (a *mikveh* lady was and still is an important job in observant communities) and keeping kosher were all important. The need for kosher meat helped maintain trade lines between the Caribbean and the South, as Marcie Cohen Ferris elucidates in her book *Matzoh Ball Gumbo*:

> *Curaçao, Cayenne, Surinam, Jamaica, and other Caribbean communities imported kosher meat, such as smoked sausages and pickled "Jew beef," from Savannah and Charleston. The islands also contributed to the growing Jewish population in Savannah and Charleston as Jews left the Caribbean for opportunities on the mainland. In Mobile, Alabama, in 1827, the local shohet Isaac Lazarus supplemented his income with the sale of "Jewish provisions, Beef, and Sausage fit for the West and East-India market" (p. 34).*

Spanish-Portuguese Jews themselves moved foods across the new expanding sphere of Western Europe—from their Iberian roots, grapes, olive oil, and garlic spread across the globe. It is possible these people were responsible for introducing tomatoes to Southern Europe and helping to popularize them in British America, including in Williamsburg, Virginia, where Dr. John de Sequeyra was credited by Thomas Jefferson for doing so, even though enslaved Africans were growing and eating tomatoes themselves. Escabeche in Jamaican foodways—a definite Sephardic contribution—and other foods remain. According to Joan Nathan in *Jewish Cooking in America*, Aaron Lopez "was one of the few American Jews active in the slave trade. A distiller of rum and manufacturer of clothing, barrels, ships, and foods, he built an extensive transatlantic mercantile empire. From the West Indies be brought commodities like sugar, molasses, cocoa, coffee, pimiento, ginger, nutmeg, allspice, pepper, and cloves to satisfy the tastes of the colonists" (p. 10).

As Ferris notes in *Matzoh Ball Gumbo*, this culture of trade assured a cosmopolitan palate:

> *Isaac Da Costa, a well-known merchant on Broad Street and "on the Bay" in colonial Charleston, had business in South Carolina and Georgia and traded a wide range of goods with the northern colonies, the West Indies, West Africa, and Britain. Among the commodities he traded were foodstuffs such as butter, cider, rice, corn, "ship bread," flour, and beer. Other Jewish merchants advertised the sale of fruit, rum, chocolate, cordial wafers, sugar, and spirits in the Charleston newspapers. Isaac Polack of Savannah traded foodstuffs along the Atlantic and in the West Indies. Polack's advertisement in the* Georgia Gazette *of March 1790 listed "green and bohea teas, old Jamaica spirits, Philadelphia beer, gin, and brandy, loaf and brown sugar, Spanish olives, and salt" (p. 66).*

Cassava, moving from Taino/Arawak and Carib foodways into the foodways of the African Atlantic, became part of the Jewish Caribbean diet, as did an array of tropical fruits that would come to make new confections and delicious preparations of charoset. Mrs. Cardozo's often shared traditional charoset, for example, included cherry jam (I bet that it originally incorporated the fruit of the indigenous Suriname cherry—a tart red tropical fruit), coconut, spices, and the dried temperate fruits that would have been brought on ships from Europe. Alongside a mixture of Spanish-Portuguese-Moorish–influenced dishes were French, Dutch, colonial Spanish, and indigenous ingredients.

As I did my research, I happened upon an amazing out-of-print cookbook, *Recipes from the Jewish Kitchens of Curaçao* by the Sisterhood of Congregation Mikve Israel (1982). Incorporated into an old Sephardi repertoire were lots of dishes rooted in West and Central Africa and the Afro-Caribbean. Much like Suriname, the influence from Africa was long and deep owing to the slave trade that lasted from the seventeenth to the nineteenth centuries. The recipes I found were from the heart of the Guinea coast and Kongo-Angola. Fritters and fried plantains for Hannukah, soup for Shabbat, stews for other holiday meals—all mixed in with recipes drawn from across the globe.

Akaras, the classic and ancient black-eyed pea fritter, so-called by the Yoruba of Nigeria and Benin (a culturally powerful and influential Diaspora culture in their own right), became kala in Creole/Papiamento.

Kala (Black-Eyed Pea Puffs)

½ pound dry black-eyed peas

2 teaspoons salt

2 hot peppers (promèntè pika)

5 to 6 tablespoons water

½ teaspoon baking powder (optional)

Oil for frying

Soak the peas 24–36 hours in water to cover. Drain, peel, and dry thoroughly. Grind the peas very fine, adding salt and hot peppers. With a mixer, beat well while adding the water slowly. The consistency should be fluffy. Fry by spoonfuls in hot oil. Makes about 25 kalas.

Fried plantain—a favorite street snack of West African roads and markets—became "banana" chips.

"Banana" Chips

____

2 or 3 very green plantains	Salt
Oil for deep-frying	

Slit the skin and peel the plantains. Slice into very thin rounds. Separate rounds and drop them individually into hot oil. When they turn golden, almost immediately, remove them to paper towels and sprinkle with salt. Store in an airtight container.

A roux-less gumbo, giambo, its name taken from the Ovimbundu and Ki-Mbundu languages of Angola, was made into a Creole okra soup complete with the addition of basil, known in West Africa as scent-leaf, and hot pepper to keep it lively.

Giambo (Okra Soup)

____

½ pound cubed salted beef	About 4 cups okra sliced into thin rounds (about 40 small okra pods)
6 cups water	
About 1 pound cleaned fish—red snapper or muldá (wahoo) (do not wash fish with lemons)	A few sprigs of fresh basil (yerba di hole)
	Hot pepper sauce or Tabasco sauce to taste

Cover the salted beef with water and bring to a boil twice, changing the water after the first boil. Reserve the first water to add to the soup.

Cook the beef with 6 cups of water using some of the reserved salted water. Bring to a rolling boil, reduce heat, and simmer until the meat is tender, about 45 minutes.

Add the fish and cook until it flakes easily. Remove the beef, debone the fish, and then cut into bite-size pieces.

Add the okra, basil, and hot pepper or Tabasco to the broth. Simmer until okra is tender. With a wire whisk or a lele stick, reduce the okra to tiny pieces and simmer until the broth thickens.

Return the beef and fish to the broth. Adjust seasonings. Serve with funchi. Serves 6.

There is stewed burr gherkin, or Stoba di Kòmkòmber, and funji (shown here as funchi), also drawn from the cultures of Angola. The burr gherkin, or kòmkòmber, is a variety of small cucumber that have spines and a stem.

Stoba di Kòmkòmber (Curaçaoan Cucumber Stew)

6 to 8 cups kòmkòmbers

About 3 pounds lamb or beef, cut into cubes

Salt, pepper, nutmeg, and garlic and onion powders, to taste

Worcestershire sauce and Maggi, to taste

About 1 pound salted beef

2 small onions, finely chopped

2 green peppers, chopped

2 garlic cloves, minced

1 14-ounce can tomatoes

1 pound cubed potatoes

1 tablespoon tomato paste

8 tablespoons margarine

1 tablespoon sugar (optional)

Remove stems from kòmkòmbers and cut each into 4 to 6 wedges. Wash and remove as many seeds as possible.

Season lamb or beef cubes with salt, pepper, nutmeg, garlic and onion powders, and Worcestershire and Maggi sauces. Put salted beef in water to cover and bring it to a boil twice, changing the water after the first boil.

Sauté the lamb or beef cubes with onion, green pepper, garlic, and tomatoes. Simmer for 15 minutes. Add the salted beef and some water if necessary, but not too much as the kòmkòmbers will later add their water content while cooking. Cook until the meats are nearly done. Add kòmkòmbers, simmer 5–10 minutes, then add the potatoes and tomato paste; cook until potatoes are soft when pierced with a fork. Add margarine and sugar, if using, and blend well. Serves 8.

Funchi (Cornmeal Mush)

1 cup cornmeal

1½ cups cold water

1 teaspoon salt

½ cup boiling water

1 tablespoon butter or margarine

Mix the cornmeal, cold water, and salt in a heavy saucepan. Stir in the boiling water and butter or margarine. Bring to a boil and cook for about 3 minutes. Continue cooking for another 3 minutes while stirring with a wooden spoon. Mixture is done when it pulls away from the sides of the pan, and it is stiff in texture. Remove from heat. Butter a mold or a deep dish, spread funchi, shake and then turn onto a serving platter; cut into slices. Serves 4–6.

And last, a dish that is also known in contemporary Nigeria, tutu:

Tutu (Cornmeal with Black-Eyed Peas)

1 pound dry black-eyed peas

8 cups water, divided

2 cups cornmeal

¾ cup sugar

2 teaspoons salt

4 tablespoons butter or margarine, plus more for serving

Cheese, to taste

In this dish, black-eyed peas were boiled, drained, and mixed with cooked cornmeal to form a porridge, here heavily sweetened.

There was already a precedent for Black cooks in Jewish households as Southern Jewish life was born. Southern Jews didn't just eat in the manner of the African Atlantic; they shared spaces with the other Diaspora that were marginalized and exiled, but over whom many of them had far more power and mobility. If these families in Baltimore or Norfolk or Charleston, Savannah, or New Orleans, or any of the port cities of the Caribbean where many had roots, kept kosher, the complexity of the Black non-Jewish cook's workload increased tenfold. Most Southern Jews would, by custom, not keep strictly kosher, but the first generation included many who did out of habit and practice. Long before modern Southern shuls had Black folks trained to assist or be themselves *mashgichim* (people who are charged with keeping a kitchen strictly kosher), Black women and men were doing this work in some of the homes and estates of the antebellum and colonial South. Jewish women who kept kosher and Black women would have worked on a far more constant and intimate basis than their white Protestant and Catholic neighbors.

The parallels between Jewish life in the American South and the Caribbean basin and some sense of inherited tradition are further hinted at by similar practices. In the earliest years of the Moses Myers estate in Norfolk, Virginia, crabs, oysters, and the like were purchased for the food rations of the "servants." Meanwhile, in Suriname, Schorsch, citing J. D. Oppenheim, says, "House slaves in Jewish homes learned the difference between kosher and non-kosher fish . . . the former, which became known as *backra fisse* (White's fish) and the latter *ningre fisse* (Black's fish) used to feed them because it could not be consumed by the ritually observant masters." The word *treyf*, pronounced as "treef," became part of the vocabulary of Maroons (freedom seekers who escaped to the rain forest outside of the plantations and cities) for things taboo. This was a complicated meeting of cultures in an arena of power imbalance, both bearing very ancient understandings of how tradition and worldview shaped food.

Whether Caribbean or Southern Jews with Black labor understood it or not, enslaved Africans and free people of color often came from West and Central African cultures where certain dietary restrictions and taboos—Islamic or traditional African—played a role in shaping their own foodways as well. Not only that, but to the extent that the cultures and cuisines from Africa they were interacting with were born in antiquity themselves and now found themselves dispersed across a wide map has profound implications for a deeper, more thoughtful understanding of these interactions. Joining these in North America were the cultures of the Senegambians—long influenced by Islam, with some elements of Jewish engagement and settlement—and the Igbo—long mythically associated with Jews. In the eighteenth century Oladauh Equiano, a formerly enslaved Igbo, wrote that the Igbo practiced circumcision "like Jews" and were "extremely clean and had many purifications and washings . . . as the Jews." When writing of his African home, he noted that "like the Israelites . . . our government was conducted by our chiefs, our judges, our wise men, and our elders." In other words, had it been another time, a more transparent, enlightened, and rich conversation could have been had about all the currents and intersections at hand, especially among women.

Jews in the American South pushed beyond the Lowcountry, the Lower Mississippi River valley, and the Chesapeake into Appalachia, middle Tennessee, Kentucky, and the Cotton Belt. When the wave of German immigration hit during the 1820s–1840s, so did a large wave of German Jews, who settled in Baltimore, Louisville, St. Louis, and beyond. They were the next layer of culture creators, along with small trickles of Eastern European Jews, leading up to the 2.5 million predominantly Ashkenazi Jews who arrived between 1880 and 1920. Significantly smaller numbers of Sephardim from the Eastern Mediterranean arrived in that period as well, their patterns similar to the Greeks, Turks, and Slavs with whom they lived in the former Ottoman Empire.

Even as each of these groups played specific roles in the evolution of American and American Jewish food culture—from peddling wares to opening small restaurants (which in the South were a real innovation)—their domestic and communal lives moved in step with non-Jewish whites. Many of their meals were prepared by Black women and men, especially women. Enslaved people became emancipated people after a civil war that knew Jewish participation and casualties on both Union and Confederate sides, and they remained in the employ of Jewish families. Black women not only worked tirelessly for Jewish families by performing labor-intensive domestic tasks, but through their influence in the kitchen, they helped Jewish families assimilate into a demanding regional culture that required familiarity and cohesiveness. Some Southern Jews went as far as moving their religious day to Sunday and playing the organ to mimic the ways of Southern Protestants.

It's no accident that I heard the same exact Shabbat meal described by two seventy-year-olds—one who still lived near Savannah, and another who was far away in Maine—who grew up in the Mikveh Israel community, both Ashkenazi. They described a Shabbat meal of okra soup, red rice, fried or barbecued chicken, challah, collard greens made with beef bacon or sausage, and peach cobbler or pie. In both cases, the cook was Black. Not all families had Black domestics, but in most cases, the spread was learned through close interaction at one point or another with a Black cook or Black associates. Sephardi Southern Jews did not usually entrust the cooking to Black domestics—probably because, in my estimation, the basic ingredients (black-eyed peas, okra, peppers, rice, tomatoes) were far too similar and prepared in adjacent ways. But for many Ashkenazi Jews, the refreshing update to their home cuisine and go at assimilation into everyday Southern culture was irresistible.

Not every dish was creolized and mixed with regional elements, but many were. People ate what was cheap or affordable and easily available—grits, black-eyed peas, leafy greens, rice and gravies, and soups. Briskets and roast chickens shared the stage with fried and barbecued meats, collards cooked in schmaltz, black-eyed peas and kishke, gefilte fish made from trout or redfish, red beans, rice, fried whiting or flounder and grits, jambalaya, gumbo, Charleston bunch soup with kneidlach, dirty matzoh, and Hanukkah beignets. Macaroni and cheese went onto Jewish tables, kugel onto non-Jewish Black tables, but the exchange was not even; many traditional Eastern European foods were not to the taste of Southern Black folk. But more than that, African American women who worked as domestics mostly kept work life in the white world and the safety and security of their own domestic Black spaces separate and distinct.

As I combed through all of these stories and recipes brought to life by Marcie Cohen Ferris, Mildred Covert, Sylvia Gerson, and Joan Nathan, among many others, I had to do a bit of reverse translation regarding things I understood from traditional Southern, Creole, and overall African Atlantic foodways. I had to try to get insight into the predominantly Black cooks who made this food possible, not because I wanted to be performative or be an expert; I simply wanted to create a food repertoire that allowed for improvisation and creativity and to advance kosher Southern cuisine. I understood that it would be important for me as an African American, Southern culinarian who was also Jewish, to have a culinary voice that could speak to those parts of who I am.

I don't always know how to feel as I work through these recipes. It feels as though I am bilingual, but it also feels as if I'm plumbing the depths of someone else's secrets. And yet this cuisine wasn't a secret; it just wasn't primarily consumed by Black people. Black people absorbed Jewish deli foods and ingredients; we liked roast chicken and brisket, but unlike other ethnic communities, we didn't seem to absorb much from the crossing of foods described here. So here I am, translating these ideas about food into my life where they can be absorbed and integrated to beautify and enhance my practice and my peoplehood.

Whenever I cook these dishes, I acknowledge the men and women who went before me. At the same time, I don't just make this "Miss Daisy" food. Sometimes, my mind goes to Brazil, Haiti, or mainland Latin America, where some of these cultural intersections and histories also exist. Sometimes I just mix up contemporary West African and Israeli food with our Southern and Sephardic or Ashkenazi Caribbean dishes. Even if I am incredibly alone in this, it still satisfies me; I am bringing people back to life, and I am helping myself really live.

This, too, is Jewish food.

Mayseh:
DRIVING MISS DAISY

I suppose it's time to confess that I didn't really have a reference point for Southern Jewish life or the intimacy of Black-Jewish relationships in the Deep South until Pulitzer Prize–winner Alfred Uhry's *Driving Miss Daisy* moved from play to film. Starring the incomparable Morgan Freeman and Jessica Tandy, not to mention the great Esther Rolle, the film is both tender and grating as it tackles change, getting older, losing control, gaining perspective, and losing grace. Like many portrayals of the civil rights era, for the early twentieth-century crowd, the film has aged with a bit of representational patina. Whether some might see it as a "white savior" movie or a "magical Negro" movie is completely unimportant to me. This movie, to be fair, was based on assumptions about the different characters' perspectives—Hoke Coleman, the driver. Daisy Werthan, the Jewish employer, and Idella, the maid (note that Idella doesn't have a last name), Boolie Werthan (Miss Daisy's son), and others were as large an audience as probably ever before for documenting the role of Black domestics in the Southern Jewish experience with all of the racial and anti-Semitic trauma that went with it.

Four of my grandparents who were products of the Jim Crow South were living when that movie came out in 1989. For my Alabama-born and -raised grandmother, Hazel Todd Townsend, movies like *Driving Miss Daisy* were bittersweet because they raised in her very complicated feelings about a Southern girlhood that seemed simple and cohesive and yet nightmarish and uncertain. Watching movies like this with her brought out the original researcher in me. I wanted to know what was real and what was made up. To my horror, the bad parts to her were never bad enough. The way that "white" others looked down upon and treated colored people was never quite as vibrant onscreen as she had lived it.

One Jewish store owner in Birmingham she recalled was particularly mean, abusive, and sexually vulgar toward Black girls, but to my maternal grandmother, his identification with whiteness was the important issue, although being a Jew clearly stood out in her memory and that of her two younger sisters. I don't remember her having any particular bad feelings toward Jews, but it was very clear that whispers about dagoes, hunkies, and hymies sat right along with crackers and peckerwoods in the vocabulary of the older Black ladies of my childhood. Although loving and accepting of all, my grandmother lived with a very keen sense that white people were inherently suspect and mean as the devil until proved otherwise. What would you think if they almost lynched your father and called your mother a "nigra gal," or claimed to be innocent after injuring your mother in a hit-and-run accident, or marched down the streets of your neighborhood wearing Klan robes? The others—the Italians, the Jews, the Poles and Hungarians, the Greeks and the like who trickled behind the old British and Celtic Southerners—usually represented in their minds two extremes: those who bought a ticket on the white supremacy train, and those who didn't—and the latter were seen as saints in waiting.

Watching my grandmother's face during *Driving Miss Daisy* was as important as watching the movie. A lot of the movie made her angry because she remembered a world where you could do all of the intimate work of helping someone exist but not share a meal with them or hug or have them call you "Sir" or "Ma'am" or Mr. or Mrs. or Miss. She openly cussed as Daisy accused Hoke of stealing a can of salmon, or as Hoke and Daisy were harassed by racist cops—were there any other kind?—on the roadside in Alabama. The scene amps up from two sharing memories to a lanky ersatz Barney Fife going, "Hey, boy, what you think you're doing with this car?" Daisy acknowledges it is her car and that she has ownership of it, and as the cop peruses Hoke's license and Daisy's registration, he asks her what kind of name Werthan is, which he mispronounces. Daisy responds, "It's of German derivation," which the cop repeats as if her secret is out and his scorn has already grown deeper. As the scene transitions and they get the hell out of Dogpatch, the cop opines, "An old nigger and an old Jew woman taking off down the road together. Now that is one sorry sight."

This movie was also my first exposure to the infamous bombing of Atlanta's premier Reform synagogue of the era, The Temple. This was one of many major moments in the history of civil rights that just didn't get much play as the country looked back twenty-five to thirty years later. Open support for civil rights by a rabbi or Jewish congregants meant the Jewish community would become a target. The scene is dramatized by Hoke telling Daisy she won't be attending Temple for a while. When she is told it was bombed, she is astonished but rebuffs Hoke's attempt to compare her grief with his own, having known many friends and family who were victims of Georgia lynchings. You're left wondering why she doesn't want to accept the bridge to understanding or why such a major event in American history, let alone American Jewish history, is something she's never heard of.

My grandmother had heard of it. The Klan formula at the time was very simple: Negro, Jew, Catholic, or sympathizer—the penalty for not knowing your place, even after the Holocaust, was death. She had already left the South by 1958 when the real event occurred, but being in Cincinnati, in close proximity to Border State Jews, it was certainly in the cycle of current events. Some Ohio Jews later went South to register Black folks to vote, and some of them trained at Miami University, where Andrew Goodman did civil rights organizing before he was murdered for his activism along with James Chaney and Michael "Mickey" Schwerner. Jews in the South once again had to wrestle with the eternal question of which "side" they were on and who had their best interests at heart, and for those encountering Jews from outside the region, it was contentious and unnerving. One woman I interviewed in Birmingham told me that Rabbi Abraham Joshua Heschel "and the people who were involved in Freedom Summer and other parts of the movement were not heroes to my parents; they were troublemakers who they and many others thought would get Jews killed." Indeed, the Conservative synagogue in Birmingham was nearly bombed, had a Black janitor not found the device just in time; and not far away, the Sixteenth Street Baptist Church was bombed, and four little girls paid the ultimate price for simply trying to be Americans.

This complex blend of art, real history, family memory, and popular culture is unique to our existence in an age of television, streaming services, movies, home entertainment, and constant recorded debate over our perceptions of ourselves and the past. It goes with us into the kitchen, and it becomes part of our conversations at the kitchen table and over the meals we prepare. This mix becomes part of who we are and how we navigate spaces. For a twelve-year-old, those scenes seared themselves in my mind for safekeeping. I cannot make my matzoh meal fried chicken—the ultimate Southern Passover dish—without thinking of Hoke gently scolding Miss Daisy for turning the heat up too much or having the chicken pieces be too close to one another; or the haunting nature of his placing a plate of food before Miss Daisy as he withdraws to the kitchen to eat his chicken separately with a plate full of rice, okra, and hot sauce.

I knew why, but I didn't understand *why*.

13

THE GRIOT FROM BLYTHEVILLE: DR. MARCIE COHEN FERRIS

I am fortunate that one of the major players in how this story unfolds is a great friend and mentor. I almost never met her. Habitually late, I just barely made it into cookbook author Joan Nathan's car as she and Marcie Cohen Ferris took me to a Hadassah event in DC where Marcie was the guest speaker. I was lucky; a long bus and Metro ride from Silver Spring to almost the other side of the Red Line did not stand a candle against an introduction that was *bashert*. Joan and Marcie remain the two greatest living documentarians of American Jewish culinary history and life—and a barely twenty-something me was in the car with them headed to a presentation on culinary history.

I hardly understood what culinary history was, but once I saw Marcie give a talk on it, I knew I wanted to study and teach it. Enrolled in the Ph.D. program in American Studies at George Washington University at the time under the stewardship of John Michael Vlach—a monumental scholar of African American folk and material culture—Marcie gave me hope that there was something useful and meaningful about doing this work. She began her presentation with her grandmother's recipe box and stories told around the table in

Blytheville, Arkansas. The pamphlet passed around that day would later become what, for many like me, is a form of scripture. The title of her classic book *Matzoh Ball Gumbo: Culinary Tales of the Jewish South* is drawn from an interview with Ms. Mildred Covert. It is a scholarly work that delights in complexities like the one expressed here:

> *Leanne Silverblaft of Indianola, Mississippi, says that "growing up Jewish in the South is hard to explain to someone who is not from here and hasn't experienced it—because it was mixed up and intertwined together. We are Jewish, but we're southern. And sometimes we feel more comfortable with southern Christians than we feel with Jews from another part of the country . . . yet we have a very strong sense of Jewishness, and we are very adamant that we want to be Jewish, and we want our children to be Jewish." While southern Jews share the same religious heritage as urban Jews in the Northeast, they bond with non-Jewish southerners through fried chicken, cornbread, and field peas. (p. 23)*

My conversation with Marcie began with an immediate, profound truth both of us acknowledge as being at the core of why we do this searching at all. Without hesitation, she said to me, "If you can't find yourself in history, it's very hard for you to feel meaning." The film *Driving Miss Daisy* was a potent cultural moment for her as well, but in a very different way than it was for me. That movie, she told me, "recognized our experience, especially in the canon of popular Jewish culture and especially American Jewish culture. We don't see ourselves as Southern Jews."

She continued: "When I was in a college folklore class, I came across Eli Evans's book *The Provincials*, a lay history of Southern Jews, and it just dawned on me, 'I think I will write about my people.' People from off think that the sum of being Southern and Jewish boils down to 'those people just happen to live there,' but that's not our history. Early on, as I presented about Southern Jewish food, I was supposed to present at someplace in New York, and they were horrified that I was going to do some *treif* nightmare. They assumed disrespect on my part that we don't know better not to live there, and they disrespect *kashrut* out of ignorance or zeal."

And yet, the overall response to Marcie's version of Southern Jewish history—told through food and treated as a living, breathing tradition—is that readers, particularly women, have been moved to see their families and their stories reflected. "I'm glad Southern Jewish readers have had a voice or seen some aspect of their experience honored and were encouraged to preserve and honor or treasure their American Jewish experience," Marcie said. "The material culture of Jewish foodways is very strong to me as a woman. I was in the kitchen with my mother a lot. I have a whole thing in me genetically that tells me how to prepare for the holidays; the cloth to wrap the challah in, the tablecloth and the special silverware, the world of women's ritual and Jewish practice. I still have my grandmother Luba's pots where she made the best chicken soup and matzoh balls. She was stylish and Bohemian with lots of Russian elegance. I cooked a lot with my grandmother—latkes for breakfast; her home definitely had that Grandma Jewish smell. She had a beautiful garden. I really paid attention to those women, to the relationships of my mother and the temple. Those women were very close. They hooted it up, they ran the Sunday school and kept it going, they were strong, and they held each other up through every challenge and struggle. I think they survived the worst of it with their pound cake.

"Blytheville—from Little Rock, it is about two and a half hours, maybe an hour from Memphis. Our temple was a small synagogue in northeastern Arkansas. Temple Israel. Materially it was very important; it was a place where we went to. I have to say, in these pivotal times, I felt very safe there. It was always a place of refuge. There wasn't a lot of overt, obvious anti-Semitism, but it was there. As a little kid, every now and then, someone would say something to me in school that hurt my feelings. Even in the fifth or seventh grade, somebody would ask me about burning in hell. They said, 'We like you, but we're worried about your soul.' But even then, I experienced that in a limited way because I was protected by the community."

What people don't understand about Southern Jewish communities like Marcie's and beyond is that their Jewish engagement and involvement and even the practice of preparing and serving food meant that there was strength and security in numbers. Keeping kosher and going to the *mikveh* and other hallmarks of traditional Judaism could be found in some communities, but for the most part, the emphasis lay in being counted, being present, and being there for one another. Jews throughout history formed communities where their skills, experience, and knowledge were needed and set them apart, but nothing set Jews on the margins more than their core identity and history and experience of marginalization. They were not the only people who found themselves trying to keep up with the elites, grandees, and intellects of Southern society, but they had an extra hurdle to jump—they were not Christians, and their ethnicity was a conundrum in a system clearly based on a binary of Black versus white.

"There were times I didn't want to be there," Marcie said. "Who wants to go to Sunday school? But to this day, I still have very important relationships that have spun out of that synagogue. I can still see the worn blue covers of the *Union Prayer Book* and hear my mother playing the organ, and we even had members of a Methodist or Baptist church who might come in and sing on the High Holidays.

"We ate a lot there. It was a window for how food played a role in Judaism and how food played a role in my Jewish life, and how that food shaped Southern Jewish life. My mother, Huddy, grew up in New England in Connecticut from Polish Jewish roots, and my father, Jerry, grew up in a nonreligious home in northeast Arkansas, with roots from Odessa and Minsk."

Matzoh Ball Gumbo and her later work, *The Edible South*, gave voice to Southern Jewish women and the Black women in their intersections with these families as bakers, domestics, cooks, kitchen managers, and a million different roles. "I remember meeting a Black man in Atlanta working for a shul," Marcie said. "Whole families from the African American community had a legacy of working with or for synagogues and their related families."

But Marcie's work has always been realistic about the origins of that relationship in the colonial and antebellum South, as her work attests: "At the center of all these culinary worlds stood enslaved African Americans. So by 1860, more than four million African American slaves were held in bondage on plantations and in the homes and businesses of middle and upper-class white southerners, including southern Jews. If a Jewish businessman needed slaves and could afford them, he bought them. Participating in slavery allowed Jews both to prosper in the local economy and to demonstrate their loyalty to the white South" (*Matzoh Ball Gumbo*, p. 95). The food, albeit remarkably rich in its backstory, was part of a larger system that wasn't, and isn't, happy or nostalgic, and Marcie asked me onstage, in front of an audience, Jew to Jew, Southern Jew to new Southern Jew, what it would mean to be an enslaved cook or domestic on Passover hearing the words, "Now we are slaves; next year may we be free in Jerusalem."

Marcie's coming of age, like that of many Southern Jews I interviewed, was textured by the coming of integration. "Growing up Jewish in the Deep South was growing up in a Black and white South and more," she said. "Those were the most significant aspects of your daily life. After civil rights, we still lived in a very segregated place. We dealt with the pushback against civil rights, as we fight today for it not to be diminished. There was a lot of realization that a lot of the legal changes were not being enforced. The boycotts against racist treatment and inequity were frequent. My mom, a just woman, helped the best she could. It got expressed in our synagogue in creative services, alternative services utilizing themes of racial justice.

"My mom was really involved in social justice. She was a stay-at-home mom but a real activist. It was a big deal having a group of integrated women in our living room. We were the only family that would put up two African American girls who came to our town with the nonprofit educational organization Up with People. My dad, a civil engineer, and his father, Jimmy, a very Russian Jew, were both involved in agriculture and flood control. My father would tell me about Black men who worked for them and were segregated by skill, got less money, and weren't allowed to perform certain jobs. He became best friends with a young Black contractor in Little Rock. It changed my dad's life in very significant ways. He was just a man, my dad. My parents set an example for us, and moral suasion and social justice became part of my Southern Jewish cultural awareness and identity."

As we spoke about her relationship to food, Marcie paused to take a long breath. "It evolves, right? How we figure out how our story relates to the whole. It's all these pieces that come together. You know, in my travels, I've been able to witness and document an entire range of responses to what it means to be Jewish and Southern. What does Southern Jewish food taste like? The best answer I can give is, it tastes like we're going to be okay. You know it's roast chicken for Shabbos—honey orange chicken or barbecued chicken and the kind of things we grew up with, like Le Sueur canned peas with mushrooms or kugels where pecans found their way in or tzimmes made with local farm-grown sweet potatoes and brisket on the holidays was the line between the South and between Jewish depending on the secrets—Coca-Cola or Eastern Carolina sauce.

"In Louisiana, I was most moved by the adaptations, the dirty matzoh, and beef-based soups—German, Central European Jewish-based soups; but then there's also Creole matzoh ball soup with the Cajun trinity [of onions, bell peppers, and celery] and tomatoes and matzoh balls with ginger in them. Everywhere in the South, there is this reflection of urban immigrant influence from Central Europe meeting the rural South. Butter beans, okra, and collard greens and field peas and snap beans—African American women's presence, everyday local seasonal Southern vegetables, and fish and grits, fried chicken in matzoh meal, black-eyed peas, and kishke—it's endless. Talismans—that's what my Southern Jewish foods are to me. They bring me back to a centered place for myself where I can reconnect to my family, to the people who raised me up."

Mayseh:

THE OTHER (WHITE) JEWS— THE KOSHERSOUL OF SOUTHERN WHITE JEWS-BY-CHOICE

One of my biggest audiences consists of white Southerners with predominantly but not exclusively Protestant origins who have fully embraced *kashrut* but are seriously invested in maintaining Southern culture—especially through food. I hear things like: "I'm from Louisiana, I'm a former Catholic, but I just have to have my King Cake at Mardi Gras time, and thank Hashem, the one I can get up here is also kosher, surprise surprise—or kosher enough." The break with nonkosher food, on whatever level, they assume is important. It's cleansing on multiple levels, and I assume from some of the things I've been told in confidence that it relates to the prejudices and cultural issues and ancestral trauma these folks were raised with. As Rabbi Chaim Frazer once told me, "You can't have a conversion without a conversion." In other words, the changes you choose to make to fit in with Yiddishkeit are significant and important.

On a practical level, these folks mostly want to know about

substitutions, but it's deeper than that: they want to know how I meld meanings. The reality is that we are all—no matter our Ancestral roots, which may connect us to Jewish peoplehood—coming from a lived experience that is at odds not only with the culture and cuisine we were raised within but also with many American Jews for whom partial or full *kashrut* observance is not a thing. Southern food is supposed to entertain and communalize, and when you first shift your religious observance and diet, your circles shrink. The question of who your people are becomes more profound than you bargained for. Fittingly enough, these conversations remind me how much white Southerners and I have in common and the kinds of things we can talk about outside of sports, Jesus, and mileage—and everybody's unspoken elephant, past Southern historical trauma and current racial flashpoints.

I Miss Cheerwine

My ideal Shabbos dinner is challah, fried chicken, rice and butter beans, and a salad. Or barbecued brisket, collard greens, rice, and big lima beans and challah.

—*Cherie*

My ideal Shabbos dinner is fried chicken, mashed potatoes, collard greens (cooked with smoked turkey), freshly boiled squash, butter beans, fresh extra-rich egg challah, cream corn, okra, sweet noodle kugel, red velvet cake with extra pecans, banana pudding, homemade peach ice cream made with fresh Georgia peaches. But this could all change tomorrow!

—*Sean*

For me, it gotta be mashed potatoes (which we prefer rather than kugel), white gravy, biscuits, hot sauce, grits, veggie chili (especially with corn chips and rice), collards, fried chicken (the plant-based version now), and waffles, and sometimes fried (kosher) fish. As a family, we tend to put hot sauce on everything. I've seen my husband throw hot sauce in his matzoh ball soup! Growing up, my grandmother told us that good food should make your nose run from the spice and clear your sinuses and that you cannot truly be a Texan unless you like spicy chili.

—*Erin*

My conversations with white Southerners who have converted to Judaism have highlighted how we come from a common culture, albeit a culture made common because of our shared African and European roots and ancestry. Most had Scots-Irish, English, German, and French roots. They came from Florida, Texas, Georgia, the Appalachian South to the Gulf Coast, and beyond. Most missed Southern foods because it hits a chord. I always like to start with favorites, and Cherie's list was classic: field peas/butter beans and rice, corn pudding, cornbread, pecan pie, collard greens, pecan pralines, grits, buttermilk biscuits, okra, fried chicken.

Sean listed all the foods he loves but can't eat regularly for health reasons or because they simply aren't kosher; it reads like a culinary *Al Chet* (the confession on Yom Kippur). "The Southern foods I can't live without—which means I make them at some point every year," he told me, "are grits (butter and salt only), biscuits, sautéed okra, hoecakes, and cooked greens (collard, mustard, or turnip greens with the turnips chopped up and cooked with the greens, G-d it's so good!). The one dish I make most often since it's one of the easiest to make healthy is my mama's red beans and rice. No added fat except what's in the sausage, so that's a plus for us.

"As for other Southern foods I'd die for, here are a few off the top of my head:

- *Banana pudding*
- *Creamed field corn (we used to cream it by hand with a metal mayonnaise jar lid that had holes poked in it with a screwdriver)*
- *Ham steak with gravy (even though I can't eat it anymore)*
- *Field peas/butter beans/pink-eyed purple hull peas*
- *Yeast rolls (smothered in butter!)*
- *Chicken and dumplings*
- *Fried catfish (I can't eat that anymore either!)*
- *Boiled shrimp (this is getting painful)*
- *Boiled peanuts*
- *Pecan pie—or ANYTHING with pecans; I love 'em!*
- *Fried steak with gravy*
- *Fried crawfish (the sadness!)*
- *Deviled eggs*
- *And that coconut cake that that one old lady at church brought on special occasions to eat after services, and it was heavenly*
- *And don't get me started on Cool Whip . . ."*

For Sean, shellfish was more of a sacrifice than pork: "The biggest loss for me, more so than any pork dish, was the seafood I had to give up—specifically fried catfish, boiled shrimp, crab, and crawfish tails. For me, there just isn't a substitution for shellfish. The other loss was my mama's fried ham steak. She'd fry up whole ham steaks and use the juices to make a gravy for rice on the side. And I loved the fried marrow from the steak bone."

Erin had a similar list of common indulgences. "Catfish is probably the only one I miss sometimes," she told me. "We used to go fishing and fry up the catfish with our friends. Fish cookouts were a big thing. Bass isn't quite the same.

"Crabs and shrimp weird me out now, even though I grew up eating them. Growing up, we also used to grill burgers, and I put cheese on mine. I was also a fan of chicken parmesan. I have basically given up all meat for *kashrut* and ethical reasons, but I sometimes eat fish.

Kosher meat is a bit of a pain to procure around here, so I prefer to just stay vegetarian. I miss fried chicken more than anything, but there are really good plant-based alternatives now."

As I listened to Erin, I couldn't relate to eating cheese on burgers—I never really enjoyed or needed that. And I'm not a fan of catfish and haven't eaten a bite of it, but I can make an awesome antebellum catfish stew.

Another interviewee, Angela's, comments helped recall that much of traditional rural Southern cooking involved catching fish, hunting, and trapping: "I was born and raised in Florida, which doesn't get enough credit for being as country as it really is. My mom was from the Appalachian coalfields, and my dad was all Alabama. I grew up eating whatever game meats my dad dragged home; my mom has more than one recipe for rattlesnake, and it was squirrel or rabbit at least one night a week. We were on the coast of Florida, so there was tons of shellfish. When my dad would get a hog or a deer, he'd trade stew meat with the fishermen at the port and bring home a sack of shrimp or crabs. My grandfather, an old Coonass from Mobile, was the only one who ever bought me a left-handed oyster shucking glove, and that's how I know I was his favorite grandchild.

"I, too, tried to make equivalencies and substitutions, thinking they would translate, and they clearly didn't. Macaroni and cheese and kugel might be cousins, but they are quite distant. Chicken and dumplings our way is not matzoh ball soup." Angela described a list of walls and boundaries that didn't help on her kosher journey that sounds very similar to mine, although I do love kneidlach and latkes.

"I was disappointed," Angela continued. "People joke about latkes being hash browns, but I truly couldn't taste a difference between a latke and a double order of Waffle House hash browns, and scattered and covered does not involve applesauce. Matzoh ball soup reminded me of my Aunt Sarah's chicken and dumplings—those firm, unleavened, rolled-and-cut dumplings that taste like flour and chicken fat, not my mom's fluffy drop biscuits with garlic and white pepper in the dough. Like, falafel? How are you gonna tell me hush puppies are a sandwich ingredient? I miss Cheerwine and couldn't vibe with Dr. Brown's Cel-Ray. I wasn't into lox. I've haaaated beets since I was a kid. There was so much in kosher/Jewish cuisine that I could not hang with. My conception of 'Jewish food,' of course, was firmly rooted somewhere between a Russian shtetl and a New York deli. I wondered if I could even be Jewish if I couldn't 'do' Jewish."

For his part, Sean had a laundry list of favorite Jewish foods although he and his husband now live in New York City:

- *"I really like cholent. I heard someone refer to it as Jewish soul food, and I kind of agree with that sentiment, seeing as how warm and comforting it is to eat."*
- *"Latkes. Cook 'em up shredded, and it's like little hash brown patties. Love 'em."*
- *"Fresh gefilte fish. I didn't think I'd like it, but I actually do enjoy it. Never from the jar, though."*
- *"Challah. Of course."*
- *"Kugel—potato or sweet noodle."*
- *"A good Everything Bagel."*
- *"Matzoh ball soup. I've made several batches of it in this quarantine alone."*
- *"Lots of Jewish baked desserts."*

Erin's list was far more taken from the global cuisine of Israel, which draws heavily on the Jewish Diaspora: "I love shakshuka, challah, kugel, falafel, tahini, babka, matzoh ball soup, matzoh brie, you name it. I love trying foods from all over the world, and the Jewish people have made their home literally everywhere and adapted the cuisine for *kashrut*. Ethiopian food is one of my favorite cuisines, and I have read that doro wot is used as a Shabbat stew. I no longer eat chicken since I started raising my own for eggs, but I used to LOVE doro wot."

Given the finicky nature of Black and white Southern approaches to what ingredient belongs in what dish, I asked about substitutions. Sean replied: "There are other dishes that require substitutions, which are usually pretty painless, like smoked turkey for ham in collard greens and fried chicken skin for pork rinds in crackling cornbread. I try to come up with kosher solutions for things frequently.

"One thing I used to do but no longer do is dairy substitutes. It works on occasion, but it usually just changes the flavor or texture too much for me to enjoy it, and I end up wishing I'd made something else instead."

(Rabbi Twitty comments: "Smoked turkey and gribenes are truly the answer to everything. I would agree—dairy should stay dairy; it's very hard to make a good pareve tasting anything, and mayonnaise is sure as hell not getting involved.")

Cherie uses stale challah to make her bananas foster bread pudding. Erin's substitutions were cultural: "I tend to do mashed potatoes in place of kugel for holiday dinners. My family also tends to pull apart the challah and eat it biscuit-style. I've seen other families do that as well. I like to eat a challah ball with some butter and honey, the way I was raised eating biscuits."

Erin reminded me that Southern food isn't just what you eat; it's how you eat it and the way you talk about it. It's the forming of the hand to break, to sop, to drag. It's how you eat it as a family, the community you form as you consume. It has its own language and scripture. And Southern food is flexible and doesn't mind company. Angela summed it up for us all: "I believe there's room to be both entirely Jewish and entirely Southern, and live and eat and celebrate both of those lived experiences. I've found creative ways to riff on those Ashkenazi traditional foods and ways to make my Southern favorites kosher."

Mayseh:
A SOUTHERN GUIDE TO *TASHLICH*

*T*ashlich is an ancient symbolic ritual among Jews where we scatter crumbs from our pockets into a body of water with fish in it. As our friends below nibble, it symbolizes parting ways with our sins. We say a few psalms, make personal commitments to change for the better, and then shift to atonement in preparation for Yom Kippur.

If you are anywhere below the Mason-Dixon Line, I invite you to a special Southern *tashlich* service. Bring your appropriate baked goods tomorrow afternoon:

If you gossip too much: deep-dish peach cobbler
If you are too affectionate and cause your partner to be late: spoon bread
If you are way too Lowcountry for your own good: rice waffles
If "it's always complicated" and you have layers of issues: Smith Island cake
If you're always getting in trouble: hot water cornbread
If you are too New Orleans for your own good: beignets
For bland sins: water challah

For really tasty sins: extra egg challah

For hardheadedness: beaten biscuits

For sins of cultural appropriation and overall racist b.s.: Aunt Jemima pancakes

For sins that even G-d doesn't understand: gluten-free buttermilk biscuits

For the sin of looking at somebody else's form: apple dumplings

For the sins of addiction: Krispy Kreme fresh off the conveyor belt

For the sin of going to funerals just for the food: caramel cake

For the sin of driving people crazy: pecan pie

For the sin of having bad taste in recipes: Frito pie

For the sin of having bad taste in presidents: Cheeto pie

For regret over a Stein vote: grasshopper pie

For the sin of always judging the hats ladies wear to services: lemon meringue pie

For the sin of being too Conch: key lime pie

For the sin of being too damn good: peanut pie

For the sin of being too eastern Kentucky for your own good: stack cake

For the sin of killing people with kindness: sweet potato pie

For the sin of writing this and laughing at my own jokes: cornbread

Happy Rosh Hashanah!

Mayseh:
HALAL SOUL CHEF SHAMBRA

Philadelphia has one of the largest African American Sunni Muslim populations in America. Although the community began largely centered in the Nation of Islam founded by the Honorable Elijah Muhammad, many also later became part of a more orthodox practice under his son Warith Deen Muhammad and other movements with a more global approach to Islam. Today the plurality of Muslims in Philadelphia have African American origins, with the community numbering around two hundred thousand. Concentrations of Muslims live in Germantown and West, North, and South Philly, and the call to prayer and *Jummah* gatherings on Friday afternoon are a key part of the city's culture, including the United Muslim Masjid founded by Philadelphia legend and creator of the sound of Philadelphia Kenny Gamble, known by his Muslim name, Luqman Abdul Haqq. As of 2018, the political and cultural clout of the community successfully advocated for Eid being an acceptable reason to be absent from work.

Philadelphia has always been an important Black urban center. Although it was north of the Mason-Dixon Line, the city was part of the trans-Atlantic slave trade, receiving African exiles from what is now Ghana, Senegambia, Sierra Leone, Kongo-Angola, and Madagascar. Many of the city's Sephardic merchants had connections with the local food and provision trade with the West Indies. Black West Indians came to Philadelphia first as enslaved labor and later as freedmen, including outliers from Haiti during and after the Haitian revolution and later after emancipation in the British Caribbean. Many of these families, and those who had sought their freedom and escaped from Maryland, Virginia, and Delaware, were prominent in the food trade—from markets to taverns to catering. Black Philadelphia produced superb catering dynasties, the Mintons, the Augustins, the Dorseys, and others, earning their notoriety from high society into the pages of W. E. B. Du Bois's landmark sociological study *The Philadelphia Negro*. During the Great Migration, old Black Philadelphia, a hotbed of abolitionist activity and free Black life, was eclipsed by folks coming north from the Eastern Shore of Maryland, central and Tidewater Virginia, and the Lowcountry of the Carolinas and Georgia.

Chef Shambra, a caterer and food entrepreneur born and raised in Philadelphia, has an identity that meets at the crossroads of all of these stories. She is a member of the large Muslim community; both of her parents made Shahadah in the Nation of Islam and later became Sunnis. Her mother's roots are from John's Island, not far from Charleston, South Carolina, and her father's family roots are from Orangeburg along the coastal plain. I spoke to her because I felt that her narrative was in many ways a bridge between us all—between Southern Jews and Southern white converts to Judaism, and a long history of African American Muslims and the story of African American Jews with diasporas and roots in the South and the Caribbean floating in between and Chava with influences from the Persian community. What did it mean to share so much and still be so different? I wanted to understand the distinctions along with the common threads.

Chef Shambra's father was a chef and food entrepreneur who owned a snack company, and she had positive images of African American youth and Muslim figures. "I remember cleaning fish with my father—scaling, gutting, and frying them up. The Nation of Islam had a fish marketing project, and whiting was very important to that. We had a restaurant later on named African Cajun Fish, which was very popular. I went to culinary school in the city." Much of her diet growing up was shaped by the dietary culture of the Nation of Islam. "Fish chowders, whole wheat bread was essential, and my father was the main distributor and baker for the Ali [navy] bean pie."

How to Eat to Live by Elijah Muhammad, the main food text of the Nation of Islam, its "*kashrut*" guide, not only shaped the diet of followers of the Nation; its influence went far beyond that, making it a signature text in the attempt to reform and represent the African American diet. Popular and influential, the book included a lot of symbolic nods to shame over slavery and the sharecropping past. To reclaim respect and authority, it was argued that "the so-called Negro" had to abandon not only pork but collard greens, cornbread, sweet potatoes, black-eyed peas, and other foods. "If you were used to using ham with your greens or peas," Chef Shambra said, "he wanted to just do away with it all and reorient you and have you cook just navy beans." *The Final Call*, the official newspaper of the Nation of Islam, published recipes for corn pudding instead of cornbread, and carrot cake and pie and carrot fluff replaced sweet potato pie and candied yams. "The yam was bad," Chef Shambra says, "but if you added sugar to your carrot fluff, you were good! Instead of modifying the preparation, he said, 'Let's do something different.' It was about making a new Black man and a new Black woman." Elijah Muhammad's approach was contemporary with the Urban League and other organizations at the time that discouraged elements of rural Southern Black culture from updating and modernizing African American life—similar to efforts in the Jewish community during the time of mass immigration from Eastern Europe.

Although Elijah Muhammad did not outlaw the patronizing of kosher butchers and admired the Orthodox Jewish commitment to *kashrut*, he was ambiguous about trusting anyone outside the community. He advocated for more of a vegetarian and pescatarian diet, with limited use of white sugar and dairy. His commitment to a nationalist approach was centered on keeping money and commerce within the Black community. He also encouraged extended fasts for his followers and a commitment to healthier eating that inspired other health food movements. "My parents had a health food store called Carrot Top," Chef Shambra remembers, "and when we were kids, they didn't use white sugar. They were very health conscious—it was a throwback to what they were taught in the Nation. We used sorghum, carob, sesame seed candy."

Chef Shambra is still committed to healthier eating, as are many in the Muslim community, but she enjoys it in balance. Fried chicken is one of her favorite South Carolina delicacies, and she also loves collard greens and smoked turkey. "With the influence of West African cousins, I've recently started adding smoked dried fish," she says. "What really makes me happy is black-eyed peas. A nice piece of fried chicken and a piece of cornbread, and I'm happy. That's what I find comforting. Summertime—give me fried fish and a really good potato salad. That's my happy plate—and don't forget the greens."

Many in the Muslim community enjoy traditional Southern food made halal. Lima beans and smoked turkey, peach cobbler, red rice, barbecued chicken, okra and tomatoes, potato salad and beef ribs, and beef hot-links are standard family gathering and backyard cookout fare. And steamed crabs. Chef Shambra continues: "My family were crab eaters; my grandmother would get a bushel of crabs, steam them at home, and sell them off the front porch through the window in a piece of newspaper. That and fresh sugarcane. My family would eat crab with plenty of Old Bay, corn, and potatoes, and because it's Philadelphia, you have to have broccoli. We had multiple crab feasts through the summer."

Philadelphia soul likes to incorporate cream cheese, borrowing subtle elements from the surrounding food cultures—Italian, Jewish deli culture, Mexican regional foodways, and cuisines from across Africa and Asia. The layers in the African American Muslim community are many. The fried fish hoagie is a staple, and the bread must be whole wheat. Chef Shambra is adamant: "In Philadelphia, it's not legit unless it's on a whole wheat roll." Tomato-based vegetarian navy bean soup, carrot pie, bean pie, and several other delicacies have become part and parcel of how Black Philadelphia eats, partly through the many eateries owned by members of the Muslim community. We all remember growing up having Akbar juice as a treat. (Akbar juice usually included orange juice, pineapple juice, grape juice, lemon juice, and carbonated water. Chef Shambra's Dad added coconut water or coconut cream.)

During Ramadan, the food becomes a mixture of the ethnic diversity of the community. *Iftar* meals, which end the daily Ramadan fast, are sponsored by different families and communities within the larger Muslim community and have affected the diet of the African American members as well. And this is reciprocal; the dishes of Southern migrants have been introduced to others. That means upside-down date cake—a play on both American/Southern upside-down cake and the customary dates that reflect the way the Prophet Muhammad was said to break his fast. Because of the trading of foods among worshippers, pomegranate syrup, tahini, tabbouleh, hummus, orange water, and quality Middle Eastern olive oil have become kitchen staples for Chef Shambra, along with a plethora of spices and spice mixtures from Islamic heartlands. "I always keep chickpeas around, but I can't get down with rosewater. I love my Indian and Pakistani brothers and sisters, but the pink milk is not for me."

When she caters *iftar* meals in her own home, Chef Shambra is prepared to feed the crowds: oxtails with black-eyed peas, green beans, and salad are staples. Carolina barbecue sauces meet whole frozen halal lambs broken down and grilled or cooked in barbecue sauce. Fried fish, macaroni and cheese, greens, eggplant bake, rice dishes, and fish and stews fill the plates of the faithful, honoring the commitment to fast during each day and commemorate the Islamic spiritual past.

Chef Shambra adds: "We recently have had a surge of Liberians, Senegalese, Ghanaians, and Nigerians, and they are sharing their foods. I catered a wedding for a family, and they allowed me to do the jollof rice, and I was really honored. By going to restaurants owned by people in my community from West Africa—our homeland—I've learned that I love sweet potato greens, jollof rice, grilled fish with yassa, peanut stews, and suya." Through DNA analysis, Chef Shambra has learned she has strong connections to the regions from which enslaved Lowcountry communities known as the Gullah and Geechee came from, areas heavily populated by Ancestors who shared her faith in Islam. Many of the foods she enjoys are staples of her Ancestral homelands of Sierra Leone, Liberia, Ghana, and Nigeria.

"After Jummah, we love our salmon or whitefish cakes, with onions and green peppers and garlic. We always have a rice dish, potato salad, carrot raisin salad."

"No coleslaw?" I joke.

"Carrot raisin salad is too goyish, huh?" Chef Shambra says, laughing loudly.

14

THE CUISINE OF
THE CHOCOLATE CHOSEN:
COOKING BLACK AND JEWISH,
A KITCHEN TABLE KIBBITZ

We're just like regular Jews. We just have better food.
And music. And style.

—*Rabbi Shais Rishon*

My kitchen is painted with different accents of blue. It's
a feng shui thing for me but also a nod to the spiritual
power of the color blue within both Jewish and Black
Southern traditions. Blue is the color of the heavens and
of spiritual protection. So that's the energy I incorporate. I also have two wooden forks that I display; it's a
nod to the African American fork and spoon home de-
cor and just makes me think of how our hands provide
the sustenance for us to maintain a sense of home. Also
in my kitchen is the eighteen cents that was the first
item to come into my apartment when I moved in. It was
good luck (eighteen cents along with sugar and a loaf
of bread). My identity as a Black Jew shows up in the
patterns on my washcloths and floor mats and in the
energy of the space.

—*Jessica V.*

Soul means food with love and resilience with it.

—*Koach Baruch Frazier, rabbinical student*

I cook what I know and who I am, and that is a Black Jewish woman.

—*Tikvah*

Yes, we exist, and it's cool, like REALLY cool. I don't know a single person who wouldn't say that there's a LOT of uncomfortable feelings regarding race on either side. Depending on how "Black" or how "Jewish" you look, your treatment outside your own community can differ. Some Black and Jewish people struggle with being the only one in their smaller communities, not being able to connect to others in their religion/culture/ethnicity/race/people, feeling unwelcome or unvalued. I grew up with it being very positive, the best of both worlds, but certainly I experienced moments of isolation, as neither parent was just how I was, or no one in temple looked like me . . . or no one at Howard [University] went to temple like me. It's a really good combination to be; like any identity, you can find common ground or parallels and draw strength and compassion from within. There's a lot of diversity in being both Black and Jewish, and an overwhelming and sobering history. It's not like we all have the same point of view, and I think a lot of it depends on how you grew up—just like any other part of your identity.

—*Rebecca Franklin*

We're not all converts. Judaism belongs to us, just like it belongs to every person who chooses to call it home. We are family.

—*Krystle*

I t's time to bring everything to the table. The kitchen table has always been a sacred and important space for me. It resonates with me that in Jewish tradition the table in the home is associated with the *mizbeach*, the holy altar in the Temple, the Beit HaMikdash, the House of the Holy, the heart of our sacred universe. This sounds lovely until you make peace with the rough work of worship and sacrifice as known at that time, but the work is real—it's not just mellifluous words and prayers and heartbreaking supplications but sacrifices, exaltations of spiritual ecstasy, clouds of incense that mix the acrid and unpleasant (galbanum) with the floral and intoxicatingly pungent. It was the original eleven herbs and spices! (Why place the odoriferous among the perfume? One tradition teaches that the galbanum represents the negativity and sin among the people, and the diversity of the spices is the diversity of the souls that join together—for good may overcome the bad, but without all the ingredients, the *ketoret*, the incense, like the people, is incomplete.)

The same goes for the Four Species that we wave on Sukkot. One has a sweet taste but no smell—the date palm. Another has no taste and no smell—the leaves of the willow. The etrog or citron has a taste and a glorious scent. The myrtle has a fragrance but isn't edible.

The theme again is that the good will overshadow the bad. The diversity is real and necessary, and without it, the Four Species, like the human species, is incomplete. We aren't allowed to forget that despite our differences, we must unite for higher purposes. The incense clouds out the gore and slaughter; the Four Species bring on rain and fertility necessary for growth and change in an otherwise arid climate. Lest we get lost in the poetry, the word for "worship" in Hebrew, *avodah*, has connotations of work and service as well as spiritual devotion; the work of repairing the wounds of the world, *tikkun olam*, is hard work.

When it came time to get everybody to the table, I had to pivot from a lovely meeting of distant friends and family in person to virtual conversations and calls. Thrilled as I may have been to not spend a fortune at the kosher supermarket, I had to figure out how to bring to you this conversation that took place over time and space. The voices you meet in this chapter are jewels in the mosaic. The goal was not babeldom, I assure you, but something more cohesive, but since part of Jewish culture is conversations with a bit of conversational overlapping, I don't feel so bad. To make sure you really hear the voices of our *mishpocheh*, coming to the table is the first step in this holy, complicated but joyous work.

Black or Jewish or Black and Jewish means food is a love language. That love isn't just invested in satiety, and it is more than anchored in survival. There are indeed signifiers of trauma and patinaed historical memories. And yet there is joy. For us, "my soul looks back and wonders how I got over" braids well with "they tried to kill us, we won, let's eat."

The micro-cuts, the microaggressions, and the daily tests of our spirit and confidence in the outside world make our kitchen tables a place to rage, vent, entertain, savor, and before and after it all, bless the Lord and be satisfied. Food is a pleasant way to inject humor into a difficult space as translators and healers. My gut sinks when I hear of the 2019 knife attack in Monsey or the 2015 kosher supermarket shooting spree in France—how do I heal that? Or maybe it's the devastating policies and rhetoric of a hopeful demagogue hellbent on white nationalist propaganda or a school board gone rogue. In the spaces in between, we don't agree among ourselves—is law enforcement our necessary ally in preventing anti-Semitic attacks, or is it policing our presence?

We have to eat to live, and life is with people. Part of the beauty of being us, Jews of color, is that we liven the concept of *hiddur mitzvah*—making the commandments beautiful—with our frabjous tables. The colors, the flavors, the seasoning, the meaning, the spirit, the togetherness, the reverence are all there. We use it all to tell about who we are and why we matter. I am overwhelmed by our endurance and the worlds we make within worlds.

I take my cues here from the work of Joan Nathan, Faye Levy, the late Rabbi Gil Marks *z'tl*, Claudia Roden, and Marcie Cohen Ferris. These pioneers desired that Jewish food be seen in its breadth and richness. The legacy of their collective passion is that Jewish food was not only no longer seen as a simplistic monolith, but it was to be documented as a way into the history, identity, and survival narratives and inventiveness of Jewish communities. Like their work, I hope all of this helps give insight into how the old and new interplay in Jewish tradition. This chapter is, I hope, for many readers, their introduction to the world of Black Jewish culinary anthropology. Lest you grow weary of the listing and cataloging, it's an important first step in being able to define elements of a culinary tradition and understand the patterns and mental architecture of how people think and feel about their food and the art of hospitality.

Jessica says: "We started attending synagogue when I was nine or ten years old. After my mother and father split up, someone suggested to my mother that she bring us into some kind of spiritual community. Judaism was what she knew. That was a complicated experience for me. It was the first time I was in a majority white community as a little Black girl. I was welcomed in some ways, tokenized in others, and marginalized as well. So, I had a lot of feelings about that. And in Black communities, where I felt more accepted, I felt like my Jewishness othered me in a way I didn't like. So not until more recently have I been redefining for myself what it means to be Jewish and Black. It's been helpful to be connected to other Black Jews who claim the fullness of their identities so unapologetically. I'm still learning that for myself and finding my way."

We Black Jews share our battle scars and triumphs with each other, and somehow we become more whole than we ever thought we could be. This can be a lonely or unsure space because of how others react to us not fitting in the boxes they are used to. I joke that making koshersoul food and shoving it in someone's mouth shuts them up before they say something stupid, but it also gives them a taste of who and why I am and why the parts of me and we fit together.

> People usually ask, "Why would you want to add to your oppression [by being Jewish]?" The answer is: they already hated me, I've got to live!
>
> —*Naftali*

Naftali is an Orthodox Jew with roots in Accra, Ghana. You don't even have to ask, "The mound of yam and plantain in the corner says 'African'? Yes." His koshersoul is built on the intersection where West African food meets African American, Caribbean, Ashkenazi, and Middle Eastern and North African Jewish food. He loves plantain latkes, Memphis-style dry rub barbecue (beef, chicken, and lamb) on Sukkot, and jollof rice. "Potato kugel goes especially well with okra stew or palava sauce," he says. Ghanaian traditional food, particularly on the coast, can involve pork, smoked fish, lots of shellfish, and ingredients that don't bear a symbol called a *hechsher* that testifies to their kosher certification. Its particular flavor often comes from a condiment called shitor made of ground shrimp, tomatoes, and peppers cooked brown. Naftali continues: "I use soy-based pastes for fish-related pastes, fatty smoked meats in place of pork products, soy milk in place of milk, beef fry for bacon; there are many, many more. The staples here are onions, potatoes, plantain, palm oil, and a variety of greens. I'm not brand loyal, but Eden miso is a lifesaver. I mix it with kosher bullion to make a pretty good substitute for Maggi cubes."

Zebulon, in his twenties, comes from a heritage based in the Great Migration. "I love being who I am, and I don't feel like I'm 'not enough' of either thing. No one can tell me that." Based in Chicago, Zebulon says: "When I think of Black food, like the food I grew up on, I think of all those down-home recipes that my great-grandmother taught my grandmother, taught my aunties, taught my mom, taught me. It means the magic we made out of what inhumane slavers called 'refuse.' It means looking at what some might call scraps and seeing the fixings for a beautifully seasoned, vibrant, flavorful, rich kind of nourishment. It means the food you eat around the table that's so good people stop fighting for twenty minutes. And Jewish food? It means the chicken soup that heals you from the first smell you get of it; going to Manny's to get a stupidly big corned beef sandwich. It means foods that survived plus got retranslated plus remixed plus reinvented plus kept circling back to This Food Is for All of Us—Past/Present/Future."

For Zebulon, turkey is key in his koshersoul. "I make a Southern breakfast my grandparents would eat but without pork—scrambled eggs with rice and a biscuit, maybe with some kosher chicken or beef sausage cooked with spices and onion. I make my greens with turkey necks—they are my ham hocks. I make red beans with turkey, too! I don't eat pork, but I will never say no to fried catfish at somebody's house, and I don't refuse food when I'm a guest because I was raised that way." Some koshersoulniks have very similar practices to American Jews who keep kosher at home but, when out, choose to eat a variety of other foods. For many Black Jews, the dietary issue can often arise from the rejection of foods that are central to the inherent authenticity or performance of non-Jewish Black identity.

Krystle, from California, has her own way of keeping kosher. "That means no pork, ever. For greens, I use smoked salt or liquid smoke instead of pork parts. I also tend to use vegan products because I have a dairy allergy. The vegan products essentially prevent me from mixing meat and dairy." For anyone balking at the lack of pork, I should remind you that the most important element is smoky and umami, not porky—porky may be a phenomenon of the antebellum South and other parts of the African Atlantic in the West, but it is not an inherently West or Central African food or flavor. The importance of this flavor element is such that liquid smoke, imitation bacon bits, kosher lamb or beef bacon, and smoked turkey wings, necks, legs, etc., fulfill this koshersoul necessity.

Shais comments that Black flavor starts with "food made by people who understand that black pepper isn't 'spicy' and that salt and onions aren't a 'seasoning.' Now, unless we're talking about matzoh, there is no 'Jewish' food. Unfortunately, people think Jewish food means food with none of the pork, twice the salt, and half the flavor. So, for example, the closest thing I get to 'fusion,' I guess, is my gefilte fish. When I have time, I get a fresh mix and season it. If not, I buy a frozen loaf, defrost it, reseason it, then boil. My go-to's are a habanero/jalapeño gefilte fish, a cilantro/lime/capers gefilte fish, and a cinnamon/honey/carrot gefilte fish—none of that terrible jarred gefilte fish nonsense. If substituting for dairy in a dairy-meat recipe, I go either with a Daiya cheese substitute or swapping out heavy creams and the like with duck fat. I don't substitute for meat. I'm a huge fan of the imitation lobster/crab deal. I have no idea if that's actually what lobster/crab tastes like, but I'm down with it. Whatever that is in kosher 'pork'-fried rice is a necessity."

For several people I interviewed, the need to substitute something for crab, lobster, shrimp, crawfish, and the like was very important. Mendel, a serious foodie with African American Jewish and Egyptian Jewish heritage, said not only does he miss bacon, but he misses crab from his nonkosher foray: "I am from Baltimore!" Tikvah, an Orthodox woman also from Baltimore, loves to make faux crab cakes and other delicacies that reflect her commitment to *kashrut* as well as to highly flavored food: "My kosher crab cakes are a hit. I use one pack of kosher fake crab meat, one can of salmon, half an onion, celery, three tablespoons of mayo, Old Bay, bread crumbs, and two eggs. Mix and form into cakes and fry in hot oil until brown on the outside.

"Yes, I make kosher oxtails that I love, collard greens, sautéed kale, faux Maryland crab cakes and seafood chowder, sweet challah rolls/bread, a pumpkin and sweet potato cholent, turkey chops, fried gizzards, liver scrapple. To be honest, it all has to be kosher, and I'm Black—so, the way I see it is, it's fusion. I cook what I know and who I am, and that is a Black Jewish woman. On Hanukkah, we have treats like homemade fried chicken, latkes—both applesauce and sour cream—and fried plantains."

The foods mentioned in my conversations with Black Jews started to develop a common grocery list. We all had our kosher brands on the shelf—Lieber's, Paskesz, Mehadrin, Millers, Mother's, Streit's, and Manischewitz. And then there was the constant reference to onions, garlic, curry powder, Kosher bouillon powder, Old Bay, plantains, sweet potatoes, cumin, seasoned salt, coconut milk, peanuts, hot sauce of various types, cornmeal, leafy greens, black-eyed peas, beans, and rice. Each one of these gives a certain smell flavor to the air in our homes. One day I just want to travel to each person's spice cabinet for a qualitative analysis.

It reminds me of a quotation from Marcie Cohen Ferris's *Matzoh Ball Gumbo* discussing Lamar White, a chef and caterer employed at the time by an Atlanta synagogue. Even though Lamar isn't Jewish, his sensibilities very much match many of our own. He grew so accustomed to eating kosher meat that he stopped eating pork and other nonkosher meats. Today he has separate refrigerators at home for *treif* and kosher products. "I started out young eating the kosher items, and the food is really good if you really know how to prepare it. When I cook, it kind of has that 'soul' taste. I know how to fix it; it tastes basically like an African American chicken. I'm seasoning it. I'm soaking it. Garlic, black pepper, Lawry's seasoned salt. You never fail when you make it."

By incorporating African American flavors and cooking methods, Lamar created a Southern and kosher culinary style distinctive to Atlanta. His food is so popular that the synagogue's catering department sells "carry out" trays of his brisket, meatloaf, barbecued chicken, kugels, prime rib, and sides of vegetables. "That way, when people cannot come to the shul that night," Lamar says, "at least I'll be in everybody's house." What makes this kosher food different from food eaten in an Orthodox shul in Long Island? "Only way I can tell you the reason why it is Southern is that there is nobody like me in those areas. I'm not in there cooking." Lamar is the secret ingredient here. His command of African American cooking traditions and his knowledge of *kashrut* create a uniquely southern Jewish culinary experience.

The foods Tikvah prepares expand the notions of Jewish food beyond their relationship to *kashrut* and temporal religious observances and reflect the foodways of Jewish cultural tribes, or *edot*—Ashkenazi, Sephardi, and Mizrahi. The innovation of the Black Jewish home cook plays against ideas of staid tradition and relies on a dynamic improvisation to clear the air—this, too, is a product of the Jewish people. The more I talk to Jews of African descent about their style of koshersoul, the more I am reminded about the subtle bits of resistance to erasure baked in, the food as our flag, the power of creating your own *minhag* (customs). And it's there to create a feeling.

One way of digging in deeper is discovering what Black food means for each person. Rebecca Franklin is a Californian by way of DeQuincy, Louisiana, via the Great Migration. One parent is of Eastern European descent, and the other is African American and Southern. For her, all the layers of geography, neighborhood, and preference overlap. She loves "gumbo burritos" and "pastrami tacos." "When Hanukkah and Kwanzaa overlap," she says, "I usually have fried chicken and red beans and rice and latkes in the fridge, so I make a sandwich out of the three. Heat up the latke and the red beans and rice; if there are greens left over, that's even better. Put it all together and sprinkle chunks of the fried chicken over it."

For Rebecca, the food that came to her from Africa and the Caribbean—through Louisiana and other parts of the South to California and South Central LA, partially flavored with classic Ashkenazi roots—does more than just gesture at notions of a melting pot or salad bowl; it's the record of an interior life for Black people that has become more enriched in our status as Black Jews. I agree with her: Black food brings deep narratives and meaning to Jewish food as we all understand it.

Rebecca says,

I think about seasoning and making substitutions in recipes that can make or break a reputation. I think about eating for survival and making meals stretch. I think about time and perspective— food that Ancestors ate in horrible times of violence, poverty, uncertainty, and uprising being the same food to celebrate today and share with others. I always felt that if the spirit of people and food can live on, if it got my family through, it may do the same for me. I feel connected to other Black people when I can contribute to our cultural meals. Sure, lots of Southern food is intertwined in a Black identity, just like it is in my family. Still, even foods that present themselves more as regional, like barbecued ribs or sweet potato pie, are unequivocally Black foods to me. Ethnicity (regions within the US, the Caribbean, Africa, etc.), class (Kool-Aid, 40s), religion (Easter dinner, Christmas dinner) all can share a space within the general heading of "Black food."

Shabbat and Yom Tov

My favorite Jewish holiday is Yom Kippur. I like it because it reminds me to engage more mindfully with the rest of the year, particularly with food. (Of course, Yom Kippur is not meant to be a diet thing.) I like break-fast afterward because it's the most mindful bit of sustenance I receive all year. Usually, it's just water, an apple, and a tiny bit of bread. The break-fast after party is also pretty fun.

—*Krystle*

In my conversations with Black Jews, I asked them to detail a menu they might serve for Shabbat. Yavilah McCoy was able to offer rapid-fire some of her family's favorite Shabbat meals. A Friday night might mean roast red snapper, collard greens, fried chicken, candied yams, red beans and rice, and plump corn on the cob. By Saturday afternoon there could be a body-and-soul-warming meal of split pea soup, barbecue short ribs, roasted mashed potatoes, garlic string beans, and a sweet side of apple cranberry crumble. Needless to say, our homes are outfitted with multiple crock pots (I have two triplets and two massive ones) and stoves with a Shabbat mode.

From the start, Black-Jewish folks will make you mourn for the poor chickens—everybody but the vegans and vegetarians makes them a Friday dish, even me. I was struck by how much many of their menus reflected influences from Black African American, African, and Afro-Caribbean traditions around Sunday dinner, the staples of modern Israeli food, and Ashkenazi "out of the box" cuisine that had been dressed up and remixed. Tikvah exclaimed, "My husband sometimes says on Shabbos night during the meal, 'I feel sorry for our boys; I pray they find someone who can cook like this'—meaning with flavor and as a Jew of color."

Our virtual roundtables and phone calls and emails were fruitful to the point where I had too many offerings for Shabbat:

Zebulon: Red beans and rice with a turkey neck, chicken soup, collard greens with smoked turkey, candied sweet potatoes, cornbread dressing, potato salad, and pound cake.

Koach: Fried chicken, sautéed Brussels sprouts, and challah.

Savay: Challah, injera, doro wat, spicy salmon, rice, schnitzel, meatballs, a few different salads, wine, and more.

Shais: A baked salmon dill dish, a pasta with sauce/broccoli/ mushrooms/olives/ground beef, orange-glazed chicken, and couscous or rice with curry.

Shais adds: "Growing up, my mother's go-to Shabbat regulars were chicken soup, a vegetable mix of some kind, mashed potatoes or rice, sometimes fried chicken, and—especially in the winter when Shabbat would get started early—spaghetti and meatballs. My favorite holiday is Pesach. Our signature Pesach meal is my five-meat meatloaf. Always a crowd-pleaser. That, or duck legs.

"How do I make the meatloaf? I don't list measurements, just ingredients, and I season by eye because, as my Black Jewish momma taught me, the blessing doesn't rest on things that are precisely measured. So, ground beef, ground veal, ground turkey, ground chicken, ground and sliced sausage [chorizo, merguez, or sweet Italian], sliced black olives, sliced baby bella mushrooms, fresh thyme/dill/rosemary/cilantro, Marsala wine, honey, onion powder, garlic powder, lemon pepper, red wine vinegar. Mix everything together. Wrap in thin-cut slices of deli meat [pastrami/turkey/corned beef]. Drizzle honey on top of the loaf and dust with paprika. Bake for about forty-five minutes at 375 degrees."

> *Tikvah: Baked Cajun chicken, honey Old Bay potatoes, sautéed kale, or balsamic glazed roast overnight for lunch.*
> *Naftali: Soup and stew and heavy meals for Friday nights, grilled or smoked stuff, and hamin/cholent for lunch on Shabbat day.*

Naftali notes: "We pull from both sides, so there isn't a 'typical.' The week starts with leftovers, but when I cook for the kids, I'm as likely to make them simple Ghanaian bean stew (like red-red) over rice. Bofrot (also known in West Africa as puff-puff) or Ghanaian doughnuts come out at Hanukkah." Meanwhile in Yavilah's home, empanadas (an older food among Sephardic Jews than in Mexico), churros, latkes, green salad, and Israeli sufganiyot fill the table on the festival of lights. For me, it's fried chicken time, scallion pancake-style latkes, plenty of salads, and beignets with as much powdered sugar as I can muster, Al Pacino in *Scarface* style.

Binah: Homemade spelt challah, Moroccan carrot salad, Israeli salad,
   tahini, eggplant salad, egg salad, baked salmon or other fatty fish,
   chicken soup, a potato kugel. Sometimes maybe chicken and rice.
Menachem: Grilled lamb. Sous vide salmon. ("Not even a question," he
   says. "I think cholent is one of the best parts of Shabbos lunch. There
   is just something about eating it in the winter.")
Asher Joy: Stewp (soupy stew). ("My stewp is a combination of root
   vegetables [sweet potato, typical potato, carrots, parsnips], leafy
   greens, lentils, beans, and spices for flavor and healing—all these
   slow cook in a crockpot.")
Yavilah: Pesach means curried matzoh ball soup, turkey wings,
   cornbread dressing, roasted broccoli rabe, and portobello mushrooms,
   vegetable soup, lamb chops, and Persian rice.

The Black Jewish year has its own culinary hallmarks. For Chava, Sukkot is gumbo time; for Naftali, it's the last bit of barbecue season, and kykyinga or suya mingles with other meats Memphis style as the family enjoys nice meals outside in the *sukkah* during the *chol hamoed*—or middle weekdays of the festival. Now Koach has added Juneteenth and a Juneteenth seder. Some people like myself also have a special seder plate and seder at the end of Passover that honors the connections between the exodus and the fight against American slavery. Jessica agrees: "My favorite holiday is Pesach. I love the tradition of the seder and the centering of conversations around liberation. It resonates on so many levels; and particularly as a Black Jew, it creates a space for my identity to show up that acknowledges the past, present, and future." Kwanzaa, which is not tied to any particular religious tradition, provides an opportunity for Black people of different backgrounds to come together or to tailor the cultural commemoration with specific references from their own experience.

What is comforting is how beautifully dense many of the delicacies my larger community prepares are, especially for the three pilgrimage holidays of Pesach, Shavuot, and Sukkot. Chava's roast head of lamb, black-eyed peas, plantains, and candied butternut squash, her gumbo, Shais's Passover meatloaf, and his cousin's Portuguese meatballs—all speak to the flash of the spirit (the late art historian Robert Farris Thompson's shorthand for the African Atlantic aesthetic wow factor) on the table, the idea that the Divine is a guest at our gatherings and delights in our *hiddur mitzvah* and keeping the spirit of the table that our Ancestors gave us. For her Shavuot table (the holiday that commemorates the giving of the Torah), she makes a traditionally dairy-based meal that includes American favorites like lasagna, home fries, and Cajun salmon.

But Shais's Shavuot macaroni and cheese is too much for me! He tells me: "My standard Shavuot recipe is a wild macaroni and cheese endeavor that I gradually evolved from my mother's recipe. Mozzarella, sharp cheddar, Havarti, provolone, gouda, pepper jack, Romano, parmesan, blue cheese, black pepper, white pepper, crushed red pepper, cayenne pepper, onion powder, garlic powder, thyme, paprika, oregano, onions, garlic, black olives, red and green bell peppers, and mushrooms. I rarely, if ever, use macaroni, and instead tend toward more ridged or curled pasta. It's an oven-baked macaroni and cheese—a layer of pasta, layer of cheese, repeat until the pan is full. Cover with foil. Bake at 425 degrees for thirty to thirty-five minutes."

"Wow, you doing too much!" I say.

"Cuz I'm doing me."

My distant cousin's macaroni and cheese sounds fun, but I like mine better—a shidduch (arranged marriage) between mac and cheese and kugel. At least it's not a play on kosher catfish and spaghetti. I don't think either of us would be able to get down with that.

Whether we are *frum* from birth, became Jews by choice, or any of the other possible combinations by which Jews of African descent grace this planet, our traditions have their own family and folk stories. To survive, they must be documented and be written down. Time is of the essence, especially when so much about us through the centuries has been marginalized and pushed to the outer realms of Jewish or Black knowledge and literacy. As Reb Shais said, "Before we are making our own *yichus*, our own *mesorah*, and telling and cooking our own story dish by dish."

That doesn't mean I have to like his macaroni and cheese, but I'm sure some of you are salivating. This is what we do: gentle ribbing and joking and sighing. Some of the koshersoul school of cooking may just be in my head, but the other part is very real, and it's the banter between us, talking food with folks who know both sides of who I am and from where I come. It's the feeling of being home—a home with many doors. As the saying goes, two Jews, three opinions—and probably more. Nobody will get the same meal at our tables; there is no standard here except for our sensibilities and patience upon patience for how the world outside of us perceives us. Our culinary DNA may just be the most varied, diverse, and rich. Sometimes it's what you might expect, and other times its none of the above. Sit at our tables, eat, listen to our stories, and we hope, you will know us.

IF I WERE A COOKBOOK

T he mark of a great scholar in Judaism is to be known eternally by the name of your greatest work. Your legacy is spelled out in the title of your labor of love. It's a little like one of my favorite modern dystopian cautionary tales, *Fahrenheit 451*, where the main character, Montag, and other refugees memorize and therefore become their favorite books, manifesting by choice as living retro bards. The custom reinforces the idea that in book form, these figures live on and on despite losing corporeal form; each one is in essence preserved not as a document of the past but as a voice worth listening to as long as there is someone to read and study their work and argue about it with a friend.

There is the *Ben Ish Chai*, the holy Rabbi Yosef Hayyim of Baghdad, who wrote an extraordinary compendium of Jewish law beloved by Mizrahi Jews everywhere. My favorite notation is the discussion of using white sugar on Rosh Hashanah as "salt." And the *Chofetz Chaim*, Rav Yisrael Meir Kagan, a leader of the Musar movement meant to shape good character and daily morals and ethics. And, of course, the *Sfas Emes*, the mystical and spiritual writings of the great Hasidic Rebbe Yehudah Aryeh Leib Alter.

During this season of COVID quarantine and unease, I attended my first virtual *shiva minyan*. In Judaism, sitting shiva means the seven-day period of mourning following someone's passing. Traditionally, it means sitting down and having others greet you and comfort you, often in a very gloomy space with everyone wearing black. It is a glimpse into the future, where people trade memories and poems over the internet, saying the mourner's Kaddish—the main prayer said around death and memorial—on little screens with voices compiling and competing in airspace.

I am not nor ever have been one to have a healthy attitude toward death. I don't wish it on myself for a long time to come, and I'm a bit queasy writing this now, even though I understand it is a necessary eventuality. I want to earn my rest, the way my grandfather did, dying one century after arriving in a world vastly different from the one he passed in, life-muscles exhausted from changing it to make it better, enacting *tikkun olam*, repair of the world. My grandfather was born into a world of Jim Crow, right after World War I, the time of another great pandemic, where nobody flew in an airplane as a mode of travel and where Black, gay, Jewish me probably existed but was completely and absolutely socially impossible. What a gift, though, to live and create the future you want, to challenge the world to be a better place; and although you leave it still imperfect, there it is, as touched by the hand of a good Southern guest, left better than you found it.

You are not allowed to pronounce yourself an improver; others do that on your behalf. Humility is the loyal spouse of death, one way or another. The greatest tragedy about death in Judaism is not so much the cessation of life but that it ends and, one might say, absolves the individual of the task of doing mitzvot. Passing on means no more chances in this shell to get up and do good and be good.

There are many opinions in Yahaduth about souls leaving the plane of the living, but let's focus on one in particular. The Jewish afterlife is a place of light—sapphire-hued and gleaming with pulses of protection and purity. Jewish heaven is a park, a place of study, and a banquet hall. In heaven, some of the sages say, everything will be kosher for the faithful; magically, all the *treif* will be holy—and, one presumes, delicious. Moses will be there, and so will Miriam—playing her timbrels—and David the King, playing his lute-harp.

At the carving station will be the Ziz—the giant bird to be served up when the Moshiach, or Messiah, comes. Also, the Behemot—the gargantuan mammal; from it, we will have endless brisket. And we will chew on the Leviyatan—the world's biggest fish. In true gefilte fish fashion, we will sit as the stuffing—a *sukkah* made of its iridescent skin, reflecting millennia of rainbows—seals on ancient covenants between the living G-d and us.

If you need a break from this incredibly noisy and non-introvert-friendly scene, there is the park—more like a park plus an orchard—and, of course, there is the study hall. Words will be repeated and sung for all time, and old friends and foes and literary Ancestors will sit side by side with their descendants, bandying about renewed arguments and conversations—but only in the most holy and loving way. Countless hands will touch books and scrolls containing the most profound secrets of the galaxy. Learning will be a mellifluous experience for all.

In those stacks are books, billions of books, but in my imagination, they are not just books; they are like the Torah—blueprints. And they are not just blueprints but priceless individual narratives; on a closer look, they are us. Our lives are the stories in G-d's celestial library. We are the ones the Creator studies and anguishes over, the reflection on the page of its glory and promises and doubts.

Some of us will be extra lucky. We will have tomes that represent us, tomes that weren't just formed by feather pen or hammered out on typewriter or tip-tapped on a laptop. We will be books. My mind no longer focused on my absence from a world that will wait for perfection, I think about the kind of book I want to be.

Maybe you will call me *The Cooking Gene*, or perhaps *Koshersoul* if I'm lucky, or something else. I guess if I had my druthers, I'd be a bunch of books. If G-d is great, and I know G-d is, maybe I'll luck up and also be a cookbook.

It isn't very Jewish to pontificate on death and posthumous honor and all that, so I'll end it here. I have onions to grow and peppers to dry and seasonings to make. I need to manifest years like Moses—to one hundred and twenty, full of joy and mistakes corrected. I have a spouse to love and pets to spoil, and lessons to teach. I have to get on with my time on this plane so one day I can settle into my spine and pages and fabulous bookmark. Until then, I have to live—and cook.

RECIPES

The recipes here represent a koshersoul community cookbook of sorts. They and the suggested menus reflect the minds of the people I interviewed and my research and preferences. However, feel free to adapt what is here to your own dietary practices and, if you choose, go meatless or dairy- or sugar-free. I support your personalizing any recipe and improvising to bring a dish to the table. The ingredients reflect the lived practice of individuals in a vast human family, not the definitive culinary markers that establish individuals as Black and Jewish or practitioners of koshersoul. And besides, you don't have to be Black or Jewish to love koshersoul.

Shabbat

Koshersoul Collards

Inspired by Matt's Four Pepper Collards, from The Lee Bros. Charleston Kitchen (Clarkson Potter, 2013).

Serves 8

¼ cup canola oil or schmaltz (chicken fat)1 cup red onion, cut into thin slices

1 long red cayenne pepper, cut into thin rings

1 teaspoon crushed garlic

1 teaspoon crushed ginger

1 tablespoon pareve kosher "chicken" consommé powder

1 teaspoon Kitchen Pepper (see recipe)

4 pounds collards, stemmed, trimmed, and cut into long, thin strips

3 cups vegetable stock (see note)

2 tablespoons lime juice

2 teaspoons coconut sugar

1 teaspoon smoked paprika

Heat oil or schmaltz in a large pot over medium heat for one minute; after a few minutes, toss in the onion slices, and soon, they will make a telltale light sizzle and begin to sweat. Add the red pepper, garlic, ginger, consommé powder, and Kitchen Pepper and slowly sweat on low heat for 10 minutes, stirring occasionally.

Raise the heat to medium-high. Add the thin strips of collard greens handful by handful, stirring as necessary. With each batch of three handfuls, quick cook for about 5 minutes. When all of the collards have been incorporated, add the vegetable stock; bring to a boil, and then lower the heat so that the pot settles into a slow bubble. Add lime juice, coconut sugar, and smoked paprika.

Cover and cook on a low simmer for 45 minutes. Remove collards with a slotted spoon and serve over cooked rice or grits.

Note: Make your own vegetable stock by covering the following ingredients with water and slow simmering for 3 hours: 2 carrots cut into rounds; 1 onion studded with cloves; 3 pieces mashed garlic; 2 parsnips cut into rounds; 1 turnip, cubed; 1 bunch parsley; 3 celery ribs, chopped; and 1 small sweet potato, cubed. Strain before use.

Tahini-Nokos Dressing

About 1 cup

½ cup tahini paste (sesame paste) with its oil, well mixed

2 finely minced garlic cloves

¼ cup vegetable stock

¼ cup apple cider vinegar or lemon juice

1 teaspoon kosher or sea salt, depending on your preference and taste

1 tablespoon Kosher Senegalese Nokos (see recipe)

Combine all ingredients together and whisk briskly until roughly blended. (You can whisk all you want if you have a strong hand, but do yourself a favor and put it all in a blender and blend until smooth if that's the texture you want.) Transfer to a small container or a small jar. May be refrigerated for 3–5 days.

Couscous (or Millet) Salad

This simple-to-make side dish pairs well with grilled or fried main dishes, and is a great choice to take to a potluck Shabbat or simchah. I always make extra couscous whenever I'm serving it for a meal so I'll have plenty left over to make this bright, textured salad the next day. Couscous is North and West African and cooked millet is endemic to the savanna regions of Africa. Couscous salads are widely popular in Israel.

Serves 4–6

2 cups COLD cooked leftover couscous (prepare according to package directions)

2 tablespoons finely chopped yellow bell pepper

2 tablespoons finely chopped green bell pepper

2 tablespoons finely chopped red bell pepper

2 tablespoons finely chopped red onion

2 tablespoons thinly sliced scallions (also called green onions)

2 tablespoons finely chopped fresh Italian parsley

2 tablespoons dried cranberries or golden raisins

¼ cup red wine vinegar

¼ cup extra virgin olive oil

1 tablespoon honey or light agave (optional)

1 teaspoon kosher salt, or to taste

½ teaspoon coarse ground black pepper, or to taste

Combine the couscous, bell peppers, red onion, green onion, parsley, and dried cranberries in a large bowl, and stir to mix well.

In a small bowl, combine vinegar, olive oil, honey or agave, salt, and pepper. Use a whisk or a fork to mix well. Add dressing to couscous or millet and stir to combine evenly and well. Serve or cover and chill for up to three days.

Notes: This is a great dish for Shabbat or Yom Tov. You can add about one cup of almonds or peanuts; chunks of tofu or tempeh, meat, poultry, or seafood to make this a more "main course" salad. You can also substitute mint, cilantro, or dill for the parsley if you're serving it as a side salad.

Use your best judgment with the spices. I add a salt-free herb or spice mix to punch up the flavor and add color. You can do a pinch of this or that, but keep it simple and keep it spare.

Tip: Use low-sodium broth for more flavor. If you have a gluten condition, substitute cooked millet.

Green Bean Salad with Lemon and Sweet Bell Pepper

Green beans are significant in both African American and Jewish foodways. Seasonally, they make a welcome addition to the table as a side dish. Classic Southern dishes are green beans cooked with smoked meat or green beans and potatoes or they can flavor stews like the Sephardic dish fassoulia, where meat, onions, and green beans make a meal. This green bean salad works well for Shabbat and holidays, when cooking isn't an option. Here roasted or steamed green beans treated with acids and oils work together to make it a more palatable vegetable when chilled for a day or two.

Serves 4–6

1 ½ pounds fresh green beans, snapped and trimmed

1 teaspoon sea salt

2 quarts water

1 bowl ice water

Dressing and Garnish

4 tablespoons extra virgin olive oil

4 tablespoons fresh lemon juice

½ teaspoon kosher salt

2 cloves garlic, sliced into thin slivers

2 tablespoons fresh, roughly chopped flat-leaf parsley

2 tablespoons thinly sliced scallions

½ teaspoon organic sugar (optional)

4 tablespoons total cubed red, yellow, and orange bell peppers (use a bag of baby bells, if possible)

Place green beans in a large pot of boiling water well seasoned with sea salt. Cook 5 minutes, then immediately drain in a colander and plunge into the ice bath until the beans are just barely warm.

Prepare the dressing while the green beans are in the ice bath. In a small bowl, whisk together the olive oil, lemon juice, salt, garlic, parsley, scallions, and optional sugar. Place the green beans in a nonreactive mixing bowl, add the chopped peppers, splash on the dressing, mix well for a minute or two, and then allow the green beans to marinate in the dressing for an hour or so. Toss well before serving.

Variation: Instead of lemon juice, use balsamic vinegar.

Caribbean Compote

Compote is something I was completely unfamiliar with until I became Jewish. This combination of fruit and sugar or honey, and perhaps wine or liquor, is a traditional Ashkenazi fruit salad served hot or chilled for Shabbat or Passover. My recipe brings together the Jewish Afro-Caribbean with the world of the shtetl to create a light dessert with a bit of a kick.

Serves 4–6

3 cups peeled, seeded, and chunked grapefruit

3 cups peeled, seeded, and chunked oranges

3 cups pineapple chunks

1 cup mango chunks (optional)

½ teaspoon allspice

½ teaspoon cinnamon

2 tablespoons vanilla

¼ teaspoon cayenne pepper

¼ cup agave syrup or ½ cup organic granulated sugar

In a large bowl, combine the grapefruit, oranges, pineapple, and mango, and set aside.

In a small bowl and using a fork, mix the allspice, cinnamon, vanilla, cayenne, and agave syrup. Stir into a smooth dressing. Add the dressing to the fruit and use a large spoon to combine gently, just enough to coat the compote evenly. Chill before serving.

Yam Kugel

Although frequently translated as "pudding," the traditional Ashkenazi dish kugel takes a thousand forms and has diversified even further in an American cuisine where casseroles and hot dishes abound. Inspired by the traditions preserved by Mrs. Mildred Covert, this side dish relies on plump, sugary sweet potatoes to bridge Southern sweet potato casserole with the Eastern European standby, kugel.

Serves 6-8

2 cups shredded raw sweet potatoes

¾ cup margarine or vegan butter, melted

¾ cup packed brown sugar

1 cup flour

1 teaspoon baking soda

½ teaspoon cinnamon

½ teaspoon ground nutmeg

½ teaspoon salt

½ cup raisins or plumped dried mango, cut into small pieces

½ cup chopped pecans (optional)

Combine the sweet potatoes, margarine, and sugar; mix well. Combine all the dry ingredients; then add to the sweet potato mixture, mixing until just moistened. Fold in the raisins or mango. Pour into a 9-inch square or round baking dish. Top with pecans if desired. Cover with foil and bake at 350°F for 1 hour. Uncover, continue baking for 10 minutes.

Black-Eyed Pea Hummus

Black-eyed peas are a strong link between the two Diaspora cuisines, probably meeting in the Nile River Valley and the Fertile Crescent. Originally from ancient West

Africa, black-eyed peas are a significant part of the cuisine of the Levant to this day, moving with African people throughout the region. Hummus, emblematic and beloved by many cultures in the Levant—is a dish that relies on the staple legume of the Arab farmer and ancient biblical standby, the chickpea. Here the black-eyed pea, loaded with mystical symbolism and its own honored place in West and Central Africa, replaces the chickpea.

Serves 4–6

1 15-ounce can black-eyed peas, rinsed and drained

¼ cup extra virgin olive oil, plus more for garnish

⅓ cup tahini

½ cup fresh lemon juice

1½ teaspoons kosher salt or Soul Seasoning (see recipe)

4 garlic cloves, chopped

1 teaspoon sweet or smoked paprika

½ teaspoon ground cumin

½ teaspoon ground coriander

½ teaspoon chili powder

1 teaspoon brown or turbinado sugar

1 teaspoon hot sauce

2 teaspoons minced parsley, for garnish

Throw everything but the parsley into a food processor and blend until smooth. Taste and add more spice, hot sauce, or whatever you think it needs. To serve, sprinkle parsley and drizzle olive oil on the top.

Berbere Brisket

Berbere is the versatile Ethiopian and Eritrean spice mixture central to dishes like Doro wat—spicy stewed chicken and many others. Ethiopian Jews have long added it to the spice-mix repertoire of Israel alongside North African harissa and Yemenite hawaij. Here, I use it with a nontraditional cut—a hunk of brisket is Eastern

European—not from the Horn of Africa, but it works!
Try it for seasoning roast chicken, lamb, or roast vegetables, or kebabs.

Serves 6–8

4½ pounds beef brisket, some fat left on

2 tablespoons Berbere Spice Mix (see recipe)

2-inch knob of ginger, peeled and finely grated

2 cloves garlic, crushed

4 tablespoons olive oil, divided

3 onions, roughly chopped

2 14-ounce cans Italian diced tomatoes

2 red onions, sliced into thick rings

2 cups chicken or beef stock

½ tablespoon brown sugar

1 sprig rosemary

Sea salt and ground black pepper, to taste

Preheat oven to 325°F. You will need a flameproof roasting pan large enough to fit the brisket. In a small bowl, combine the Berbere Spice Mix, ginger, garlic, and 2 tablespoons olive oil. Rub into both sides of the brisket.

Heat the remaining olive oil over high heat in the roasting pan. Sear the brisket for a few minutes on each side until well browned. Remove from the pan and set aside. Add the chopped onion to the roasting pan, adding a splash of oil if needed, and sauté for about 15 minutes or until the onions are soft. Add the tomatoes and toss through. Turn off the heat, remove the tomato mixture from the roasting pan, and set it aside.

Place the red onion in the roasting pan and lay the browned brisket on top. Pour the tomato mixture on top of the brisket.

Stir the brown sugar into the stock and pour it around the brisket. Add the rosemary and season well with salt and pepper. Cover tightly with aluminum foil and bake for 3½ hours, or until the brisket is fork-tender.

If you are not serving the brisket immediately, remove it from the oven, allow it to cool, and refrigerate. When chilled, remove the excess fat from the sauce, slice the meat, and place in an oven-proof serving dish, piling the red onion on top. To serve, reheat gently at 325°F for 30 minutes or until heated through.

Cachopa

Cape Verde, a collection of islands off the coast of West Africa, was colonized by the Portuguese in the Age of Exploration. Today's Cape Verdean diaspora is rediscovering its many Jewish roots. Worked by forced labor from West Africa, the Cape Verdean people are a mixture of Africa, Iberia, and all the worlds in between, including Jews who sought refuge from the Inquisition. Cachopa, one of the island's signature dishes, scaled-down here, makes an excellent Shabbat stew or replacement for cholent.

Serves 4–6

Olive oil, as needed

1 medium onion, chopped

2–4 garlic cloves, peeled

2 bay leaves or two teaspoons of powdered bay leaf

6 cups chicken or vegetable broth

2 cups canned hominy, drained

2 cups canned light kidney beans, drained

½ cup frozen large lima beans, drained

1 kosher sausage, sliced

¼ pound kosher beef or lamb bacon, diced

¼ cup fresh green beans, sliced lengthwise

2 cups cabbage or kale, coarsely chopped

1 plantain, peeled and sliced

2 cups fresh white potatoes, peeled, cut into small chunks

2 cups sweet potatoes, peeled, cut into small chunks

2 cups winter squash, peeled, cut into small chunks

1 chicken, cut into 8 serving pieces

Salt and pepper, to taste

2 cups tomatoes, quartered

½ cup Sofrito (a seasoning paste of equal parts sautéed garlic, onion, and tomato paste), to taste

Cilantro, chopped, for garnish

In a stockpot, combine 2 tablespoons olive oil, onion, garlic, and bay leaves. Saute until fragrant over medium high heat and the onion is translucent.

This should take 5–7 minutes. Add 6 cups of broth. Add hominy and kidney and lima beans. Bring to a boil. Simmer on a low heat until nearly fork-tender, or for about 45 minutes to an hour.

In a separate large pot or skillet, brown the kosher sausage and bacon to render a little fat, then add the sliced green beans, the chopped cabbage or kale, plantains, potatoes, sweet potatoes, and winter squash. Lightly saute, removing the meat and vegetables when wilted and softened, and set aside.

Season the chicken with salt and pepper, then saute in the same pot you browned the kosher sausage and bacon, adding a little bit of olive oil until lightly browned. Add the chicken, tomatoes, and the kosher sausage and kosher beef or lamb bacon and set aside vegetable mixture to the stockpot of hominy and beans. Cook on low heat for approximately an hour, skimming the top and stirring occasionally.

Add the sofrito to the pot, simmering for 20 minutes longer. Turn off the heat and let rest, covered, for at least 30 minutes. Serve in large bowls garnished with a little cilantro.

Note: This recipe works really well with a crockpot for Shabbat afternoon.

Swahili Roast Chicken

Roast chicken (*gebratener hindle*), a signature Shabbos dish, is a standby in Ashkenazi cuisine. Because chicken is such a neutral flavor, you can season it a million ways reflecting whatever taste or cultures you want to bring to the table. Better yet, you can follow Rabbi Gil Marks's (*z'tl*) lead and make it Syrian Shabbat worthy, serving this roast chicken (*dajaaj*) with basmati rice cooked with cinnamon stick potatoes, pasta, or eggplant. Here is a favorite recipe I culled together from researching one of my late grandmother's favorite dishes that she learned in Kenya in the 1960s.

Serves 4–6

4½-pound chicken

2 tablespoons softened pareve margarine or vegan butter, plus extra for basting (coconut oil works too)

3 garlic cloves, crushed

1½ tablespoons minced fresh ginger

1 teaspoon kosher "chicken" consommé powder

1 teaspoon Kitchen Pepper (see recipe)

2 teaspoons curry powder

1 teaspoon dried thyme

1 tablespoon finely chopped fresh parsley

4 tablespoons thick coconut milk

2 teaspoons tomato paste

Kosher salt, to taste

Remove the chicken giblets, rinse the chicken inside and out, and pat dry.

Put the vegan butter or margarine and all remaining ingredients in a bowl and mix to form a thick paste. Rub underneath the skin of the chicken, then rub the remainder of the mixture over the skin, legs, and wings of the chicken and into the neck cavity. Place the chicken in a roasting pan, cover loosely with foil, and marinate overnight in the refrigerator.

Preheat oven to 375°F. Cover the chicken with clean foil and roast for 1 hour; then turn the chicken over and baste with the pan juices. Cover again with foil and cook for 30 minutes. Remove the foil and rub the breast with a bit of extra margarine or vegan butter, and roast for a further 10–15 minutes or until the meat juices run clear and the skin is golden brown. For a full-on Kenyan-style meal, transfer to a platter and serve hot or warm with basmati rice, chapati, roasted sweet potato, Sukuma wiki, and kachumbari (see recipe.)

Kosher-Cajun Rice Dressing

One of the many reasons you need to hunt down the cookbooks of Mildred Covert and Sylvia Gerson is that they are a triple volume of treasures of Southern Jewish cooking. These jewels have a Southern kosher answer to virtually anything you can imagine alongside rich congregational cookbooks from across the South. Black domestics and chefs and synagogue sisterhoods crafted an entire genre of Southern cuisine locked primarily in its generation and time but unbelievably important in documenting relationships and flavors of a part of America negotiating culture and identity. Mrs. Covert was not shy about telling me how much of the story behind the recipes relied on the knowledge and skills of Black women and Black non-Jews, and (white) Ashkenazi Jewish women in dialogue with one another. Here is my adaptation of her dirty-rice–style dressing.

Serves 4

1½ pounds kosher ground beef or ground turkey

½ cup chopped onion

¾ cup chopped celery, including some leaves

2 teaspoons Creole Seasoning (see recipe)

½ teaspoon cayenne powder

1 teaspoon dried thyme

1 cup kosher "chicken" broth

1 cup sliced scallions

½ cup chopped parsley

4 cups cooked white rice

In a large pot, cook ground beef with onions and celery, stirring often. Add salt and pepper to taste. When the meat begins to sizzle and brown, add Creole Seasoning, cayenne, thyme, and chicken broth. Cover and simmer for 20 minutes or until almost all of the liquid has evaporated.

Remove from heat; stir in scallions and parsley. Add cooked rice. Stir until well mixed. Bake, covered, until the rice dressing is fragrant and heated through for 20–25 minutes at 350°F. Serve in a casserole dish.

For Ashkenazi Passover: Instead of rice, use matzoh softened in broth or water for 5 minutes.

Basic Southern Fried Chicken

Serves 4

4- to 5-pound fryer, cut into 8 pieces

Juice of 2 lemons

1 teaspoon Soul Seasoning (see recipe)

1 teaspoon kosher chicken consommé powder

¼ teaspoon black pepper

¼ teaspoon cayenne pepper

1 teaspoon paprika

¼ teaspoon garlic powder

1 teaspoon poultry seasoning

Flour for coating the chicken

Vegetable oil for frying

Place chicken pieces in a large bowl of lemon juice and turn to coat the pieces well. In a small bowl, combine the Soul Seasoning, consommé powder, black pepper, cayenne pepper, paprika, garlic powder, and poultry seasoning. Stir with a fork to mix them evenly. Add the chicken pieces to the bowl a couple at a time, sprinkling the spice mixture over the chicken and turning to coat the pieces evenly. Let stand for 30 minutes; cover and refrigerate overnight.

To fry the chicken, heat oil to medium high in a heavy skillet or Dutch oven, preferably cast iron. (I usually go with a range of 350°F to 375°F.) To test the oil, add a pinch of flour, it should bloom at once. The oil should almost cover the chicken. Add the chicken, cover, and cook 15–20 minutes. When golden brown, turn, and be mindful to make sure the heat is even and not too intense. You don't want raw chicken inside and a burned outside.

Finish cooking uncovered, turning as needed, until brown and crisp on all sides. Drain on paper towels. Chicken is done when pieces reach 165°F with an accurate thermometer.

Naftali's Kosher Shitor
(Ghanaian Pepper Sauce)

In Naftali's own words:

"For Friday, I sometimes make our challah: I make Ghanaian sugar bread roll dough and put them in a pan together to bake them, so they pull apart. Instead of the traditional butter, I use pareve margarine or kosher certified vegan butter. There is always a green salad or Ghanaian-style salad—which is a meal in itself with lettuce, hard-boiled eggs, beans, tomatoes, onions, and peppers. Shabbat can mean ground-nut (peanut) soup with rice mash or omo tuo, or kontomire (taro leaves— you can substitute a mix of mature spinach and collard greens) and with palava sauce. My palava sauce uses palm oil, smoked beef instead of stockfish, and instead of a Maggi cube, we use the kosher "chicken" bouillon with kosher certified miso paste. For *egusi* (melon seeds indispensable to palava sauce), we grind the melon or pumpkin seeds ourselves.

For Shabbat day, we might do *waakye* (wa-chay), Ghanaian rice and beans (black-eyed peas), fried plantains, and fried tilapia—all served with homemade kosher shitor. Sometimes for Shabbat or holidays, we do chicken marinated in suya spices and red-red, which is black-eyed peas stewed with palm oil, savories like onion and pepper, and tomato. For the umami of the stockfish, I substitute equal parts miso and MSG.

Like any African cook, I usually really have no idea about my actual measurements for these; I cook them how my mom did it."

About 2 cups

1 large yellow or red onion, chopped

1 15-ounce can plum tomatoes

2 tablespoons ginger paste

2 tablespoons garlic paste

4 habanero peppers, seeded and chopped

2 tablespoons vegetable oil

2 tablespoons palm oil

2 tablespoons red miso paste

2 tablespoons dried mushroom powder

2 tablespoons dried seaweed flakes

2 tablespoons red chili flakes, more to taste

2 tablespoons smoked paprika

1 teaspoon salt, to taste

1 teaspoon black pepper, to taste

Add onions, tomatoes, ginger paste, garlic paste, habanero peppers, and 2 tablespoons vegetable oil to a blender. Blend until smooth. In a large Dutch oven, add the palm oil and gently heat. Sauté the onion and tomato mixture 10–15 minutes, stirring often.

Add miso paste, mushroom powder, and seaweed flakes and continue cooking on low for 5 minutes; then add red chili flakes and smoked paprika and salt and pepper. Cook for 25 minutes. Turn off heat and continue stirring to thicken. When cool, transfer the shitor to a bowl and serve with fried or roasted plantains, suya or kebab, fried fish, fufu, and the like.

Jamaican Jerk Chicken Spaghetti

4–6 servings

4 boneless, skinless chicken breasts

1 teaspoon kosher salt

1 teaspoon black pepper

Marinade

1 small red onion

4 cloves garlic

2 tablespoons chopped flat-leaf parsley

1 tablespoon (or more) chopped fresh ginger

Juice of 2 limes or 2 to 4 tablespoons bottled lime juice

½ teaspoon cinnamon

1 teaspoon dried thyme

1 teaspoon allspice

2 tablespoons vinegar, preferably malt

1½ tablespoons turbinado sugar, coconut sugar, or organic brown or blond sugar

2 tablespoons dark rum (optional)

Sauce

2 cups grape tomatoes, washed and sliced in half

1–2 tablespoons olive oil

To Finish

1 cup or more chicken broth

2 tablespoons margarine or olive oil

½ teaspoon nutmeg

2 tablespoons soy sauce

1–2 orange habanero peppers, seeded

4 scallions, chopped

½ cup canola oil

1 cup chopped bell peppers (mixed green, red, yellow, orange) (optional)

1 cup chicken broth

1 16-ounce box of spaghetti or linguine—preferably whole wheat or high fiber

Chopped flat-leaf parsley and scallions for garnish

Place the chicken in a bowl, rub with the salt and pepper, and prick all over with a fork. Blend the marinade ingredients, from the red onion to the canola oil, until puréed. Pour purée over the chicken and marinate 4–6 hours.

Begin the sauce by breaking down the tomatoes. I do this by placing 1–2 tablespoons olive oil in a pan over medium heat, adding a little garlic (add the optional bell peppers here), and then adding the tomatoes, stirring occasionally. The tomatoes will start to break down in about 20 minutes. Adjust the heat accordingly and watch them like a hawk. Don't let them burn; make sure you stir and squish them until they give up their liquid and soften significantly.

Remove the chicken from the marinade and set aside. Add ½ cup of the reserved marinade to the tomatoes, as well as the chicken broth. Let the sauce develop, bubble, and *take care to avoid burning it*! Turn heat to low and stir occasionally.

Food safety alert: Because you are using a marinade that raw chicken has been in, sustained heat is the only way to make sure you kill any bacteria. The process should take about 20 minutes from boil to simmering over low heat.

Sear the chicken for 5–7 minutes on each side. Loosely cover with foil and place in a preheated 375°F oven for about 20 minutes.

Prepare the spaghetti or linguine according to instructions on the box.

Remove the chicken from the oven (make sure you don't overcook it!) and allow to rest for 5 minutes, then slice thinly. Place the chicken in the sauce. Add the margarine or olive oil to the pasta and toss with the chicken and sauce. Garnish each plate with plenty of parsley and scallion.

Ginger, Cumin, and Garlic Roasted Vegetables

Serves 4–6

5–6 small potatoes—red, purple, or yellow—cut in half

3 large carrots, peeled and cut into chunks

1 parsnip, peeled and cut into chunks

2 sweet potatoes, peeled and cut into chunks (use whatever color you like; I like white or yellow in this dish)

1–2 bell peppers, cut into equal sections or chunks

1 handful fresh green beans, snapped

4 cloves garlic, smashed, peeled, and roughly chopped

2 tablespoons grated raw ginger

4–6 tablespoons olive oil

½ teaspoon cumin

½ teaspoon powdered ginger

1 teaspoon black pepper

1 tablespoon kosher or sea salt

3 tablespoons fresh chopped parsley

Preheat oven to 425°F. I prefer to roast vegetables on the middle rack.

Combine vegetables in a bowl with seasonings and oil; toss a few times, and place in a single layer on a flat cookie sheet or pan covered with foil.

Place the pan in the preheated oven and roast for about 20 minutes, undisturbed. Then give the vegetables a check to make sure they are browning evenly and are becoming tender. You might decide to turn some over and let the other side cook for another 20 minutes.

I always toss finished veggies with chopped flat-leaf parsley and throw them in a serving bowl. They can rest, but not for too long; they go to sleep fairly early but should be warm.

Senegalese-Inspired Chicken Soup

Senegal was my first experience with West Africa. I've been there twice, and each time has been momentous and spiritually clarifying. I noticed people touching doorposts on my second trip as they left domestic spaces, and I was intrigued. The town I was in, a resort town called Saly-Portudal, was settled long ago by Portuguese settlers, and lo and behold, a significant number were Jews fleeing the Inquisition.

The food culture of Senegal, based on halal tradition and incorporating indigenous, Francophone Noir (French West African) Islamic, French, and Vietnamese cultures, is constantly evolving. The traditional Ashkenazi Goldeneyoikh (golden chicken soup) is varied here with Senegalese flavors that remind one of Yemenite-style chicken soup served on Shabbat and holidays.

Serves 6

1 medium red onion, diced

4 tablespoons olive oil

1 teaspoon minced garlic

1 teaspoon fresh minced ginger

1 teaspoon suya spice

½ teaspoon of turmeric

½ teaspoon of chili powder

1 teaspoon ground cayenne

1 teaspoon black pepper

2 teaspoons ground coriander

1 pound raw boneless chicken, diced (you can also use leftover roast chicken or leftover rotisserie breasts)

5 cups chicken stock (or vegetable broth)

1 teaspoon thyme

2 cups crushed plum tomatoes

Salt, to taste

¼ cup peanut butter

1 cup thinly sliced scallions

⅓ cup chopped peanuts, green onion, and 3 tablespoons flat-leaf parsley for garnish

Cook diced onions in olive oil until soft and translucent. Add garlic and cook for 2 minutes. Add ginger, suya spice, turmeric, and chili powder, cayenne pepper, black pepper, and coriander and fry for an additional 2 minutes. If dry, add a small quantity of olive oil until moist.

Add the diced chicken to onions, garlic, and seasonings and sauté. (If using leftover cooked chicken, just add and mix together.)

Add stock and scrape the bottom of the pan very well with a wooden spoon. Add thyme, crushed tomatoes, and salt. Simmer for 30 minutes. Stir often and scrape the bottom every few minutes. Do not boil.

Combine peanut butter and half of the liquid soup stock in a blender or food processor and purée, adding small quantities of broth as necessary if too thick. When smooth, add the purée to the remaining soup and stir well. If the soup seems too thick, add broth to taste.

Add scallions to soup, cooking 5 minutes more, remembering to reserve a few tablespoons for the finished soup. Garnish with remaining scallions, the chopped peanuts, and parsley.

Rivka Campbell's Jamaican Rice and Peas

Rivka worked her tuchus off to bring me to the fine city of Toronto, Canada, through two snowstorms. Her Jamaican roots show through and through in this recipe recorded in her own words. She is brilliant, spicy, and forthright, and she, among other Afro-Caribbean Jews, guards well a rich heritage with so many more stories to tell. Rivka recommended that bammy—cassava flour bread—could be the hoecake on an Afro-Caribbean seder plate along with raw sugar cane, callaloo, Scotch bonnet peppers, and other items indicative of the Caribbean story. Having Trinidadian roots myself, I intend to do both in years to come!

Serves 4–6

1½ cups dried kidney beans or gungo peas (pigeon peas) (You can also use a large can of drained kidney beans—but why?)

1 13½-ounce can coconut milk

Enough water combined with coconut milk to yield 4 cups of liquid (Use the liquid from boiling the beans.)

3 cloves garlic, chopped

2 stalks scallion, chopped (you can also use a small chopped onion, or both)

5 pimiento seeds (allspice) or ½ teaspoon allspice (if using whole seeds, remove after cooking)

Black pepper and salt, to taste (better to use less salt and have "fresh" rice because I will add it later)

5–6 sprigs fresh thyme

1 Scotch bonnet pepper, whole (be careful not to pierce it because then the whole pot will end up too spicy—"Hawt like fiyah")

2 cups long-grain rice, rinsed and drained until water runs clear

Coconut milk from fresh coconut

Rinse and soak the beans or peas overnight and drain; then boil 1–1½ hours, until soft.

Combine all ingredients except the rice in a large pot. Bring to a boil. Add rice and boil on high 2–3 minutes. Turn heat to low and cook covered for 15–20 minutes until the water is absorbed. Remove from heat and let stand for 10–15 minutes. Remove the Scotch bonnet, scallions, allspice, and thyme.

Old-school tip: Do not lift the lid while cooking and do not stir/disturb with a fork. (I seriously don't know the rationale—it's a Jamaican ting.)

Instead of canned coconut milk, here are two other options: Grate a coconut, put in a blender with 2 cups hot water, and blend until fine. Pour over a cloth on a sieve or container and let it sit until cooled. Then squeeze the coconut. Pour water over again and squeeze again. Let it sit in the fridge for about 3 hours. It will separate; use the thinner liquid.

Coconut milk for creamed coconut: 3½ ounces creamed coconut and 1½ cups hot water. Often, I just add a couple extra tablespoons to the liquid if I am using coconut milk. I love extra coconut in my rice and peas.

Peach Rice Kugel and Peach
Noodle Kugel Variation

Rice kugels, according to my friend Leah Koenig, were once widespread in Lithuania and parts of Poland. I loved the idea and made my first one with some Southern additions, like peaches, and it was a hit. I then did it again with apple butter and was almost accosted for the recipe. Peach noodle kugel has long been a Shabbat and Yom-Kippur break-fast staple of mine, especially good with the dairy additions of a cup of sour cream, real butter, and a topping of frosted cornflakes!

Serves 8-ish

2 cups cooked fresh peaches or canned peaches—but the good kind in a jar is preferred

3 large eggs

1 teaspoon sea salt or kosher salt

½ cup turbinado sugar (organic granulated sugar is also okay)

1 tablespoon vanilla extract (*Tip*: If you have it, add 1 teaspoon of vanilla bean powder, which I love for color and appearance.)

1 teaspoon cinnamon

½ cup golden raisins

1 cup rehydrated dried peach bits (optional)

2 cups cooked long-grain white rice—cooked until very soft, mushy is okay

8 tablespoons room temperature butter (use vegan butter or margarine for pareve)

½ cup peach preserves (optional)

1 tablespoon turbinado or brown sugar

Preheat oven to 350°F. Butter a deep quart-size baking dish and set aside. Peel, slice into wedges, and cook fresh peaches in a large pot with enough water just to cover. Cook on high heat being careful not to let it boil over. Turn off heat then drain. (I have an allergy to peach fuzz and the area near the kernel, so you can omit this if it seems too much.) In a medium bowl, beat together eggs, salt, and sugar. Stir in vanilla extract, cinnamon, golden raisins, rehydrated peaches, cooked fresh or canned peaches, cooked rice, 6 tablespoons of the butter, and the peach preserves.

Pour into the buttered dish; dot with remaining 2 tablespoons butter. Sprinkle with 1 tablespoon turbinado or brown sugar. Bake 40–60 minutes; serve hot.

For Peach Noodle Kugel variation: Omit raisins. Replace rice with 4 cups of wide egg noodles (a little over 8 ounces dry should do). Follow directions, checking kugel for doneness at about 40 minutes.

Red Rice

There is something very satisfying about this recipe for red rice. Number one, it is rooted in my maternal origins going back to the Mende people of Sierra Leone brought to South Carolina to grow rice during enslavement that I revealed in *The Cooking Gene*. The Mende women are superb cooks, and I was lucky to travel there in early 2020 to receive my Mende name—Ka-Ngenda—meaning born in the morning and see how this Lowcountry favorite began in the cast-iron pots of the forest country and swampy lowlands of Mende-land.

It's critically important to acknowledge the fine print of this particular cultural history. Red rice—with roots in Senegal, Gambia, Guinea, Sierra Leone, and Liberia—owes a lot to my Mende, Temne, Mandinka, Fula, and Kru ancestors. For more than 300 years, red rice became a beloved Jewish dish in the Lowcountry and shared the Jewish South with "pink rice" (*arroz kon tomat*), a tomato and onion pilau from the Ottoman Jewish world brought at the turn of the twentieth century—and by the way, there were Black cooks there, too!

Serves 4–6

¼ pound lamb bacon, diced small or sliced thin

1 medium onion, trimmed, split lengthwise, peeled, and chopped

1 medium green bell pepper, stemmed, seeded, and chopped

1 cup long-grain rice, washed and drained (converted rice is okay)

2 cups canned plum tomatoes, with the juice, chopped; or 2 cups fresh, chopped, juicy red tomatoes

1 14-ounce can tomato paste

1 cup basic meat or chicken broth

1 tablespoon Worcestershire sauce (non-fish if serving with meat)

1 teaspoon kosher or sea salt

½ teaspoon each ground cayenne pepper, black pepper or Kitchen Pepper (see recipe), and poultry seasoning, or to taste

Put the lamb bacon in a deep Dutch oven and turn the heat to medium. Fry, uncovered, until the fat is rendered and the bacon is crisp. Spoon off all but 2 tablespoons of fat. (A neutral vegetable oil is a good substitute for the fat.) Add the onion and bell pepper; sauté until translucent, 5–7 minutes.

Add the rice and stir and sweat for about 5 minutes, scraping any loose grains sticking to the pan. Add the tomatoes with their juice, tomato paste, broth, Worcestershire sauce, salt, cayenne pepper, Kitchen Pepper, and poultry seasoning.

Loosely cover, reduce the heat as low as possible, and simmer for 25 minutes. Take it off the heat and allow it to rest for 15 minutes before serving.

Okra Soup

Okra is an ancient member of the mallow family indigenous to sub-Saharan Africa. It was brought along the Gold and Silk Routes and made the Middle Passage with our Ancestors during the trans-Atlantic slave trade and moved eastward with the Portuguese to Macau. In Middle Eastern cooking, it is known as bamia. The Jews of the Levant, Ladino-speaking Jews in the Balkans and other parts of the Ottoman Empire, and Jews from Egypt to Persia to India were familiar with it. Bamia is stewed, sometimes pickled, and frequently paired—as in West Africa—with tomatoes in one-pot dishes.

Unsurprisingly, okra soup became a Jewish dish in the New World wherever European Jews settled and were culturally impacted by the presence of the African diaspora and the civilization of the African Atlantic.

Serves 4–6

¼ cup pareve margarine or vegan butter

1 tablespoon olive oil

1 small onion, diced and dusted with flour

2 tablespoons finely chopped flat-leaf parsley

1 clove garlic, minced

1 sprig fresh thyme

1 teaspoon salt

½ teaspoon black pepper (or to taste)

½ teaspoon red pepper flakes

4 cups vegetable broth (you can also use chicken or beef broth—vegetable broth keeps the recipe kosher and vegetarian)

3 cups water

1 28-ounce can tomatoes with juice (or 3½ cups peeled and diced fresh tomatoes)

2 cups small, thin pieces of fresh okra or frozen okra pieces

In a Dutch oven, heat the margarine and oil until melted. Add the onion and finely chopped parsley; gently cook until the onion is translucent and soft. Add the garlic and cook for a minute more until fragrant.

Add the thyme, salt, black pepper, and red pepper flakes and cook for another minute or so. Add the broth, water, and tomatoes and cook on a medium simmer for 30 minutes.

Add the okra and cook another 20–25 minutes, or until the okra is tender.

Serving suggestion: Ladle into bowls over a ¼-cup lump of warm cooked rice.

Gullah-Geechee-Inspired Beef Stew

Serves 4–6

3 pounds beef short ribs

1 teaspoon seasoned salt or Soul Seasoning

1 teaspoon Kitchen Pepper (see recipe)

1 teaspoon sweet paprika

½ cup flour

¼ cup lamb bacon drippings or schmaltz or vegetable or coconut oil

1 cup diced red onions

1 cup diced green pepper

2 stalks celery, cut into thin slices

½ teaspoon crushed red pepper

4 cups beef broth (low sodium)

2 cups tomato sauce

2 fresh bay leaves

4–5 sweet potatoes, peeled, halved, and cut into chunks

1 rutabaga, peeled, halved, and cut into chunks (white- or yellow-fleshed preferred)

3 carrots, peeled and cut into 1½-inch pieces

Green onion/scallion slices and minced fresh flat-leaf parsley for garnish (optional)

In a large bowl, season the short ribs with the seasoned salt or Soul Seasoning, Kitchen Pepper, and sweet paprika. (Don't get cute and use smoked or hot paprika—it won't taste right!)

In a large Dutch oven, heat the oil/fat of your choice over a medium-high heat or until a cube of bread gently toasts and browns in it. Discard the bread, and brown the short ribs on all sides, being careful not to let them burn.

Remove the short ribs from the oil and discard a third of the remaining fat in the pan (the surface stuff only!), then add the onions, bell peppers, and celery. Scrape up all of that browning goodness at the bottom of the pan and gently sauté for 5–7 minutes. Add the broth and the tomato sauce and cook uncovered on medium bubbling heat for about 5 minutes.

Add the short ribs and boil, uncovered, steadily for about 15 minutes. Skim off any scum that rises to the top. Drop in the two fresh bay leaves, reduce the heat, and simmer gently for about 2½ hours until the short ribs are super tender.

Fish out the bay leaves and discard; add the sweet potatoes, rutabaga, and carrots. Simmer for another 35 minutes until the vegetables are tender and infused with the flavor of the stock.

Adjust seasoning and serve over rice with garnishes.

Rosh Hashanah–Yom Kippur–Sukkot

Apple Barbecue Sauce

Put this sauce on chicken or salmon or sliced pot roast, lamb, or brisket, or eat it with spicy roasted vegetables.

About 2 cups

2 tablespoons pareve oil of your choice

½ cup chopped Vidalia onion or any sweet onion

¼ cup minced celery

¼ cup minced carrot

1 tablespoon minced garlic

1 teaspoon crushed, minced ginger

1 teaspoon kosher or sea salt, or to taste

½ cup tomato paste mixed with ½ cup apple juice or apple cider

½ cup grated Granny Smith or Honeycrisp apple (unpretty apples are great for this!) or ½ cup applesauce

½ cup apple butter

½ cup apple cider vinegar

¼ cup low-sodium soy sauce

¼ cup brown mustard

½ cup light brown sugar

1 teaspoon Kitchen Pepper (see recipe)

1 teaspoon sweet paprika

1 teaspoon small coarse black pepper

1 teaspoon seasoned salt of your choice

Add oil to a medium saucepan and sauté the onions, celery, carrots, garlic, ginger and salt. When it sizzles, reduce heat to medium low, stirring often until onion and celery are translucent. Be attentive! Don't let them burn. This will take 5–10 minutes.

Meanwhile, combine the tomato paste with the apple juice and stir to mix well into a thick, smooth tomato sauce. Set aside.

When the onion mixture is ready, add the tomato paste mixture, along with all remaining ingredients, to the saucepan. Increase the heat to medium high and quickly bring to a boil, stirring often. Then reduce the heat to medium low and cover. Let the barbecue sauce cook for 45 minutes, stirring every 5 minutes or so. Taste and adjust the seasonings.

Cool to room temperature and use or transfer to a covered container. May be refrigerated for up to 5 days.

Cushaw or Sweet Potato Pumpkin

Serves 6–8

1 medium-size cushaw, 10–12 pounds

2 sticks pareve margarine, divided

½ cup sugar

Pinch salt

1 tablespoon honey

2 teaspoons vanilla extract

2 eggs

Honey for drizzle

Cut cushaw into pieces, remove seeds and skin, and boil until tender. Drain and peel.

Heat 1½ sticks margarine in a pan over medium heat and stir in sugar until the mixture is brown. Add salt, honey, vanilla extract, and cushaw; cook for 25 minutes. Remove from heat.

Beat eggs and stir into cushaw. Place in a casserole dish and pour the remaining melted margarine over the top. Drizzle honey over the top and bake for 30 minutes in a 325°F oven. You can substitute butternut squash.

Hanukkah

Louisiana-Style Latkes

Serves 4–6

2 cups peeled and shredded Yukon gold or russet potatoes

1 tablespoon grated onion

1 tablespoon chopped celery

2 tablespoons chopped green onion

1 small garlic clove, minced

1 pinch dried thyme

½ teaspoon cayenne pepper—powder or flakes

3 eggs, beaten

2 tablespoons all-purpose flour, matzoh meal, or potato starch

1½ teaspoons salt

½ cup peanut oil for frying (use canola or vegetable oil if you have allergies)

Creole Seasoning (see recipe)

Wring the shredded potato in cheesecloth; repeat several times to extract as much moisture as you can. In a medium bowl, stir all the ingredients except the oil together.

In a large, heavy-bottomed skillet over medium high heat, heat the oil until hot—between 350°F and 375°F. Place a heaping tablespoon and a half of the potato mixture into the hot oil, pressing down on it to form ¼- to ½-inch-thick patties. Brown on one side, turn, and brown on the other. Drain on paper towels.

Serve hot with an extra dusting of Creole Seasoning and a few slices of green onion. You can also serve with applesauce, sour cream, and maybe some sweet chili sauce (sugar, vinegar, salt, garlic, chili, pepper).

Yam Latkes

Serves 8

2 pounds sweet potatoes	2–3 tablespoons flour
4 tablespoons softened butter or pareve margarine	Oil, for frying
Salt and pepper, to taste	Cinnamon (optional)
2 eggs, lightly beaten	Cayenne (optional)
1 large onion, finely chopped	Applesauce (optional)

Peel sweet potatoes, cut into 1-inch-thick slices, and cover with cold tap water. Bring to a boil, add salt to taste, and cover. Cook until tender, about 30 minutes.

Drain potatoes and return to pot. Mash well with butter or pareve margarine, and season with salt and pepper to taste. Add eggs and blend. Stir in onions. Add flour.

Coat the bottom of a large, heavy-bottomed frying pan with 3–4 tablespoons oil and heat until moderately hot, or until one drop of batter sizzles when dropped into the hot oil. Drop one large serving spoon of potato purée into the hot oil and see if it holds its shape. If not, add a little more flour to the mixture.

Drop large spoonfuls (2 tablespoons sounds about right) of purée into the oil and fry over moderate heat for 3–4 minutes on each side until nicely browned, turning carefully with a spatula. Add more oil as needed with each batch. Sprinkle with cinnamon and a pinch of cayenne, if desired. Serve with applesauce.

Koshersoul Spring Rolls

Soul Rolls were something I heard about first in North Carolina at Mertz Heart and Soul, a restaurant in Charlotte. The rolls take different forms at different soul food restaurants and food trucks, but I wanted to figure out how to make them not only kosher but koshersoul. Most versions contained pork, cheese, or sometimes shellfish. I made koshersoul rolls for Andrew Zimmern on *Bizarre Foods America*.

One year, just before Sukkot, I gave myself a field trip to Boro Park. I was buying new tzitzit and just checking out the neighborhood. I wandered into a spot with a sign that said "pastrami egg rolls." It was delicious, but it needed something more. As soon I got home, pastrami met collards, and koshersoul spring rolls were born. As anyone who has been to Disney World can attest, the beauty of a spring roll is that it can tell any story you want it to as long as the flavors are right.

Here's my rap in a wrapper.

Serves 5

1 tablespoon sesame oil

1 tablespoon minced garlic

1 tablespoon minced ginger

5 scallions, chopped and shredded

1 cup minced kosher pastrami

1 bunch collards, stems removed and cut into thin strips

2 tablespoons vegetarian hoisin sauce, vegetarian oyster sauce, or half-and-half

1 tablespoon rice vinegar or apple cider vinegar

1 teaspoon pareve kosher chicken consommé powder

½ teaspoon crushed red pepper flakes

1 teaspoon cornstarch

½ package spring roll wrappers or egg roll wrappers (about 10)

Egg yolk to moisten spring roll wrapper

Vegetable or canola oil for frying

Hoisin-Ginger Dip

4 tablespoons pomegranate vinegar or cider vinegar

2 tablespoons vegetarian hoisin sauce

1 teaspoon minced fresh ginger

1 teaspoon thinly sliced scallions

In a hot wok or large sauté pan, add the sesame oil, followed by the garlic and ginger; stir and cook for just under 1 minute, being careful not to let it burn. Add scallions and pastrami; cook, stirring, on medium heat for 5 minutes.

Add thin strips of collard leaves and cook for another 7 minutes on medium heat, making sure the greens are cooked and wilted, you can add a little water here if you like.

Add hoisin sauce, rice vinegar, consommé powder, and pepper flakes; adjust seasoning to taste. Add cornstarch and stir to thicken. Set aside and cool for 15 minutes. While the filling cools, whisk together the dip ingredients, to make a smooth sauce. Transfer to a small serving bowl, and sprinkle sliced green onion on top.

To make each roll, lay out one wrapper with the corner facing you; place about 2 tablespoons mixture in the wrapper. Moisten edges with egg yolk and fold the bottom corner up over the filling; fold in both sides and continue rolling.

Heat 3 cups of oil in a frying pan or deep wok to about 350°F; you can use a bit of spring roll wrapper to test the heat. (If the spring roll wrapper browns, the heat is correct.) Once hot, place rolls in the hot oil, three at a time, being careful not to overcrowd the pan. Cook until golden brown and then turn over and finish cooking the other side. Remove to plate with paper towels to drain. Repeat to fry the remaining rolls. Serve hot or warm with Hoisin Ginger Dip.

Collard Green Kreplach Filling

Kreplach (a filled pasta triangle or bundle) are one of the many reasons I am grateful for the Silk Routes. Stuffed and wrapped foods flowed along these paths. So sambusak (a Middle Eastern filled fried or baked turnover), samosas (their Indian descendants), sambusa (the Somali version of samosa), and empanadas make up one line. On another line are spring rolls. Egg rolls also owe some of their genealogy to this many-branched tradition. Kreplach and wontons, often served in a sauce or soup or stew, have the same filled dumpling thing that makes them versatile and tasty.

Kreplach are served explicitly on holidays like Purim, the final meal before the fast on Yom Kippur, and Hoshanah Rabbah during Sukkot and Shavuot. Many Jewish foods are associated with mystical teachings, and kreplach are no different. One belief noted by the late Rabbi Gil Marks is that practitioners of Kabbalah associated wrapped foods with being surrounded by Divine mercy, kindness, and protection. Because the ingredients inside were minced or "beaten," Purim became significant since Haman was beaten by those he tried to destroy, we the Jewish people.

2 cups filling

3 tablespoons extra light olive oil

1 cup scallions, thinly sliced

1 cup button or shitake mushrooms, finely chopped

1 cup thinly sliced, chopped collard greens, stems removed

1 garlic clove, minced

⅓ cup kosher "chicken" consommé broth

1 tablespoon non-fish Worcestershire sauce or apple cider vinegar

1 teaspoon Soul Seasoning (see recipe)

¼ teaspoon red pepper flakes

In light olive oil, sauté scallions over medium heat until softened, about 3 minutes. Add mushrooms, collards, and garlic. Sauté on medium heat for 8 minutes. Add consommé broth, Worcestershire sauce or vinegar, Soul Seasoning, and red pepper flakes and cook for an additional 2 minutes. Cool before using it as a filling in your favorite kreplach recipe.

Sour Apple Slaw

Makes 12 servings

8 cups shredded green cabbage
(½ medium head)

1½ teaspoons salt

¼ cup cider vinegar

2 tablespoons maple syrup

1 teaspoon Dijon mustard

½ teaspoon ground pepper

3 medium Granny Smith apples,
julienned or shredded

3 cups spinach leaves, thinly sliced

2 scallions, sliced

1 teaspoon minced fresh flat-leaf
parsley

1 teaspoon minced fresh tarragon,
dill, or parsley

Toss cabbage and salt in a colander and set over a large bowl. Let the cabbage wilt for 30 minutes, then plunge it into a bowl of cold water. Drain and pat dry.

Whisk vinegar, maple syrup, mustard, and pepper in a large bowl. Add the cabbage, apples, spinach, scallions, parsley, and tarragon; toss to coat well.

Kwanzaa/New Year's

Cash Collards with Sukuma Wiki Variation

Serves 4–6

4 tablespoons olive oil

4 cloves fresh garlic, peeled, smashed, and chopped

1 medium yellow onion, chopped

1 small fresh fish pepper or cayenne, diced (optional)

5 cups collard greens or kale, washed, stemmed, and cut into thin strips

Salt and black pepper, to taste

1 cup fresh winter vegetable stock (cook collard stems, onion, garlic, carrot, turnip, parsnip, and herbs with a few pinches of salt for several hours until a complex, rich broth emerges)

2 tablespoons freshly chopped oregano, marjoram, or parsley

Heat olive oil in a large skillet and toss in garlic and onion; sauté until onion is translucent. Toss in diced fish pepper, if using, and then add collard strips, 1 cup at a time. Cook each cup 2–3 minutes before adding the next; when all have been added and have cooked down, add the fresh vegetable stock and cook 10–15 minutes. Top with freshly chopped herbs and serve over rice or with black-eyed peas or other cowpeas.

For Sukuma Wiki: After onion add 2 cups of red, orange, or yellow bell peppers cut into thin strips, 2 cups of chopped fresh tomatoes or canned plum tomatoes, and ½ teaspoon of curry powder. Omit herbs.

Senegal Meets Lowcountry Kwanzaa Salad

Serves 4–6

2 pounds white, yellow, or orange sweet potatoes, peeled and cut into ½-inch cubes

1 teaspoon kosher salt

1 teaspoon black pepper (I like coarse ground)

1 pound red or white baby potatoes, peeled and cut into quarters

Juice of 1 lemon, divided

2 tablespoons–¼ cup peanut butter (depending on your taste)

¼ cup apple cider vinegar

2 tablespoons olive oil

1 teaspoon hot sauce or hot pepper flakes

1 tablespoon sugar

1 tablespoon sesame seeds, preferably lightly toasted (we call it *benne* from Wolof and Bamana!)

1 clove garlic, minced

1 teaspoon minced fresh ginger, or 1 teaspoon powdered

4 tablespoons minced scallion

Place the potatoes in a pot; cover with water, salted to taste. Bring to a boil, then reduce and cook until potatoes are tender. This process should not take more than 15–20 minutes. Test potatoes with a fork between 10 and 20 minutes of cooking. Drain potatoes and toss with about a third of the lemon juice and allow to rest and cool.

In a medium-size bowl, whisk together until smoothly blended the peanut butter, remaining lemon juice, apple cider vinegar, olive oil, hot sauce or pepper flakes, kosher salt, pepper, sugar, sesame seeds, garlic, and ginger.

If you like your potato salad fresh, mix the dressing with the potatoes, stir it up, and toss it with the minced green onion. If you like it developed—as I do—mix the potatoes with the dressing and place them covered in the refrigerator. When brought to the table, garnish or toss with the green onion.

Hoppin' John

Serves 8

1 cup dried red field peas

2–3 kosher smoked turkey wings

4 cups kosher chicken broth

1 cup uncooked rice

4 slices kosher lamb or beef bacon, fried (reserve drippings)

1 medium onion, chopped

1 teaspoon Soul Seasoning (see recipe)

1 teaspoon poultry seasoning

Boil the peas and turkey wings in the broth until the peas are tender. Combine the peas and 1 cup of the pea liquid with the rice, kosher bacon and reserved drippings, onion, Soul Seasoning, and poultry seasoning. Put the mixture in a rice steamer or double boiler and cook for 1 hour until the rice is done.

Akaras (Black-Eyed Pea Fritters)

Serves 3–4

2 cups dried black-eyed peas	1 cayenne, Scotch Bonnet, or habanero, halved, with seeds removed
1 onion, chopped	
1 teaspoon Suya Spice (see recipe)	⅔ cup water
1 teaspoon of kosher "chicken" consommé powder	Oil, for deep frying

Cover and soak the black-eyed peas in a deep bowl with cold water overnight. Drain them and then rub them between the palms of your hands to remove the skins. Return the shelled peas to the bowl of water, and the skins will float to the surface. Discard the skins and soak the peas again for 2 hours. Drain.

Place peas in a blender or food processor with the onion, Suya Spice, consommé powder, hot pepper, and a little water. Blend until a batter is formed. Move to a large bowl and whisk for a few minutes.

Heat the oil in a large, heavy saucepan to 375°F and fry small scoopfuls of batter until golden brown, about 4 minutes, turning to make sure each side is cooked.

Yassa Chicken

Yassa au Poulet is my favorite Senegalese dish. It's pungent, tangy, and savory and gives you the best of grilling and braising—the smoky flavor and the tenderness of cooking the meat with the sauce. It makes for a great Friday night dish, especially in the summertime.

Serves 4–6

⅔ cup lemon or lime juice

2 tablespoons white wine vinegar

2 tablespoons Dijon mustard

2 tablespoons West African Wet Seasoning (see recipe)

3 onions, sliced

2 garlic cloves, crushed

4 tablespoons peanut or vegetable oil, divided

2 chickens, cut into 8 pieces

1 sprig thyme

1 green chili, seeded and finely chopped

2 bay leaves

2 cups chicken stock

Mix the lemon juice, vinegar, Dijon mustard, West African Wet Seasoning, onions, garlic, and 2 tablespoons oil. Place the chicken pieces in a shallow dish and pour the lemon mixture over them. Cover with plastic wrap and let marinate for 3 hours to overnight. Reserve some of the marinade or make up a new batch, if you prefer.

Fry or grill the chicken until it's browned and almost done, then set it aside.

Add the marinated onions to a Dutch oven or large pot with the remaining oil. Sauté for 3 minutes, then add the marinade, thyme, chili, bay leaves, and half the stock. Let it come to a boil. Add the chicken to the liquid then cover the pan and simmer gently over medium low heat for 35–45 minutes. Add more stock, if necessary, as the sauce evaporates. Serve hot.

African Peanut and Curry Base
(for Chicken, Fish, or Vegetables)

———

Serves 4–6

2 teaspoons Suya Spice (see recipe)

1 lemon or lime

1 heaping tablespoon smooth peanut butter

1 teaspoon Kitchen Pepper (see recipe)

3 tablespoons vegetable oil

1 onion, finely chopped

2 garlic cloves, crushed

3 tablespoons curry powder, preferably Madras

1 14-ounce can chopped tomatoes

2 tablespoons chopped fresh ginger

1 green pepper, seeded and chopped

About 2½ cups chicken, vegetable, or fish stock

1 tablespoon fresh flat-leaf parsley or cilantro, finely chopped

Salt and freshly ground black pepper, to taste

If using chicken (2½ pounds of boneless chicken) or fish (2 pounds): Season chicken pieces or a whole red snapper or fish of your choice with salt to taste and Suya Spice and place in shallow bowl. Halve the lemon or lime and squeeze both halves all over the flesh. Cover loosely with plastic wrap and let marinate for at least 2 hours for chicken or 30 minutes for fish.

Make the sauce: Heat the oil in a large saucepan and fry the onion and garlic 5–6 minutes or until onion is soft. Reduce heat and add the curry powder and cook for 5 minutes. Stir in the tomatoes and peanut butter, mixing well. Add the green pepper, ginger, and stock. Stir well and simmer gently for 10 minutes.

For chicken: Cut the chicken into bite-size pieces and cook in the sauce for 20–30 minutes. Stir the parsley or cilantro into the sauce and adjust salt and pepper to taste. Add a little extra stock if necessary

For fish: Cut the fish into pieces and gently lower into the sauce. Simmer for 20 minutes or until the fish is cooked, then, using a slotted spoon, transfer the fish pieces to a plate. Stir the parsley or cilantro into the sauce and adjust salt and pepper to taste. Add a little extra stock if necessary. Return the fish to the sauce and cook gently to heat through; serve immediately.

For vegetables: Use a mixture of cubed potatoes, sweet potatoes, carrots, plantain, mushrooms, or whatever you like. Remember to blanch or parboil veggies as necessary to speed up the cooking time. Add parsley or cilantro to the sauce and adjust salt and pepper as necessary. Cook 20–30 minutes to desired softness.

Jollof Rice

Jollof is the transnational dish of West Africa. It has many different forms from Senegal to the Gambia to Sierra Leone and Liberia, Togo and Benin, Ghana and Nigeria. Still, this recipe provides a basic outline of the pilaf that covers most bases. Party rice Jollof can be amended as you like and can be either a side or a main dish. I also use this in rice-stuffed vegetables (think bell peppers and onions) from Mizrahi and Sephardi cuisines for extra flavor or stuffed cabbage (*holishkes*), rolled collard leaves, or stuffed grape leaves (*dolmades*).

Serves 4–6

2 tablespoons vegetable oil

1 large onion, chopped

2 garlic cloves, crushed

2 tablespoons tomato paste

1½ cups long grain white rice

1 green pepper, seeded and chopped

2½ cups vegetable or chicken stock

1 teaspoon seasoned salt or Jollof rice seasoning

Heat the oil in a saucepan and fry the onion and garlic 4–5 minutes until the onion is soft. Add the tomato paste and simmer over medium heat for about 3 minutes, stirring constantly.

Rinse the rice in cold water, drain well, and add to the pan with the green pepper and a pinch of salt. Cook 2–3 minutes, stirring constantly to prevent the rice from sticking to the bottom of the pan. Add the stock, cover, and simmer for about 15 minutes.

When the liquid is nearly absorbed, turn off the heat. Keep the pan covered and steam over low heat until the rice is tender.

Kachumbari (Kenyan Tomato and Onion Salad)

Salatim are an essential part of Israeli cuisine thanks in part to the number of people who have made *aliyah* with origins in North Africa and the Middle East and the culinary impact of Israeli Arabs and the Palestinians. Kemia in North Africa or mezze in the rest of the Middle East are appetizers and small-plate dishes that rely on seasonal ingredients and pantry staples. Hospitality demands that if someone were to stop by, they might sample some salad, bread, condiments, tea, sweets, and then decide whether they can stay for the main meal, to which they will inevitably be invited by their host.

African and African Diaspora cuisines, although heavy on hospitality, aren't as appetizer and small-plate oriented. However, the table is likely to have a few home-made condiments and relishes that go with the usual meal of a main dish—usually a soup, stew, or main protein consumed with sauces or sides that enhance its flavor. Kachumbari, born at the intersection of African and South Asian cuisines, is such a condiment and can serve as a salad or a flavor enhancer. It pairs perfectly with the East African dishes included here, from *sukuma wiki* to roast fish or plantains or the Swahili roast chicken and any rice or rice pilaf that goes with them. I also enjoy taking ground turkey; or chicken, lamb, and beef; and now plant-based "meat," and serving kachumbari (instead of the more traditional tabbouleh) with several other salads and hummus and pita for a quick and satisfying meal meant for a small crowd.

Serves 4–6

2 red medium onions, very thinly sliced

4 tomatoes, very thinly sliced

½ cucumber, peeled and sliced

1 carrot, peeled and sliced

Juice from 1 lemon

Salt and freshly ground black pepper, to taste

½ teaspoon red chili flakes

½ teaspoon garam masala or curry powder

Place the sliced onions, tomatoes, cucumber, and carrot in a bowl. Squeeze lemon juice over the salad. Season with salt, pepper, chili flakes, and garam masala or curry powder and toss together to mix. Allow flavors to develop for 30 minutes or more, and then serve as a salad or relish.

Variation: For a little extra zing at Pesach, add a tablespoon or two of chrain or beet horseradish.

Pesach/Passover

West African–Inspired Brisket

The number one question is: What makes this a "West African–inspired" brisket. The question is imbued with an air of "What am I missing here?" Although West African food is not very well known in the West, its influence and impact are already here thanks to the foodways of the African Atlantic. West and Central African-born tastes are so well sown into the cuisines of the Americas that the flavor elements that are key to the region may get lost in the perception of indigeneity. However, the forwardness of hot chilis; the trinity of (sweet or hot) peppers, onions, and tomatoes; the presence of garlic, ginger, and turmeric; and the overall tendency toward piquant sauces and gravies that help it pair well with rice or fufu (tubers or plantains pounded into a smooth loaf) help explain why this very Jewish brisket speaks Pidgin rather than Yiddish.

Serves 6–8

1 teaspoon ground ginger

1 teaspoon is ground turmeric

1 tablespoon paprika

1 teaspoon coarse black pepper

1 teaspoon cinnamon

1 teaspoon chili powder

1 teaspoon cayenne pepper

1 tablespoon kosher salt

5 pounds brisket

4 garlic cloves, peeled and minced

4 tablespoons extra virgin olive oil, divided

3 onions, peeled and diced

3 bell peppers—green, red, and yellow—seeded and diced

1 10-ounce can diced tomatoes (kosher for Passover!)

1 tablespoon brown sugar

2 cups chicken, beef, or vegetable stock (kosher for Passover!!!)

1 teaspoon prepared horseradish

| 2 bay leaves | 2 large red onions, cut into rings |
| 1 sprig fresh thyme or 1 teaspoon dried thyme | 2 or 3 cups of white-fleshed sweet potatoes (optional) |

Heat oven to 325°F. Combine the ginger, turmeric, paprika, black pepper, cinnamon, chili powder, and cayenne pepper with salt. Save about 2 teaspoons for the vegetables. Sprinkle the brisket with this mixture and rub in the minced garlic. Heat 3 tablespoons olive oil in a large Dutch oven or pot. Sear the beef all around. Remove from the Dutch oven and set aside.

Add the diced onion and bell pepper to the oil in the pan and season with the reserved 2 teaspoons of seasoning. Sauté until the onion is translucent, add the tomatoes, mix, and cook for about 5 minutes.

Add the brown sugar and stock, horseradish, bay leaves, and thyme. Pour out of the pan into a bowl. Place the red onion rings in the bottom of the pan and sprinkle with the remaining tablespoon of olive oil. Place the brisket on top of them. Pour the vegetables and stock over the brisket. Two to three cups of cubed sweet potatoes, especially white-fleshed or yellow varieties, is a nice addition.

Cover and bake in the preheated oven for 3½ hours until the brisket is fork-tender. Remove the brisket, cool, and refrigerate. Once the brisket is chilled, remove excess fat and then slice—always against the grain. Place the sliced brisket in a pan or pot, cover with sauce. Heat for half an hour or more in the oven at 300°F or until heated through.

Matzoh Meal Fried Chicken

Serves 8

1 teaspoon kosher salt	¼ teaspoon cinnamon
2 teaspoons poultry seasoning	2 kosher chickens, preferably fryers, cut into breast, wing, leg, and thigh portions
2 teaspoons coarse ground black pepper	
¼ teaspoon ground ginger	4 eggs, for egg wash
	3 cups matzoh meal

1 teaspoon (sweet) paprika

¼ teaspoon allspice

¼ teaspoon ground cloves

KFP cooking oil, or if you are Sephardic like me, corn or peanut oil

Combine the salt and seasonings together in a bowl. Wash chicken and pat dry. Season the chicken with the spice mixture and set aside for a few hours.

Prepare the egg wash by beating eggs with a fork and mixing with a little water. Place the egg wash in a shallow dish. Place matzoh meal in another dish. Set up a rack over a baking sheet lined with paper towels. Dip each chicken piece in egg wash then the matzoh meal and set it on the rack. Let sit for about 15 minutes so the coating can set. Heat oil as in the Basic Southern Fried Chicken recipe above (minus the test with the bread). Fry for about 8 minutes per side, and turn to brown all around, another 4 minutes per piece. Use your best judgment: Crispy and golden brown on the outside doesn't mean done on the inside. To test, you should aim for 165°F degrees or higher for white meat and 175°F or higher for dark meat. The appearance of the chicken and the doneness of the meat inside are the two factors you have to balance when frying chicken.

As pieces are finished cooking, remove them with tongs and place them on a paper-towel-lined platter to drain. Serve hot or warm.

Passover Barbecue Lamb Rub
(for Shoulder, Breast, or Ribs)

——

¾ cup

1 teaspoon kosher beef or chicken bouillon powder

1 teaspoon black pepper

1 teaspoon ginger

1 small onion, finely chopped

2 tablespoons garlic, finely chopped

2 tablespoons olive oil

2 tablespoons white balsamic or pomegranate vinegar

2 teaspoons sweet, hot, or smoked paprika (or a mix, according to your taste)

½ teaspoon cinnamon

1–2 tablespoons prepared white horseradish

1 tablespoon brown sugar

Mix all the ingredients together, transfer to a covered container. Refrigerate up to 3–4 days.

Mrs. Cardozo's Famous Seven-Fruit Haroset from Suriname

Serves 6–8

8 ounces chopped raisins

8 ounces chopped dried apples

8 dried chopped prunes or dried cranberries (check for Pesach certification)

8 ounces chopped dried apricots or dried mango

8 ounces chopped dried pears

1 tablespoon sweet kosher wine to moisten (I suggest blackberry)

1 tablespoon cinnamon

8 ounces unsweetened shredded coconut

8 ounces nuts of your choice, grated (optional for nut allergies)

¼ cup turbinado sugar

2 tablespoons cherry jam or chopped brandied cherries (non-chametz)

In a large bowl, combine the first five ingredients and just barely cover the chopped fruit with water. Let the mixed fruit sit overnight in the refrigerator and then drain the bowl once the fruit is plumped.

In a large saucepan, combine the wine, cinnamon, coconut, nuts, and sugar and cook on low heat for 15 minutes. Add the dried fruit and cherry jam to the sauce and gently cook for another 10 minutes. Do not allow it to burn. Remove from the heat, let it cool, and place in a container. Keeps for 3–5 days.

Charleston Bunch Soup

Charleston vegetable bunches were sold by Black women on the streets of the city, carried in sweetgrass and pine baskets on their heads. Rich in the leafy greens of African tradition and tubers and okra when available, the resultant bunch soup and its potlikker or stock was used in sauces and braises, giving a rich, full-bodied taste to the rice, poultry, game, and seafood dishes of the region. Through the enslaved of Charleston's elite, it became a part of the city's Jewish society, once the largest Jewish community in the early colonies.

Serves 6–8

3 pounds chicken feet or wings

Enough pareve "chicken" or vegetable bouillon broth to cover chicken

1 parsnip, sliced

1 white turnip, sliced

¼ white cabbage, shredded

¼ red cabbage, shredded

½ rutabaga, sliced

4 large carrots, cut into chunks

2 large onions, quartered

1 28-ounce can tomatoes

1 handful stemmed and chopped collard greens

1 stalk celery, cut in chunks

2 teaspoons poultry seasoning

1 teaspoon or more kosher salt

1 teaspoon Kitchen Pepper (see recipe)

In a large stock pot, cover the chicken with broth, plus 2 inches. Bring to a boil over medium-high heat then lower to a simmer. Cook, covered, for 2 hours or until the chicken is tender. Skim any scum from the top of the pot as the chicken cooks. Remove wings and feet from the hot stock then add the vegetables, poultry seasoning, salt, and Kitchen Pepper and bring to a rolling boil, covered, for at least 45 minutes to an hour. The vegetables should be very tender. Strain the soup—season to taste. You can serve this soup with matzoh balls, rice, or by itself with cornbread.

Matzoh Balls

No book has informed my Jewish cooking more than Joan Nathan's *Jewish Holiday Kitchen*. Her recipe inspires my matzoh ball recipe here in *Koshersoul*. I prefer schmaltz to vegetable oil, but if you want pareve or vegetarian matzoh balls, use the latter and use pareve "chicken" consommé broth. I consistently use "chicken" because the leading brands of kosher broth are pareve since chicken is considered meat, so they neutrally name it consommé, but that's the flavor you need.

There is a saying in Yiddish cooking that a stuffed matzoh ball or one that isn't plain has a *neshamah*, or a soul. I hope these count.

Should serve about 6; makes around 20 matzoh balls

4 tablespoons chicken broth

4 tablespoons schmaltz (rendered chicken fat) or vegetable oil

1 teaspoon salt, or to taste

¼ teaspoon grated Kitchen Pepper (see recipe)

¼ teaspoon ginger

2 tablespoons minced scallion

1 tablespoon chopped parsley

2 pinches cayenne pepper

1 cup matzoh meal

4 large eggs

In a large bowl, combine all the ingredients except the eggs. Stir in one egg at a time with a wooden spoon until all four eggs are incorporated. Refrigerate a few hours or overnight.

Bring an 8- to 10-quart pot of salted water to a boil. Wet your hands with warm water and form the mixture into balls the size of walnuts. Drop into the boiling water, cover, and simmer for 30 minutes. The matzoh balls should be fluffy and float on top. Remove with a slotted spoon to bowls of hot chicken soup.

Okra Gumbo

About 6 servings

6 cups kosher pareve "chicken" broth, divided

⅓ cup plus 3 tablespoons canola oil, divided

1 large yellow or red onion, diced (small)

1 green bell pepper, diced (small)

1 yellow bell pepper, diced (small)

8 stalks celery, diced (small)

6 cloves garlic, minced

1 teaspoon tomato paste

½ cup potato starch

1 14½-ounce can diced tomatoes

6 cups sliced okra, fresh or frozen

1 teaspoon dried thyme

2 tablespoons Creole Seasoning, or more to taste (see recipe)

1 scallion, sliced thinly on a bias, for garnish

Bring the broth to a boil and set aside on low heat. Add 3 tablespoons canola oil to a heavy-bottomed pot or Dutch oven over medium heat. Add onion, bell peppers, celery, and garlic; stir and cook until the onion softens and becomes translucent, approximately 5 minutes.

Add tomato paste and cook for 1 minute, until the paste has darkened in color. Remove the vegetables and set aside in a bowl. Add the remaining ⅓ cup canola oil to the same pot and heat over medium heat for about 30 seconds. Next, make a roux by whisking in the potato starch, stirring constantly until it gently browns and has a slightly nutty aroma, approximately 15 minutes. You want it to be a dark blond or caramel color without burning it. Reduce the heat as necessary.

Maintaining the reduced heat, add 1 cup of the broth. The roux will sizzle a bit, so be careful. Whisk the mixture until smooth. Add the cooked vegetables and tomatoes. Stir the mixture until combined. Add an additional cup of vegetable broth. Stir in the okra, the thyme, and the Creole Seasoning. Finally, add the remaining 4 cups of broth. Cover and continue to simmer for 1½ hours, stirring occasionally. Taste and adjust the seasonings, if necessary. Dish up two to three matzoh balls per bowl, garnish with scallions, and serve hot.

Creole Seasoning

About 1 cup

2 tablespoons onion powder

2 tablespoons garlic powder

1 tablespoon finely powdered bay leaf

1 tablespoon dried oregano

1 tablespoon dried basil

1 tablespoon dried thyme

1 tablespoon black pepper

1 tablespoon white pepper

1 tablespoon cayenne pepper

5 tablespoons sweet paprika

1 tablespoon smoked paprika

2 tablespoons kosher salt

1 tablespoon MSG (optional)

Mix all ingredients. Can be stored and kept in a cool, dry place for about 6 months.

Southern Matzoh Dressing

I was inspired by the Dirty Matzoh Dressing recipe from Anne Zoller Kiefer by way of her mother, Mrs. Myrtle Zoller, and their housekeeper and cook, Mrs. Vinnie Williams of New Orleans in Marcie Cohen Ferris's *Matzoh Ball Gumbo*. This recipe is similar to what I do with my late mother's cornbread dressing, for which I can hardly wait!

8–9 servings

9 unsalted matzot, broken up

1 stick (8 tablespoons) pareve margarine or vegan butter, divided

1 large yellow onion, chopped

2 celery stalks, finely chopped

3 garlic cloves, minced

1 teaspoon dried rubbed sage or a few chopped fresh sage leaves

1 teaspoon Soul or Creole Seasoning

2 teaspoons powdered kosher consommé broth

1 medium bell pepper (green, orange, red or yellow) finely chopped

½ cup chopped fresh flat-leaf parsley

1 teaspoon of poultry seasoning

½ teaspoon black pepper, coarse ground preferred

½ cup chicken or vegetable stock

1 large egg

Optional: ½ cup chopped blanched pecans or 1 cup sauteed mushrooms

Preheat the oven to 350°F. Grease a 9-by-9-inch glass baking dish or casserole.

Place the matzot in a large bowl and cover with cold water. Let soak until softened, about 10 minutes. Drain in a fine-mesh strainer, pressing out the water and breaking up the matzot with your hands onto a separate plate. Dry the bowl, then return the matzot to the bowl.

In a medium skillet, melt all but 1 tablespoon of the pareve margarine or vegan butter. Add the yellow onion, celery, garlic, bell pepper, and sauté until tender or about 6 to 8 minutes. Stir in parsley and add the sage, poultry seasoning, Soul or Creole Seasoning, and powdered broth. Scrape the mixture into the matzot.

Add the optional ingredients, stock, and egg, and mix well. Transfer to the prepared baking dish and dot with the remaining 1 tablespoon pareve margarine or vegan butter.

Cover with foil and bake for 45 minutes. Uncover and bake until the top is slightly browned and crisp, about 15 minutes longer.

Note: Chopped blanched pecans or sauteed mushrooms make this even better, especially if you have a vegetarian or vegan Passover seder. Change out the matzot for 2 cups of crumbled pareve cornbread and you have a slamming Southern-style cornbread dressing for life cycle events, Rosh Hoshanah, Yom Kippur pre-meal or break-fast, Sukkot, Simchat Torah, Purim, etc. If it is an all-cornmeal cornbread, you can even have it on Pesach per your custom or rabbinical authority.

Shavuot

Mango Chai Syrup (for Cheesecake, Blintzes, and Ice Cream)

About 3 cups

4 cups chopped ripe or frozen mango

¾ cup granulated sugar

½ cup water (you can substitute a thin, light, organic juice of your choice)

Small cheesecloth bag of chai spices: a small stick of cinnamon, a few whole cloves, dried allspice berries, a cardamom pod, and a small piece of ginger

Pulse mangoes in a blender until liquefied. Bring mango pulp, sugar, and water to a boil in a heavy saucepan over medium heat, stirring until sugar is dissolved. Reduce heat and simmer on a steady low temperature, covered, stirring occasionally, until mangoes are very soft, about 45 minutes.

Add the cheesecloth with the spices and allow to steep for about 15 minutes. Strain the syrup into a bowl using a fine-mesh sieve, softly pushing the pulp against the mesh. Save the separated solids for blintzes. Cool, transfer to a covered container, then chill until ready to drizzle over your cheesecake, blintzes, or ice cream.

Collard Green Lasagna

Hey, just substitute thinly sliced collards for spinach in your favorite veggie lasagna recipe. It's that simple—no thrills here. Just a fun, Southern, soulful substitution. Spice up those greens with red pepper and thin strips of caramelized onions.

Green Cymlings and New Potatoes in Crème Fraîche with Chervil

Serves 4

2 cups young cymling (pattypan) squashes

2 cups baby new potatoes

Vegetable stock, chicken stock, or plain water, to cover

Sea salt, to taste

1 tablespoon mint

2 tablespoons thinly sliced scallions

1½ cups crème fraîche

½ teaspoon sea salt

½ teaspoon cracked pepper

2–3 tablespoons chopped chervil (you can substitute fresh flat-leaf parsley or dill)

Halve the young cymling squashes. They should be small and pale green or just barely white and soft to the cut. Large white pattypans are good for seed only, so don't even try it!

Place the potatoes in a pan and cover with stock or water with a bit of sea salt. Bring to a boil, then simmer 10–15 minutes until just tender. Add the cymlings and cook until they are also just tender. Drain the stock.

Add the mint and onions. Stir at a low temperature for 2–3 minutes.

Take the pan off the heat and stir in the crème fraîche. Season with sea salt and cracked pepper. Add the chopped chervil at the last moment and serve immediately.

Yam Biscuits

2 dozen biscuits

2 cups flour

⅔ cup sugar

2 tablespoons baking powder

1 teaspoon salt

½ cup vegetable shortening

2 cups mashed cooked white or yellow sweet potatoes

¼ cup milk

Preheat oven to 425°F. Sift the flour, sugar, baking powder, and salt into a bowl. Cut in the shortening until the mixture is the consistency of cornmeal. Stir in the sweet potatoes and milk.

Turn the dough out onto a floured board and knead lightly. Roll out to ½-inch thickness and cut with a biscuit cutter. Place biscuits on a greased cookie sheet. Bake 12–15 minutes, until they've risen nicely and are lightly browned on top. Transfer to a serving plate or basket and serve hot.

Koshersoul Mac and Cheese Kugel

Serves 6–8

1 pound elbow macaroni, cooked

1 teaspoon dark brown sugar

1 teaspoon garlic powder

1 teaspoon onion powder

1 teaspoon coarse Kitchen Pepper (see recipe)

1 cup whole milk

1 12-ounce can evaporated milk

3 eggs

½ cup butter, cut into small pieces

1 cup cream cheese

½ cup plumped golden raisins or dried cranberries (optional)

1 cup sour cream

2 cups shredded sharp cheddar cheese

2 cups cubed mild cheddar cheese

2 teaspoons pareve kosher chicken broth

1 cup shredded mild cheddar cheese

Paprika, to taste

Preheat oven to 350°F. Put cooked macaroni in a 9-by-13-inch dish and set aside.

In a small bowl, combine the brown sugar, garlic powder, onion powder, and Kitchen Pepper. In a larger bowl, whisk together the milk, evaporated milk, and eggs. Place the egg mixture in a saucepan, add the butter and cream cheese, and stir well over low heat until the ingredients are combined.

Add the raisins or cranberries, sour cream, shredded and cubed cheddar cheeses, and chicken broth to the macaroni. Pour the milk/egg/butter/

cream cheese mixture over the pasta. Add the brown sugar and spice mixture and toss well to incorporate.

Bake for 30 minutes or until the top is lightly brown. Remove from the oven, turn the oven off, sprinkle 1 cup shredded cheddar cheese and paprika on top of the kugel, return to the oven, and allow to crust over for another 15–20 minutes.

Juneteenth/The Cookout

Peach-Balsamic Vinaigrette

Makes one cup

¼ cup olive oil

¼ cup of water

¼ cup peach jam

¼ cup white balsamic vinegar

1 garlic clove, finely minced

½ teaspoon coarse black pepper

½ teaspoon kosher salt or flavored salt of your choice

½ teaspoon dried, crushed rosemary OR bruise a small sprig of fresh rosemary and let it steep in the dressing for 30 minutes, then remove

Combine all ingredients in a bowl and whisk together. Or combine in a jar, cover, and shake well. Let rest for 30 minutes, whisk or shake well again, and serve with a fresh vegetable salad of your choice. Or transfer to a covered container and chill until needed. You can also use as a marinade for chicken.

Watermelon and Feta Salad

Serves 4–6

6 cups cubed, seeded watermelon

6 ounces feta cheese, crumbled

⅓ cup minced red onion

2 tablespoons chopped flat-leaf parsley

1 tablespoon minced chives

2 tablespoons thinly sliced mint

2–3 tablespoons preserved lemon, chopped (optional)

½ cup extra virgin olive oil

¼ cup champagne or white wine or chive vinegar (search Afroculinaria.com)

Kosher salt and coarse black pepper, to taste

Toss all ingredients together in a large bowl. What the heck, throw in a pinch of red pepper while you're at it. Serve at room temperature, or cover and chill until shortly before serving time.

Yiddishe Ribbenes

This recipe is my answer to making a uniquely Ashkenazi barbecue using spices and flavorings found in an area as diverse as the Baltics to the Balkans. Even the wood used to give a smoky taste—cherry, oak, and apple—are deliberate. This recipe requires *flanken* short ribs, also known in the Jewish world as "Miami ribs," not the stout, chunky short ribs that are widely known. Long and flat-ish, their thinness makes them ideal for grilling, unlike the thick-cut short ribs, which require long, slow cooking, such as braising. You could also use the same marinade or mixture with beef back ribs, chicken, lamb, goat, etc., but the cooking method will change according to the type or thickness of the meat. I hope this recipe adds to the fun or re-imagining the Afro-Atlantic art of barbecue as part of Yiddishkeit.

Serves 4

2 pounds short ribs, flanken style

1 teaspoon black pepper

1 teaspoon ginger

2 teaspoons paprika

½ teaspoon cinnamon

1 teaspoon kosher beef or chicken bouillon

1 small onion, finely chopped

2 tablespoons garlic, finely chopped

2 tablespoons vegetable oil

2 tablespoons white vinegar

1–2 tablespoons prepared white horseradish

1–2 tablespoons brown deli mustard

1 tablespoon brown sugar

Sprigs of fresh parsley, marjoram, or chives, for garnish (optional)

Flake salt, to taste

Wash the meat and pat it dry. Mix together the pepper, ginger, paprika, and cinnamon and rub into the meat. Mix together the rest of the ingredients (except the garnish herbs), pour over the meat, and marinate 4–6 hours.

Prepare your grill according to the manufacturer's instructions. If using a pellet smoker/grill, consider using a mixture of oak and cherry or cherry and apple pellets. If using a charcoal grill or smoker, use oak and cherry or cherry and apple wood chips or packets to get a smoky flavor.

Grill meat over medium heat, 5–7 minutes per side. Wrap loosely in foil and allow to rest for 10 minutes; check for doneness. If you want, garnish with fresh herbs, or use sprigs to mellow with the flanken ribs as they rest in the foil. Sprinkle with flake salt to finish, but use sparingly.

Mrs. Covert's Stuffed Kashered Krab

Serves 6

1 egg, beaten

1 cup milk, use soy milk for pareve

6 slices toast, cubed

2 tablespoons minced onion

2 tablespoons minced celery

2 tablespoons minced green bell pepper

1 clove garlic, minced

2 tablespoons butter

2 cups shredded kosher surimi

2 tablespoons finely chopped parsley

1 teaspoon Creole Seasoning (see recipe)

¼ cup bread crumbs

6 thin lemon slices

Paprika, for garnish

Combine the egg and milk in a bowl. Add the toast and let stand.

Sauté the onion, celery, bell pepper, and garlic in the butter. Add the surimi, parsley, Creole Seasoning, and the toast mixture. Mix thoroughly.

Place mixture in six ramekins or aluminum crab shells, and sprinkle with bread crumbs. Dot with butter and place lemon slices on top. Garnish with paprika. Bake at 350°F for 15 minutes or until browned.

Creole Okra and Tomatoes

Serves 8–10

½ cup pareve margarine

1 large onion, minced

½ bell pepper, diced

1 quart sliced okra

4 fresh tomatoes, coarsely chopped

1 teaspoon, Soul Seasoning or Creole Seasoning, or to taste (see recipes)

1 teaspoon Kitchen Pepper, or to taste (see recipe)

Melt margarine in a large skillet or heavy-bottomed pot; add onion and sauté over medium heat until transparent. Add bell pepper, okra, tomatoes, Soul Seasoning, and Kitchen pepper. Lower heat, cover, and simmer for 20 minutes. Stir occasionally. Serve hot.

Macaroni Salad

Serves 6–8

1 cup Duke's mayonnaise

2 tablespoons kosher dill pickle juice

2 tablespoons Creole mustard

¼ cup diced sweet pickles

1 small onion, minced

2 tablespoons chopped pimiento

1 medium green bell pepper, diced small

½ teaspoon Soul Seasoning, or to taste (see recipe)

½ teaspoon Creole Seasoning, or to taste (see recipe)

¼ teaspoon coarse black pepper or Kitchen Pepper, or to taste (see recipe)

3 cups cooked elbow macaroni or medium macaroni shells

1 cup chopped pastrami or kosher salami cubes (optional)

Mix mayonnaise, dill pickle juice, mustard, sweet pickles, onions, pimiento, green pepper, and Soul Seasoning, Creole Seasoning, and black or Kitchen

Pepper to taste. Add to macaroni and toss. Add cold cuts, if desired, to the macaroni mixture and gently toss once more. Refrigerate until ready to serve.

Black Eyed-Peas with Tomatoes, Sephardic Style

This recipe is adapted from a recipe in Marcie Cohen Ferris's *Matzoh Ball Gumbo*, included in the Congregation Or Ve Shalom's sisterhood's synagogue cookbook, *The Sephardic Cooks*.

6−8 servings (4 cups)

2 tablespoons olive oil

1 large red onion, chopped

3 garlic cloves, minced

1 medium fresh tomato, chopped

½ teaspoon dried thyme or oregano

¾ teaspoon kosher salt

½ teaspoon freshly ground black pepper or Kitchen Pepper (see recipe)

1 teaspoon ras-al-hanout spice blend

1 15-ounce can kosher black-eyed peas

1¼ cups low-sodium vegetable stock

In a large, heavy saucepan, heat the oil over medium heat. Add the onion and garlic and cook, stirring often, until tender, about 4 minutes. Add the tomato, thyme or oregano, salt, pepper, and ras-al-hanout and cook, stirring often, until the tomato starts to soften, about 2 minutes.

Stir in the black-eyed peas and vegetable stock; bring to a boil. Reduce the heat to low, cover, and simmer until the peas are tender, about 30 minutes. Taste and adjust the seasoning, if necessary. Serve the peas hot or warm.

Three Sisters Stir-Fry

Inspired by the Indigenous Lenni Lenape people of New York, the original Manhattanites.

Serves 6

6 tablespoons sunflower oil or light olive oil

2–3 tablespoons chopped garlic scapes (stems) or chopped chives (or chopped wild garlic bulbs, or ramps) (cut down if using ramps) (scallions are a good substitute)

2 cups thinly sliced summer squash, of any type

2 cups sliced string beans (cut lengthwise, slice straight down the bean)

6 ears corn, kernels sliced off the ear

A few pinches fresh herb or herbs of your choice—think parsley, sage, rosemary, or tarragon, which go great with corn

1 tablespoon maple syrup

Kosher salt, to taste

Pepper, to taste (optional)

Cut and prepare all vegetables ahead of time. Heat the oil in a pan until just hot and throw in your garlic scapes or chives. Then add the squash, then the beans, then the corn and herbs. Stir-fry 8–10 minutes and season with maple syrup and salt and pepper to taste.

Corn Salad

A simple, Southern-inspired corn salad.

Serves 6

6 ears raw corn, kernels sliced off the ear

2–3 fresh heirloom tomatoes, cubed

1 bunch parsley, chopped

½ cup olive oil

¼ cup cider vinegar

2–3 green onions, chopped

6–7 pods fresh okra (if available), sliced (optional)

1 small hot pepper, finely chopped (about ¼ teaspoon)

Maple syrup or cane syrup , to taste

Kosher salt, to taste

Pepper, to taste

In a large bowl, combine the corn, tomatoes, green onion, okra (if using), hot pepper, and parsley, and toss to mix. In a small bowl, combine the olive oil, cider vinegar, maple syrup, salt, and pepper. Whisk to mix well. Pour the dressing over the vegetables and toss to coat. Serve at room temperature or chill for 2 hours and serve cold.

Lamb Bacon Baked Beans

Serves 4

1 28-ounce can vegetarian, kosher-certified baked beans (I prefer Bush's brand)

¼ cup Kansas City–style barbecue sauce of your choice

¼ cup water or low-sodium vegetable broth

¼ cup spicy brown mustard

¼ cup maple or cane syrup

1 teaspoon Soul Seasoning (see recipe)

1 teaspoon smoked paprika

1 teaspoon dry mustard

½ teaspoon black pepper or Kitchen Pepper (see recipe)

1 small white onion, minced

2 cloves garlic, minced

4 slices kosher lamb or beef bacon, cooked and diced

Heat oven to 350°F. Drain all liquid from the can of baked beans. Place the beans in a large bowl and add the remaining ingredients; stir to combine. Transfer to a greased ceramic casserole dish and bake 30–45 minutes until warm and bubbling.

Seasonings and Condiments

The following preparations, along with the above recipes for barbecue sauce, curry sauce, and Passover rub, can be used to make your own koshersoul creations. Use them to flavor kebabs, shawarma, bourekas, kugels, cholents and adafina, briskets, chickens, roasts, roasted potatoes and other vegetables, salads, latkes, vegetarian dishes, and the like.

Kitchen Pepper

½ *cup*

1 teaspoon coarsely ground black pepper

1 teaspoon ground white pepper

1 teaspoon red pepper flakes

1 teaspoon ground clove

1 teaspoon ground mace

1 teaspoon ground Ceylon cinnamon

1 teaspoon ground nutmeg

1 teaspoon ground allspice

1 teaspoon ground ginger

Mix all ingredients thoroughly; store in a cool, dry place. Keeps for 6 months.

Soul Seasoning

¾ *cup*

2 tablespoons onion powder

2 tablespoons garlic powder

1 tablespoon Kitchen Pepper (see recipe)

2 tablespoons sweet paprika

1 tablespoon smoked paprika

1 tablespoon kosher salt or sea salt

1 tablespoon celery seed

1 tablespoon cayenne pepper

1 tablespoon MSG (optional)

2 teaspoons raw sugar (optional)

Mix all ingredients thoroughly; store in a cool, dry place.

Suya Spice

⅓ cup

1 teaspoon garlic powder	1 teaspoon onion powder
1 teaspoon ground ginger	1 teaspoon black pepper
1 teaspoon ground cinnamon	1 teaspoon sea salt
1 teaspoon chili powder	1 teaspoon ground allspice
1 teaspoon paprika	1 teaspoon ground cayenne
1 teaspoon smoked paprika	1 crushed kosher bouillon cube
1 teaspoon ground nutmeg	

Mix all ingredients thoroughly; store in a cool, dry place. Many versions also contain finely ground unsalted peanuts; here use ½ cup if you so choose.

West African Wet Seasoning

1½ cups

1-inch piece roughly chopped fresh turmeric, or 2 teaspoons powdered turmeric

½ bunch flat-leaf or curly parsley (not cilantro), roughly chopped

2 stalks celery, leaves and all, roughly chopped

3 green onions, sliced

7 cloves fresh garlic, smashed

2 fresh shallots, roughly chopped

1 small red onion, sliced

1-inch piece ginger, roughly chopped

1 small Scotch bonnet pepper (spicy), or 1 medium red bell pepper (not spicy), chopped and stem removed

1 crushed small kosher beef bouillon or pareve consommé cube

1 tablespoon canola oil

Add all ingredients to a food processor and pulse until the mixture is fully puréed. Scrape down sides, and process again. Repeat until the mixture is more or less smooth.

You can prepare in large batches and freeze in ice cube trays, or in snack bags in amounts of 2 inches each. After the ice cubes of seasoning are frozen, remove the cubes from the trays and store them in snack bags.

Berbere Spice Mix

¾ cup

1 tablespoon sweet or hot paprika

1 tablespoon garlic powder

1 tablespoon onion powder

1 tablespoon chili powder

1 tablespoon sea salt

½ teaspoon ground ginger

½ teaspoon ground cinnamon

½ teaspoon ground cardamom

½ teaspoon dried basil

½ teaspoon ground cumin

½ teaspoon chili flakes

½ teaspoon ground fenugreek

Combine all the ingredients in a jar; seal and shake well. You can store this in an airtight container for up to 6 months.

Senegalese-Inspired Rof (Green Hot Sauce)

¾ cup

½ small red onion, chopped

2 scallions, chopped

1 bunch parsley, roughly chopped (about 2 cups)

3–4 cloves garlic, smashed

1–2 small green hot chilies

½ teaspoon freshly ground black pepper or Kitchen Pepper (see recipe)

½ seeded Scotch bonnet pepper

1 teaspoon kosher salt

1 tablespoon canola oil

Put all ingredients in a food processor and blend well. This will keep 3–4 days covered, in the refrigerator, or you can freeze it and use as needed.

Kosher Senegalese Nokos

1½ cups

6 cloves garlic

2 small yellow onions, chopped

4 scallions, chopped

1 teaspoon dried pepper flakes or 1 seeded habanero pepper

½ teaspoon finely ground black pepper or Kitchen Pepper (see recipe)

1 tablespoon kosher "chicken" consommé powder

2 tablespoons kosher red miso

1 green bell pepper, seeded and chopped

Put all ingredients in a food processor and blend well. This will keep 3–4 days covered, in the refrigerator, or you can freeze it and use as needed.

MENUS AND OTHER KOSHERSOUL IDEAS

I really want you to build up your library. Not every menu idea included here is in this book. You may want to mix and match what you put on your table. You may wish to go down a rabbit hole search for everyday koshersoul or a multicultural Jewish table.

Kosher

Kosher is technically a discipline and a standard, not a style, even if I am clearly using it as a signifier for "Jewish." In English, "kosher" has connotations of being clean or cleared and "okay," taking some of its cues from its original meaning in Hebrew of being "fit" or "proper." Kosher doesn't even solely refer to food but to an entire approach to Jewish living and choices, akin to the way "diet" not only refers to food but to one's entire eating structure. On one level, you do kosher because G-d says so, on another it's because it is a bond with other Jews who follow kashrut, and still another, it's just what you know. It also helps shape Jewish food in the following sense: sure, you could add parmesan cheese to a meat dish, but if you did, would it stop tasting "Jewish?" Over the centuries, Jewish flavors developed as migrations and exile, tastes from Eretz Israel that never died in galut, and scriptural proscriptions decided what was added or subtracted along with local influences and available ingredients.

Even if you don't keep kosher yourself and never will, if you want to bring these recipes to life in your kitchen in the spirit they are intended, knowing what kosher actually is, is critical. Lise Stern has an excellent book called *How to Keep Kosher* and I encourage you to read it. Books that go deeper into halakhic (Jewish law-based) perspectives on keeping kosher like *The Kosher Kitchen* by Binyomin Frost are also essential to understand how to keep kosher in your home and the fine-print aspects that those who keep kosher observe. Doing your homework is vital since Jewish communities have small but significant discrepancies. For example, during Passover, Sephardim may or may not eat kitniyot or foods considered too much like chametz that are forbidden to Ashkenazi Jews. At the same time, some Hasidic Jews will not even touch gebrokhts or matzah products that have touched liquid until the eighth day of Passover. Some communities will not eat meat and fish at the same meal even if there is a palate cleanser; other even rarer holdouts still consider poultry pareve. Most important, consult a rabbi when in doubt.

Jewish

"Jewish" (food) isn't ten Ashkenazi dishes with sort-of common cultural currency in America. Jewish is an exhaustingly expansive body of foodways across nearly four millennia and every inhabitable continent. Jewish food as a global whole is rather outstanding since it embraces and transforms ingredients and the meaning behind the foods to fit the paradigms and priorities of Jewish civilization. If you need some texts that genuinely exemplify this, try Rabbi Gil Marks's *The Encyclopedia of Jewish Food* or *The World of Jewish Cooking* and *The Book of Jewish Food* by Claudia Roden. Goulash is a Jewish food and goulash in its Hungarian context or koylitsch (Russian and Polish braided bread) and berches (German potato bread) or dabo (Ethiopian honey bread) as forms of "challah" have very different connotations, as does "Moroccan" Jewish and "Moroccan" Muslim.

Faye Levy has so many wonderful contributions to Jewish food writing, and you need to get her *1000 Jewish Recipes*, and even *Jewish Cooking for Dummies*, among her many other treasures. *Leah Koenig's The Book of Jewish Food* by Phaidon follows the tradition of serious archival volumes of Jewish recipes and her *Little Book of Jewish Sweets*. Researching Sephardic cooking from Syrian food (Poopa Dweck's *Aromas of Aleppo* to Copeland Marks's *Sephardic Cooking*) is just scratching the surface. For the Island of Rhodes see Stella Cohen (*Stella's Sephardic Table*); for Morocco see *I Thought I'd Never Taste This Again* by Dr. Mercedes Castiel. If you're looking for the deep gastronomic roots of Sepharad, see one of my most beloved historical cookbooks, *A Drizzle of Honey*, by David M. Gitlitz and Linda Kay Davidson, which details the dishes of Jews arrested and imprisoned by the Inquisition. Another great book is Jane Cohen's 2000 work, *The Gefilte Variations*, which helps you see outside the box on traditional Jewish recipes across the Diaspora.

Ashkenazi regional food histories are beginning to increase in earnest. For German-Jewish food see Gabrielle and Sonya Groppman's *The German Jewish Cookbook*. For a comprehensive look at Hungarian Jewish foodways see *A Taste of the Past* or *Jewish Cuisine in Hungary* by Andras Koerner. One of the great books that inspired my journey was *In Memory's Kitchen*, by Cara De Silva. The best cultural approach to Yiddish foodways is the survey *Rhapsody in Schmaltz: Yiddish Food and Why We Can't Stop Eating It* by the esteemed Michael Wex.

Joan Nathan is one of my great muses for Jewish foodways. Perhaps no other American Jewish food personality has done more to document the personal relationships between Jews and their food worldwide and in an American context. She has personally inspired me to seek stories, not just recipes—to know the feelings, not just the facts—that undergird Jewish culinary knowledge and creativity. *The Jewish Holiday Kitchen*, *Jewish Cooking in America*, *The Foods of Israel Today*, and *King Solomon's Table* are indispensable.

Middle Eastern

I think it's worth defining Middle Eastern tradition in food by those who successfully communicate it on paper. Claudia Roden, once again, does it with grand expertise in her many approaches to Middle Eastern cooking, my personal favorite being *The New Book of Middle Eastern Food*. Adeena Sussman's *Sababa* is fresh and comprehensive concerning the Israeli table. Michael Solomov's *Zahav* is another viewpoint, seeing Israeli food as part of and distinct from other Mediterranean cuisines. The edited volume, *On the Hummus Route*, gives you an understanding of how one food could be so personal and political to different groups. Anything by Israeli chef Yotam Ottolenghi, including *Jerusalem* and *Ottolenghi*, needs to be in your kitchen cookbook library.

Ottolenghi's longtime business partner, Sami Tamimi, and Tara Wigley have an excellent volume in *Falastin*. To understand common cultural roots and divergent definitions and understandings, I believe you have to educate yourself on what Palestinian food means and what Israeli food is. For me, *The Gaza Cookbook* by Laila El-Haddad and Maggie Schmitt, *The Palestinian Table* by Reem Kassis, and *Zaitoun* by Yasmin Khan are other fundamental texts key to exploring the culinary Venn-Diagram.

I encourage you to go deep on Iranian, Chinese, Ethiopian, Latin American, Yemenite, Bukharan, Georgian, and other Jewish foodways. More and more books are coming out from these communities, providing new chapters in Jewish identity and memories of traditions that we can't afford to be lost to time.

Newish Jewish

Newish Jewish is actually old Jewish brought back to life. Jeffrey Yoskowitz and Liz Alpern's *Gefilteria Manifesto* does that, as does *The Mile End Cookbook* by Noah and Rae Bernamoff. *Jew-ish*, by TikTok chef Jake Cohen, is described by the author as a love letter to his husband, Alex, mixing their Ashkenazi and Mizrahi heritages, and *52 Shabbats*, by Faith Kramer, updates one of the oldest Jewish culinary rites—the Friday night Shabbat meal. For the full picture of Jewish food with a new generation's eyes, see *The 100 Most Jewish Foods*, edited by Alana Newhouse.

Southern Jewish

Koshersoul is impossible without the scholarly work of Dr. Marcie Cohen Ferris (*Matzoh Ball Gumbo: Culinary Tales of the Jewish South*) and the preservation work of the late Mrs. Mildred Covert and Sylvia Gerson. Get everything of theirs you can get your hands on. Titles are in the bibliography. Many Southern Jewish congregations have excellent community cookbooks, and each one is another piece of the mosaic.

Soul

There are so many parts of "soul" I could cover, but to be restrained and economical, I'll stick to the basics.

"Leave no stone unturned;" These are words passed down from the Grande Dame of Southern cooking, Chef Edna Lewis, to James Beard award–winning author and culinary historian Toni Tipton-Martin, author of *Jubilee* and *The Jemima Code*, to me. That's why I'm venturing to start the imperfect process of telling these stories of

Black people who are Jewish and love the food they cook to articulate their journeys.

The Black culinary perspective of *Koshersoul* is at once African American, African Atlantic, and Pan-African. That's because all three are central to how I and many others see the bigger picture of global African-centered or influenced foodways. "Soul food," as African Americans know it, has a better view from a higher vantage point, where we can see more connections and possibilities than from a purposely narrowed lens. But Black food is more than just soul food or the canon of soul food dishes one could find at a meat and three. Soul is the intellectual and aesthetic construct—the memory, the feeling, and the skills that power African American, Afro-Latin, and Afro-Caribbean foodways, along with the verve and style that Black chefs bring to other cuisines they interpret.

In that vein, get *Black Food* by Bryant Terry and *Between Harlem and Heaven* by Chef JJ Johnson with Alexander Smalls. The former is a one-of-a-kind survey of Black food as Black culture, and the latter a unique lens on Afro-Asian crossroads and fusions across time. Books like Todd Richards's *Soul* and Nicole Taylor's *Watermelon and Red Birds: A Cookbook for Juneteenth and Black Celebrations* and Matthew Raiford's *Bress 'n' Nyam* illuminate this narrative of Black food as dynamic and responsive. Top Chef's Gregory Gourdet's *Everybody's Table* non-inflammatory plant-based approach adds to this mix with touches of his Haitian roots.

The masters have left their mark—Edna Lewis (*The Edna Lewis Cookbook*, *The Taste of Cooking*, *The Pursuit of Flavor*, and *The Gift of Southern Cooking* with Scott Peacock), Mama Dip (*Mama Dip's Kitchen* and *Mama Dip's Family Cookbook*), Leah Chase (*The Dooky Chase Cookbook*), Sylvia (*Sylvia's Soul Food* and *Sylvia's Soul Food Family Cookbook*), Dori Sanders (*Dori Sander's Country Cooking*), and Cleora Butler (*Cleora's Kitchens*) and the new elders, Robbie Montgomery (*Sweetie Pie's Cookbook*), Dora Charles of Savannah fame (*A Real Southern Cook in Her Savannah Kitchen*) and my prolific friend and teacher Sallie Ann Robinson (*Gullah Home Cooking the Daufuskie Way, Cooking the Gullah Way* and *Sallie Ann Robinsons' Kitchen*). Jocelyn Delk Adams (*Grandbaby Cakes*) and Alice Randall and Caroline Randall Adams (*Soul Food Love*) are pushing the traditional canon forward, as is our lovely Carla Hall (*Carla's Soul Food*) and Jerome Grant's *Sweet Home Café*. You must read Jessica Harris, Howard Paige, Adrian Miller, and Frederick Douglass Opie—the goal is to get a broad and diverse view of opinions about Black food history.

Going Home

One of my favorite beginner's texts on African cooking is definitely getting hard to find; *A Taste of Africa* by Rosamund Grant was the first African cookbook I ever owned, sweetly gifted by my mother. If you want an excellent survey to cook from, see *The Groundnut Cookbook* by Duval Timothy, Folayemi Brown, and Jacob Fodio Todd or *The Soul of a New Cuisine* by master chef Marcus Samuelsson. Check out *The Ghana Cookbook* by Fran Osseo-Asare and Barbara Baëta and *Zoe's Ghana Kitchen* by the vibrant Zoe Adjonyoh. For Eastern Africa, please read *In Bibi's Kitchen* by Hawa Hassan.

For the Caribbean and Latin America, Haiti, Brazil, Jamaica, Barbados, Trinidad and Tobago, Guyana, and Suriname are all critical. One of my great inspirations in creating menus here was *Original Flava* by Craig and Shawn MacAnuff and *Provisions: The Roots of Caribbean Cooking* by Michelle Rousseau and Suzanne Rousseau.

If you want an account of the African American path to soul food, please consider my first book, *The Cooking Gene*. Not just because I'm proud of it, but because I set out not to retell rehashed narratives but to reveal how the complex story of African American food works its way from Africa to America from slavery to freedom within a large African American family. I describe what each West and Central African bloc brought to African American food and how the culture of our food developed over the centuries. I also examine how people today contribute to our food's interpretation and how it impacts our sense of self, our health, and mirrors other parts of our genealogical journeys. Food was central rather than peripheral to our origin story as a people. I also incorporate part of my journey in Judaism into my story and my meeting with Mrs. Mildred Covert and what I learned from the experience.

From a practical standpoint, other paths into soul are essential for koshersoul, like the excellent vegan cookbooks by Bryant Terry (*Afro-Vegan* or *Vegan Soul Kitchen*) or *Sweet Potato Soul* by Jenne Claiborne, several exciting new editions. Vegan soul cooking helps introduce a more expansive repertoire into koshersoul cooking with pareve desserts, side dishes, and vegetarian recipes. Vegan soul also shares values with eco-kashrut, like minimizing harm and hurt done to animals, eating to protect health and the body, looking at fair trade practices, and overall environmental awareness.

Health and Celebration versus Everyday

This is an important public service announcement.

Anti-Blackness and Anti-Semitism can manifest in how we experience and look at food. Both original sins of the West have tainted perspectives on Black and Jewish culinary traditions. Black food is sometimes seen as a pathology, yet another bad Black choice, a gastronomy of slaves, and a consistent urban underclass. Kashrut is seen as a product of superstition, and kosher slaughter is an antiquated ritual born out of an archaic faith. (Ashkenazi) Jewish food and Black food is killer mama food where the matriarchy smothers you in the unhealthy.

Miss me with all of it. This book is about Black-Jewish joy, celebration, and amplification without the need to explain or justify any of the three or beyond. I want you to understand that the need for balance, self-care, and times of indulgence are not only part of Jewish and Black traditions but inherent in this book. The Torah warns us about too much of a good thing, and I take that to heart. Sometimes you can eat so much of a treat that it stinks in your nostrils. (Numbers 11.)

Most of these recipes included here are for special occasions, not everyday consumption. In writing *Koshersoul* over the years, the call for vegan or vegetarian versions of recipes has frequently been made, but that's more for faux meat and mock proteins than actual plant-based cuisine that explores the flavors of the two Diasporas in concert with one another. There is a reason why I try to present menus that are as diverse and can be changed to fit different diets. What I say here is not the first or final word. I want you to make your own choices and make the best choices you feel you can make for your health and continuity with your sense of cultural or personal identity.

I purposely included recipes here with varied applications—i.e., sauces and spices that can flavor raw, grilled, or roasted vegetables. There aren't a lot of dessert recipes here because other people can do them better, and if you know kashrut, you know what will or will not work with meat or a dairy meal. I did want to acknowledge some of the favorite dishes of African American cuisine and the Diaspora, and so I have. I also recognize those who clamor on about the absence of pork as if it is some heresy. Just as I respect the history and legacy of halal foodways, I am seeking the same respect for keeping kosher in the soul tradition; besides pork isn't really that big a deal in most of West Africa!

In other words, make your own culinary midrash. Be creative and innovative; add your imagination, thoughts, and voice to this work. Don't treat it as scripture; love it as commentary. Share the food with friends and family. Life is with people.

Menus

Recipes included in this volume are in italics

West African Shabbat Dinner

Dried Mango Bits Challah
(Make a raisin challah but use
dried mango.)*
Senegalese-Inspired Chicken Soup
West African–Inspired Brisket
Jollof Rice

Roast Plantain and *Naftali's*
Kosher Shitor
Greens
Fresh papaya, mango, guava,
pineapple

* substitute plumped diced dried mango bits for raisins

Pan African Shabbat Dinner

Mango Challah or Coco Bread
Challah*
Couscous (or Millet) Salad
*Sukuma Wiki (East African Collard
Greens)*

Yassa Chicken or Swahili Roast Chicken
Basmati or Jasmine Rice
Fresh papaya, mango, guava,
pineapple or Sugar-Dusted Puff-Puff
or Mandazi

Caribbean Shabbat Dinner

Coco Bread Challah
*Rivka Campbell's Jamaican Rice
and Peas*
Stewed Oxtails

Fried Plantains
Jamaican Steamed Cabbage or Callaloo
Pikliz
Caribbean Compote

Sunday Dinner on a Friday Night Shabbat Dinner

Challah Rolls
Mrs. Covert's Stuffed Kashered Krab or
Baked Salmon Cakes
Basic Southern Fried Chicken
Koshersoul Collards

Charleston Bunch Soup with Sweet
Potato Dumplings
Rice—white or brown
Yam Kugel or Sweet Potato Pie (see
The Cooking Gene)

Lowcountry Shabbat Dinner

Challah Rolls
Okra Soup or *Charleston Bunch Soup*
Gullah-Geechee-Inspired Beef Stew
Peach Rice Kugel

Red Rice
Basic Southern Fried Chicken
Pecan Pie or Pralines

Michael's Ultimate Afro-Ashkefardi Shabbat Dinner

Beigl Family Challah (from Joan Nathan's *Foods of Israel Today*)

Green Salad with *Tahini-Nokos Dressing*

Black-Eyed Pea Hummus

Charleston Bunch Soup with Kreplach (use Collard Green filling)

Kasha Varnishkes with Caramelized Onions

Basic Southern Fried Chicken

Potato Kugel or Potato Bourekas

Yiddishe Ribbenes

Pareve Peach Cobbler or Apple Crisp (see *The Cooking Gene*) or Coconut Milk Pound Cake

East Africa Shabbat Dinner

Coco Bread Dough Challah or Chapati

Potato Samosa

Sukuma Wiki (East African Collards)

Swahili Roast Chicken

Roast Green Bananas with *Peanut Sauce*

Basmati Rice

Kachumbari

Mandazi

Vegivore Shabbat Dinner

Challah or Vegan Challah

Black-Eyed Pea Hummus

Ethiopian Collards or *Koshersoul Collards*

Ginger, Cumin, and Garlic Roasted Vegetables

Couscous (or Millet) Salad

Green Salad with *Peach-Balsamic Vinaigrette*

Yam Kugel

Fresh fruit

Shabbat Lunch

Saturday Lunch: Creole Style

Challah Rolls

Cornbread

Red Beans and Rice or Turkey Grillades and Grits

Okra Gumbo

Green Salad

Coconut Milk Rice Pudding or Challah-Based Louisiana Bread Pudding or Banana Pudding

Saturday Lunch: Jamaican Style

Challah

Rivka Campbell's Jamaican Rice and Peas

Jerk Chicken

Jamaican Cabbage and Carrots

Jamaican Sweet Potato Pudding

Saturday Lunch: Cold Southern Style

Challah Rolls or Pareve Biscuits

Cold Picnic-Style Fried Chicken

Potato Salad or *Macaroni Salad* or Coleslaw

Deviled Eggs

Okra or Watermelon Pickles or Chow-Chow

Roasted Sweet Potatoes with *Soul Seasoning*

Saturday Lunch:
Warm Southern Style

Challah Rolls or Challah or Pareve
Drop Biscuits

Chicken and Dumplings
Kale Salad
Peach or Apple Cobbler

Purim Meal

Challah

Senegalese-Inspired Chicken Soup with
Collard Green Kreplach

Black-Eyed Pea Hummus and
Crudités

Deep-Fried or Barbecued Turkey Breast

Green Salad with *Tahini-Nokos*
Dressing

Hamantaschen filled with Apple
Butter, Rum Raisin, Peach Jam,
or broken Benne Seed Wafers

Pesach Seder 1

Matzoh Ball Gumbo
Matzoh Meal Fried Chicken
Potato Kugel with *Creole Spice*
Green Salad with *Peach-Balsamic*
Vinaigrette

Koshersoul Collards
Creole Okra and Tomatoes
Southern Matzoh Stuffing or
Kosher-Cajun Rice Dressing

Pesach Seder 2

West African–Inspired Brisket
Senegalese-Inspired Chicken Soup with
Matzoh Balls
Plantains and *Naftali's Kosher Shitor*
Kachumbari

Koshersoul Collards
Roasted Sweet Potatoes and/or
Basmati rice
Fresh pineapple, mango, citrus, peeled
sugarcane, or *Caribbean Compote*

Maimouna

Couscous Salad
Moroccan Carrot Salad
Green Salad

Beignets, Mandazi, or Puff-Puff/
Bofrot
Fresh fruit

Shavuot

Challah
Green Cymlings and New Potatoes in
Crème Fraîche with Chervil
Collard Green Lasagna
Shais's or Michael's *Macaroni and*
Cheese

Cheesecake with Mango-Chai Syrup
or Pound Cake
Fresh fruit

Juneteenth Barbecue Menu

Macaroni Salad

Lamb Bacon Baked Beans

Corn Salad

Mrs. Covert's Stuffed Kashered Krab

Red Rice

Yiddishe Ribbenes with *Apple Barbecue Sauce*

Turnip Greens

Texas Caviar (black-eyed peas, Fresh tomato, onion, bell pepper salad)

Barbecued Lamb Shoulder (use *Passover Barbecue Lamb Rub*)

Barbecued Chicken (use rub recipe)

Hibiscus-Lime-Strawberry Punch

Deviled Eggs with Pimento and Paprika

Watermelon and Feta Salad

Red Velvet Cake

Rosh Hashanah Dinner

Round Challah

Black-Eyed Peas with Tomatoes

Ginger, Cumin, and Garlic Roasted Vegetables

Roasted Salmon Heads or Head of Lettuce Wedge Salad with *Peach-Balsamic Vinaigrette* or *Tahini-Nokos Dressing* with Scallions

Sautéed Beet Greens

Red Rice

Roasted Butternut Squash or Yellow Squash

Moroccan Carrot Salad or Roasted Carrots Glazed with Date Syrup

Suya Spice Roasted Potatoes and Sweet Potatoes with Leeks

Barbecued Lamb Shoulder or Barbecued Chicken with *Apple Barbecue Sauce*

Apple Crisp or Apple Turnovers

Sukkot

Challah

Chicken and Sausage Okra Gumbo

Rice

Three Sisters Stir-Fry

Yiddishe Ribbenes or *Suya Spice*–Rubbed Barbecue Lamb, Chicken,

Goat, Beef, or Fish or *Jerk Chicken Spaghetti*

Peanut Sauce Stewed Vegetables

Cushaw or Sweet Potato Pumpkin

Apple Crisp

Sigd Break-Fast Meal

Injera or Pita

Vegetable Wot or Doro Wat (Ethiopian Chicken Stew)

Berbere Brisket

Rice

Gomen (Ethiopian Collard Greens)

Hanukkah Meal

Challah

Sour Apple Slaw

Louisiana-Style Latkes or *Yam Latkes*

Kosher "Crab" Cakes or Salmon Croquettes

Akaras (Black-Eyed Pea Fritters) or Hush Puppies

Jollof Rice or *Red Rice*

Kachumbari

Koshersoul Spring Rolls

Beignets, Bofrot/Puff-Puff, Mandazi

Kwanzaa Karamu/New Year's Meal

Hoppin' John with Plain Rice

Cash Collards

Senegal Meets Lowcountry Kwanzaa Salad

Okra Soup or *Creole Okra and Tomatoes*

African Peanut Sauce Chicken or *Swahili Roast Chicken* or *Yassa Chicken*

Fresh mango, watermelon, guava, citrus, or papaya, or Sweet Potato Pie

Bofrot/Puff-Puff, Beignets, Mandazi

The Rabbis say; Whoever eats without saying a blessing is like someone who robs from the Holy One.

Thank You for the many blessings You bestow upon us.

We thank You for the earth and soil from which our food and our roots spring.

We honor and thank our Ancestors who worked the soil of the South, the Caribbean, Brazil and many other lands with very little in return.

We remember our freedom from Mitzrayim—the narrow place that caused us pain

Thank You for the many hands that grew the food from the soil You provided.

We offer thanks to the hands that prepared the food and those who serve it, passing down recipes from generation to generation and making new traditions with a renewed spirit.

We Thank You for food in a world where many know hunger or limited access to good and nutritious sustenance and we will do our part to work to defeat it.

Barukh Atah Adonay Eloheynu Melekh Ha'olam, shehakol nihyeh bid'varo.

Blessed are You, our God, Ruler of the universe, at whose word all came to be.

—COURTESY OF RABBI SANDRA LAWSON

MORE KOSHERSOUL IDEAS

1.   *Add some chopped preserved lemon to your potato salad; it's salty, so add carefully, and don't add other salty ingredients until you've tasted it.*

2.   *Try making Yerushalmi kugel (usually made with black pepper) with Kitchen Pepper.*

3.   *Barbecue sauce can be your secret ingredient in cholent.*

4.   *Make ma'amoul with peach jam or cooked persimmon or guava.*

5.   *My black-eyed pea hummus seasonings make a great homemade Middle Eastern/Levantine–style all-purpose seasoning for meats, dressings, vegetables, roasted potatoes, salads, etc.*

6.   *Harissa paste and sauces like ʒ'hug can be used in place of or in conjunction with Southern, African, or Afro-Caribbean hot sauces.*

7.   *Kosher lamb bacon is so damn good and gives you a lot of the flavor that "beef frye" or "facon" don't entirely offer.*

8.   *For rice-stuffed vegetable dishes like peppers or stuffed cabbage, use Jollof rice, dirty rice, Hoppin' john or rice, peas, etc.*

9. *I don't have a ton of kosher surimi recipes, but I encourage you to try to make kosher Brazilian acaraje, "krab" gumbo, "shrimp" and grit cakes, and other treats. Besides, when it comes to a cake or a roll or a this or that, Old Bay is kosher .*

10. *Seeded okra stuffed with feta and fried is fire.*

11. *Sambusas (Somali samosas) are fantastic with onion, meat or meat substitutes, and other savories. Kosher ground turkey, lamb bacon, pastrami, fried/curried/roast or BBQ chicken or BBQ beef, suya all work with your choices of veggies and spices.*

12. *Traditional pickles like watermelon rind, pickled okra, chow chow, Haitian pikliz, black-eyed pea, sweet potato, or okra salad make great additions to salatim to pass around the table.*

13. *Collard greens make an excellent substitute for cabbage in traditional stuffed cabbage.*

14. *Apple butter in noodle kugel is tasty as heaven.*

15. *You can do brisket a million ways; try Piri-Piri from Angola and Mozambique for something spicy—marinate it, then saute up some onions, garlic, bell peppers that have been sliced thin, dry the meat, sear, and bake as per the recipes in this book. Jamaican Jerk seasonings and many other styles of seasonings can be substituted. Brisket debris and gravy of all kinds is great on grits.*

16. *Kedjenou, a chicken stew from Cote D'Ivoire, served with rice, millet, quinoa, or sweet potatoes, makes an excellent Shabbat dinner. So do Caribbean curry or brown-stew chicken, fish, beef, or goat.*

17.   *Your charoset creativity is up to you. As long as the ingredients are Passover compliant, we could use another Southern-, Caribbean-, or African-inspired charoset recipe or seventy. A Ugandan version from the Abuyadaya calls for peanuts or cashews, honey, bananas, apples, and sweet wine. To make the African American seder plate version, combine one part finely chopped pecans or peanuts with one part light molasses (not blackstrap) and add a pinch of cinnamon and moisten lightly with wine.*

18.   *Ditto for your cocktail and mocktail game. I tried palm wine and Manischewitz . . . nah. I'll leave that to the mixologists.*

Bonus: Rebecca Franklin makes a homemade matzah shaped like the continent of Africa called the "Afrikoman." Have fun with that!

AUTHOR'S NOTE

T his book is, admittedly, a hybrid. There are elements of personal memoir, and elements of a food book—recipes and all. Not all of the narratives directly correlate with food and cooking, and if you are at all familiar with my work, that's okay. We have come to segregate food and cooking as if they are apolitical—disconnected from history, culture, and identity—or are just another form of entertainment and distraction. That's just what some people want. If they want their food media that way, there are plenty of other places to get that content.

This project is something I've wanted to do for twenty years. I was a prisoner of youth and inexperience and the ominous clouds of ineffability. There are still things that don't get blotted out in this book. We could take a million side roads into the minutiae of Black-Jewish relations, but I'm not sure that defines my existence. I am not here to assuage or be combative; this book is not a platform: it's a place in my soul, and you are a guest, a witness to my vulnerability. I didn't come to serve anyone's interests or take orders. Welcome to my table.

Bricolage is the word here. Oppressed and marginalized people rarely have linear histories in which everything is neatly packaged. The bits, the pieces, the mosaic that makes up these fascinating histories may not be accessible using casual research or without probing epistemological journeys that take away from the basic questions asked here: What energy, past, history, relationships, moments and anecdotes do I and other Jews who are Black bring into the kitchen? How do we use food to make ourselves in the image of what we identify with and want to project? How do we navigate the complexities of an intersectional identity when we are the guides, the teachers, or trailblazers?

I couldn't begin to answer those questions and produce a dusted-off history of Black Jews in the United States, the Americas, the African Atlantic, Europe, or Africa our mother. I quickly figured out that *Koshersoul* did not need to be a one-stop shop for all of the concerns, skepticism, suspicions, overeager curiosity, and debates people usually want to bring to this rodeo. We have collectively developed a hunger for the salacious and words that overreach for attention. I've tried my best not to do that here, preferring, as it were, to tell my own story on my own terms and relate tidbits of other people's lives in the hopes that they could join this conversation at their comfort level and not be at the mercy of people who need to vet and validate them in a perverse social biopsy. Everybody's story isn't, and shouldn't be, told here.

For example, although many of my interviewees are drawn from mainstream Jewish communities, there is an established, evolving Black Jewish culture in the Hebrew-Israelite (not the guys screaming on the street) tradition. The movement's cultural cues border on syncretic fusion like the gospel-ish intonations and stylings and sermonizing and koshersoul stylings, which are closer to home. The clothing of festive times ranges from Shabbat best to African dress worn to services and on holidays at home. The movement infuses social and political issues with a greater collective emphasis on African American community life and Black nationalism. I don't jump into the fight over who is who and what is what; all I know is that the culture is poorer if we don't acknowledge the diversity of Black Jewish life. This book is not the place to fight any battles over assumptions about religious or ethnic authenticity.

In the future, I hope to write more extensively on Black Jewish cultural history and traditions. *Koshersoul* is a first effort at tackling contemporary foodways in a part of African American and American Jewish peoplehoods that don't often receive attention or awareness. I hope that you enjoy (or enjoyed) my offering and that it inspires you to greater empathy and an urge toward better dialogue, culinary creativity, and hospitality. I wrote this in the spirit of starting a conversation and reinvigorating the work of making an America and a world where we embrace differences, celebrate similarities and connections, and create new traditions that honor us all.

ACKNOWLEDGMENTS

The hardest part of a book to write is the acknowledgments. There are literally too many people to name.

I am grateful to Hashem.

I am in awe of my Ancestors.

I am thankful for blood and found family and my *mishpocheh*—the global diaspora of Jews of African descent, the African Diaspora, and the entire Jewish people.

Gregg Du'Bois Holliday/Shemmie—thank you for never being too far and being a teacher and friend for more than twenty years. You are my pilpul.

Tony Westbrook, cuz Rabbi Shais Rishon, our warrior Shahanna McKinney Baldon, Naftali Quartey, Tema Smith, Chava, Koach Baruch Frazer, Rebecca Franklin, Elisheva, Shevi/Diana, Karen/Chana, the incredible Yavilah McCoy, Rabbi Sandra Lawson, and all of my interviewees—thank you for being role models and shining lights. Thank you for your extraordinary patience and contributions and encouragement.

Marc Steiner—thank you for opening gates. #hocksandlox

Dr. Pamela Nadell—I told you I'd thank you in a book one day—thank you!

Joan Nathan—thank you for your wisdom and encouragement and for introducing me to Marcie.

Jeffrey Yoskowitz, Liz Alpern—I appreciate you.

Josh Parel and Family—thank you for this journey.

Jane Ziegelman—thank you for your inspiration and for introducing me to the amazing Jason Yarn, our mutual agent.

Thank you, my Harper and Amistad folks, Bill Strachan and the powerhouse, Tracy Sherrod.

Thank you, Rabbi Ruth Adar and Rabbi Ruth Abusch-Magder, Deborah Brodie, and families!

Thank you, Rabbi Luxemburg, Rabbi David Spey, and Rabbi Gerry Serota for paying attention.

Thanks for the hospitality, Rabbi Backman! Thank you, Manela family—I haven't forgotten!

Thank you, Elliot and Katie and Keith and Jessica and so many others!

Thank you, Jewish Social Services, for keeping a roof over my head when times were rough.

Ina Pinkney, thank you for giving me the history and career guidance and for your spirit.

As always, Phil Lueck, you are my fire, thank you for your careful eye and advice.

Nancie McDermott for her keen eye and Laura Kumin for her ongoing support.

Thank you, Rachel Herman—#WhiteGirlNumberOne—and Becca Carin and Ben Goodman; I'm proud that you are Hebrew school teachers. Thank you, Kim Roberts and Cantor Eschler.

Garrett Matthews, thank you for helping me keep this book alive during the awful pandemic.

Thank you, Be'chol Lashon and Buber Camp Alumni, Rabbi Denise Eger, Rabbi Michelle Goldsmith, Tammy Gelbart, the Jaffe family, Rabbi Dena Bodian, and so many more. . . .

Thank you to my husband, Taylor, who survived this with me. It happened in the time it was supposed to happen because a man plans but G-d laughs.

GLOSSARY

African Atlantic: The Atlantic facing part of the African Diaspora, including the Americas, West and Central Africa, and parts of Western Europe

ahavah: Love

aliyah: To be called to bless or read from the Torah, or to "make Aliyah," move to Israel, literally "to go higher"

alter kaker: Old fogies in Yiddish, literally "old crappers"; not polite

Ashkenazi: The Jewish Diaspora from Central and Eastern Europe

avodah: Worship, labor, service

bashert: Fated, intended

bocher: Yeshivah student, young man of full learning age

brachot: Hebrew and Aramaic blessings

Chabad: The outreach arm of the Lubavitch Hasidic sect; an acronym for *(Ch)ochmah*, wisdom—*(B)inah*, understanding—*(D)a'at* knowledge

chametz: Leavened bread, sourdough, leavening removed before Passover

chaver: Friend, brother in learning

cheder: Small school where Hebrew reading and Jewish literacy are taught to the young

devekus: Hasidic term for spiritual union, literally "gluing," with the Divine Presence

dhimmi: Protected minority religion status among old Islamic empires

eruvim (*sing: eruv*): Boundaries, mixtures, liminal spaces

faygeleh: Yiddish for homosexual; literally "little bird"

frum: Yiddish for very observant, ultra-Orthodox

Gemara: Commentary on the Mishnah that forms the other major piece of the multivolume Talmud

haftorah: Prophetic reading paired with the weekly Torah reading

Haggadah: Booklet used to tell the story of Passover

Hashem: Literally "the Name"; nickname for G-d

havurot: Small or informal community of Jews assembled for the purpose of Jewish celebration and observance, usually unconnected or loosely connected to a movement

hechsher: A symbol showing rabbinical approval for kosher foods

hiddur mitzvah: To make one's religious observance beautiful or aesthetically pleasing

hineni: "Behold," I am here, I am present; phrase uttered by Abraham in G-d's presence

kashrut: Kosher law and practice

kavvanah: Focus and mindfulness in prayer

keshet: Rainbow

kiddush: The sanctification over the wine that begins Shabbat and many Jewish holidays *kippa:* Yarmulke, head covering worn to show reverence for the Lord

kippa s'ruga: Knitted kippa or yarmulke, frequently worn by modern Orthodox Jews

kishkes: Intestines

Ladino: The language of the Sephardi diaspora out of Spain and Portugal. A mixture of old Spanish, Hebrew, Aramaic, and elements of Turkish, Greek, and other languages

l'dor v'dor: From generation to generation

Maafa: "The Great Disaster," from Swahili, Pan-Africanist term for the ongoing collective project of global anti-Blackness, including the slave trades, colonialism, and structural racism

maror: Bitter herbs used during Passover/Pesach

mashgiach: Kosher supervisor

mayseh: A tale, an anecdote

mechitzah: Gate, separation between men and women during services

mechiyah: A joy

mellah: North African Jewish quarter

mesorah: Tradition, path

mezuzot: Parchment containing the *Shema* hung on the doorpost in accordance with Deuteronomy

mikveh: Ritual bath

minhagim (sing: minhag): Customs practiced by different Jewish communities, sects, and families

Mishnah: First and oldest collection of oral traditions in Jewish law and lore forming the core texts of rabbinical knowledge of how to observe the written Torah

mishpocheh: Family, kin, people

mitzvah (*pl: mitzvot*): Commandment

Mizrahi: Jews from the Middle East into Central Asia and beyond

mohel: Person charged with ritual circumcision as required by Jewish law

neshamah: Soul

oneg: Casual festive gathering held on Shabbat

salatim: Salads eaten before and during a meal

schmaltz: Chicken fat

Sephardi: Jews of Iberian descent and related communities from North Africa, southeastern Europe, Turkey, and other areas of the Mediterranean

shandeh: Shame, scandal

Shema: Deuteronomy 6:4: "Hear ye O Israel, the Lord our G-d is One!"

shiva minyan: Prayer quorum gathered to say the Mourner's Prayer and comfort a family in grief

Shoah: The Holocaust

Shulchan Orech: A popular version of the code of Jewish law redacted into daily rules and laws

shvitz: To sweat or perspire; stress

sukkah: Small booth, hut, or shed built to live in during Sukkot

tallit: Prayer shawl worn during prayer or daytime services or on Yom Kippur

tallit katan: Small tallit worn like a shirt under other garments— usually with strings exposed

tashlich: Rosh Hashanah ritual where sins are symbolically tossed into a river, a ditch, a stream, or the sea *tefillin:* Small leather boxes tied to the head and the arm in fulfillment of the commandment to bind the *Shema* upon the body

tikkun olam: To repair the world

treyf: Literally "torn," not kosher

tsuris: Troubles

tuchus: Behind, buttocks

tzedakah: Righteous giving and deeds

Tzedek: Justice

tzitzit: Specially knotted ritual strings worn on the four corners of the *tallit gadol* or *tallit katan*

Yahaduth: Judaism in Hebrew

yichus: A respected pedigree or bloodline

BIBLIOGRAPHY

Adams, Maurianne. *Strangers and Neighbors: Relations Between Blacks and Jews in the United States*. Amherst: Univ. of Massachusetts Press, 1999.

Admony, Einat, and Janna Gur. *Shuk*. New York: Artisan, 2019.

Apisdorf, Shimon. *Kosher for the Clueless but Curious*. Baltimore: Leviathan, 2005.

Armstrong, Karen. *A History of God*. New York: Alfred A. Knopf, 1994.

Arnow, David. *Creating Lively Passover Seders: A Sourcebook of Engaging Tales, Texts and Activities*. Woodstock, VT: Jewish Lights Publishing, 2011.

Asch, Chris Myers, and George Derek Musgrove. *Chocolate City: A History of Race and Democracy in the Nation's Capital*. Chapel Hill: Univ. of North Carolina Press, 2017.

Ausubel, Nathan. *The Book of Jewish Knowledge: An Encyclopedia of Judaism and the Jewish People, Covering All Elements of Jewish Life from Biblical Times to the Present*. New York: Crown, 1979.

Baldwin, James. *Collected Essays*. Edited by Toni Morrison. New York: Literary Classics of the United States, 1998.

Baptist, Edward E. *The Half Has Never Been Told: Slavery and the Making of American Capitalism*. New York: Basic Books, 2014.

Benjamin, Richard, and David Fleming, eds. *Transatlantic Slavery: An Introduction*. Liverpool: Liverpool Univ. Press, 2010.

Berger, Maurice. *White Lies*. New York: Farrar, Straus, and Giroux, 1999.

Berlin, Adele, and Marc Zvi Brettler. *The Jewish Study Bible*. New York: Oxford Univ. Press, 2004.

Berman, Paul. *Blacks and Jews: Alliances and Arguments*. New York: Delacorte, 1994.

Bernamoff, Noah, and Rae Bernamoff. *The Mile End Cookbook*. New York: Clarkson Potter, 2012.

Bernstein, Ellen. *Ecology and the Jewish Spirit: Where Nature and the Sacred Meet*. Woodstock, VT: Jewish Lights Publishing, 1998.

Biale, David. *Cultures of the Jews: A New History*. New York: Random House, 2002.

Bober, Phyllis Pray. *Art, Culture, and Cuisine: Ancient and Medieval Gastronomy.* Chicago: Univ. of Chicago Press, 1999.

Bonder, Nilton. *The Kabbalah of Money: Jewish Insights on Giving, Owning, and Receiving.* Boston: Shambhala, 1996.

Borowitz, Eugene B., and Frances Weinman Schwartz. *The Jewish Moral Virtues.* Philadelphia: Jewish Publication Society, 1999.

Bresciani, Edda. "Food Culture in Ancient Egypt." In *Food: A Culinary History*, edited by Albert Sonnenfeld, 38–45. New York: Penguin, 1999.

Brodkin, Karen. *How Jews Became White Folks: And What That Says About Race in America.* New Brunswick, NJ: Rutgers Univ. Press, 2010.

Bruder, Edith. *The Black Jews of Africa.* New York: Oxford Univ. Press, 2008.

Bruce, Lawrence. "Oh My America: Lenny Bruce and the Golden Age." *Jewish Currents*, August 2, 2012. https://jewishcurrents.org/o-my-america-lenny -bruce-and-the-golden-age.

Buhle, Paul, and Robin D. G. Kelley. "Allies of a Different Sort: Jews and Blacks in the American Left." In Salzman and West, *Struggles in the Promised Land*, 197–230.

Cardozo, Miriam Irma Lopes. *As I Lived It.* Self-published, 2010.

Carson, Clayborne. "Black-Jewish Universalism in the Era of Identity Politics." In Salzman and West, *Struggles in the Promised Land*, 177–196.

———. *Civil Rights Chronicle: The African-American Struggle for Freedom.* Lincolnwood, IL: Legacy, 2003.

Chireau, Yvonne. "Black Culture and Black Zion: African American Religious Encounters with Judaism, 1790–1930, an Overview." In Chireau and Deutsch, *Black Zion*, 15–32.

Chireau, Yvonne, and Nathaniel Deutsch, eds. *Black Zion: African American Religious Encounters with Judaism.* New York: Oxford Univ. Press, 2000.

Coates, Ta-Nehisi. *We Were Eight Years in Power.* New York: One World, 2017.

Cohen, Sarah Blacher, and Joanne B. Koch. *Shared Stages: Ten American Dramas of Blacks and Jews.* Albany: Univ. of New York Press, 2007.

Cohen, Yaniv. *My Spiced Kitchen: A Middle Eastern Cookbook.* Salem, MA: Page Street, 2019.

Cooper, John. *Eat and Be Satisfied.* Northvale, NJ: Aronson, 1993.

Council, Mildred. *Mama Pip's Family Cookbook.* Chapel Hill: Univ. of North Carolina Press, 2005.

Courlander, Harold. *A Treasury of Afro-American Folklore.* New York: Smithmark, 1996.

Covert, Mildred L., and Sylvia P. Gerson. *Kosher Cajun Cookbook.* Gretna, LA: Pelican, 2006.

———. *Kosher Creole Cookbook.* Gretna, LA: Pelican, 1982.

———. *Kosher Southern-Style Cookbook.* Gretna, LA: Pelican, 1993.

Crew, Spencer R. *Field to Factory: Afro-American Migration 1915–1940.* Washington, DC: Smithsonian Institution, 1987.

Curtin, Philip D. "Ayuba Suleiman Diallo of Bondu." In *Africa Remembered*, edited by Philip D. Curtain, 17–59. Madison: Univ. of Wisconsin Press, 1967.

Davis, David Brion. "Jews in the Slave Trade." In Salzman and West, *Struggles in the Promised Land*, 65–72.

DiAngelo, Robin. *White Fragility: Why It's So Hard for White People to Talk About Racism*. Boston: Beacon, 2018.

DiAngelo, Robin. *Nice Racism: How Progressive White People Perpetuate Racial Harm*. Boston: Beacon Press, 2021.

Diner, Hasia R. "Between Words and Deeds: Jews and Blacks in America, 1880–1935." In Salzman and West, *Struggles in the Promised Land*, 73–86.

Diouf, Sylviane A. *Servants of Allah: African Muslims Enslaved in the Americas*. New York: New York Univ. Press, 1998.

Dobrinsky, Herbert C. *A Treasury of Sephardic Laws and Customs*. Hoboken, NJ: Ktav, 1988.

Dolader, Miguel-Ángel Motis. "Mediterranean Jewish Diet and Traditions in the Middle Ages." In *Food: A Culinary History*, edited by Albert Sonnenfeld, 224–246. New York: Penguin, 1999.

Dornenburg, Andrew, and Karen Page. *Becoming a Chef*. Hoboken, NJ: John Wiley & Sons, 2003.

———. *Culinary Artistry*. Hoboken, NJ: John Wiley & Sons, 1996.

———. *The Flavor Bible*. New York: Little, Brown, 2008.

Deutsch, Nathaniel. "The Proximate Other: The Nation of Islam and Judaism." In Chireau and Deutsch, *Black Zion*, 91–118.

Ehrlich, Elizabeth. *Miriam's Kitchen*. New York: Penguin, 1997.

Eichstedt, Jennifer L., and Stephen Small. *Representations of Slavery: Race and Ideology in Southern Plantation Museums*. Washington, DC: Smithsonian Institution, 2002.

El-Haddad, Laila, and Maggie Schmitt. *The Gaza Kitchen: A Palestinian Culinary Journey*. Washington, DC: Just World Books, 2016.

Eliach, Yaffa. *There Was Once a World: A 900 Year Chronicle of the Shtetl of Eishyshok*. New York: Back Bay Books, 1999.

Eltis, David, and David Richardson. *Atlas of the Transatlantic Slave Trade*. New Haven: Yale Univ. Press, 2010.

Evans, Eli N. *The Provincials*. Chapel Hill: Univ. of North Carolina Press, 1973.

Farb, Peter. *The Land, Wildlife, and Peoples of the Bible*. New York: Harper & Row, 1967.

Farrow, Anne, Joel Lang, and Jenifer Frank. *Complicity: How the North Promoted, Prolonged, and Profited from Slavery*. New York: Ballantine, 2005.

Feibleman, Peter S. *American Cooking: Creole and Acadian*. New York: Time-Life Books, 1971.

Ferris, Marcie Cohen. *The Edible South: The Power of Food and the Making of an American Region*. Chapel Hill: Univ. of North Carolina Press, 2014.

————. *Matzoh Ball Gumbo: Culinary Tales of the Jewish South*. Chapel Hill: Univ. of North Carolina Press, 2005.

Fishkoff, Sue. *Kosher Nation*. New York: Schocken, 2010.

Fowler, Damon Lee. *The Savannah Cookbook*. Layton, UT: Gibbs Smith, 2008.

Gates, Henry Louis Jr. "My Yiddishe Mama." In *The Henry Louis Gates, Jr. Reader*, edited by Abby Wolf, 12–15. New York: Basic Civitas, 2012.

Giammellaro, Antonella Spanò. "The Phoenicians and the Carthaginians: The Early Mediterranean Diet." In *Food: A Culinary History*, edited by Albert Sonnenfeld, 55–68. New York: Penguin, 1999.

Gilbert, Sandra M., and Rojer J. Porter. *Eating Words: A Norton Anthology of Food Writing*. New York: W. W. Norton, 2015.

Gitlitz, David M., and Linda K. Davidson. *A Drizzle of Honey: The Lives and Recipes of Spain's Secret Jews*. New York: St. Martin's Press, 1999.

Glinert, Lewis. *The Joys of Hebrew*. New York: Oxford Univ. Press, 1992.

Goldberg, Betty S. *Chinese Kosher Cooking*. Middle Village, NY: Jonathan David, 1989.

Goldenberg, David M. "The Curse of Ham: A Case of Rabbinic Racism?" In Salzman and West, *Struggles in the Promised Land*, 21–52.

————. *The Curse of Ham: Race and Slavery in Early Judaism, Christianity, and Islam*. Princeton, NJ: Princeton Univ. Press, 2003.

Goldstein, Eric L. *The Price of Whiteness: Jews, Race, and American Identity*. Princeton, NJ: Princeton Univ. Press, 2006.

Greenspoon, Leonard J., Ronald A. Simkins, and Gerald Shapiro. *Food and Judaism*. Omaha: Creighton Univ. Press, 2005.

Gropman, Gabrielle Rossmer, and Sonya Gropman. *The German-Jewish Cookbook*. Lebanon, NH: Brandeis Univ. Press, 2017.

Goucher, Candice. *Congotay! Congotay!: A Global History of Caribbean Food*. New York: Routledge, 2015.

Gross, Aaron S., Jody Myers, and Jordan D. Rosenblum. *Feasting and Fasting*. New York: New York Univ. Press, 2019.

Gurock, Jeffrey S. *Orthodox Jews in America*. Bloomington: Indiana Univ. Press, 2009.

Halio, Hank. *Ladino Reveries: Tales of the Sephardic Experience in America*. New York: Foundation for the Advancement of Sephardic Studies and Culture, 1996.

Hall, Robert L. "Food Corps, Medicinal Plants, and the Atlantic Slave Trade." In *African American Foodways: Explorations of History and Culture*, edited by Anne L. Bower, 17–44. Urbana: Univ. of Illinois Press, 2007.

Hammer, Jill. *The Jewish Book of Days*. Philadelphia: Jewish Publication Society, 2006.

Hauck-Lawson, Annie, and Jonathan Deutsch. *Gastropolis*. New York: Columbia Univ. Press, 2009.

Haynes, Bruce D. *The Soul of Judaism: Jews of African Descent in America*. New York: New York Univ. Press, 2018.

Helou, Anissa. *Feast: Food of the Islamic World*. New York: HarperCollins, 2018.

Holloway, Joseph E., ed. *Africanisms in American Culture*. Bloomington: Indiana Univ. Press, 2005.

————. "The Origins of African American Culture." In Holloway, *Africanisms in American Culture*, 18–38.

Hondius, Dienke. "Black Africans in Seventeenth-Century Amsterdam." *Renaissance and Reformation/Renaissance et Réforme* 31, no. 2 (2008): 87–105.

I in, Priscilla Mary. *Bountiful Empire: A History of Ottoman Cuisine*. London: Reaktion, 2018.

Jacobs, Louis. *What Does Judaism Say About?* Jerusalem: Keter, 1973.

Jones, G. I. "Olaudah Equiano of the Niger Ibo." In *Africa Remembered*, edited by Philip D. Curtain, 60–98. Madison: Univ. of Wisconsin Press, 1967.

Jordan, William Chester. "The Medieval Background." In Salzman and West, *Struggles in the Promised Land*, 53–64.

Joselit, Jenna Weissman. *The Wonders of America: Reinventing Jewish Culture, 1880–1950*. New York: Hill & Wang, 1994.

Kadden, Barbara Binder, and Sorel Goldberg Loeb. *Teaching Torah*. Denver: Alternatives in Religious Education, 1984.

Kahn, Yasmin. *Zaitoun: Recipes from the Palestinian Kitchen*. New York: W. W. Norton, 2018.

Karr, Mary. *The Art of Memoir*. New York: HarperCollins, 2015.

Katz-Hyman, Martha B., and Kym S. Rice. *The World of a Slave: Encyclopedia of Material Life of Slaves in the United States*. 2 vols. Santa Barbara, CA: ABC-CLIO, 2011.

Kaufman, Jonathan. "Blacks and Jews: The Struggle in the Cities." In Salzman and West, *Struggles in the Promised Land*, 107–122.

Kendi, Ibram X. *Stamped from the Beginning: The Definitive History of Racist Ideas in America*. New York: Nation Books, 2017.

Koenig, Leah. *The Jewish Cookbook*. London: Phaidon, 2019.

————. *Little Book of Jewish Sweets*. San Francisco: Chronicle Books, 2019.

Koerner, András. *Jewish Cuisine in Hungary: A Cultural History with 83 Authentic Recipes*. Budapest: Central European Univ. Press, 2019.

————. *A Taste of the Past: The Daily Life and Cooking of a 19th-Century Hungarian Jewish Homemaker*. Lebanon, NH: Univ. Press of New England, 2004.

Kolatch, Alfred J. *The Jewish Book of Why*. Middle Village, NY: Jonathan David, 1981.

————. *The Second Jewish Book of Why*. Middle Village, NY: Jonathan David, 1985.

Krant, Jigal. *TLV: Recipes and Stories from Israel*. Melbourne: Smith Street Books, 2019.

Labendz, Jacob Ari, and Shumly Yanklowitz. *Jewish Veganism and Vegetarianism.* Albany: State Univ. of New York, 2019.

Lange, Nicholas de. *Atlas of the Jewish World.* Oxford: Andromeda, 1984.

Lee, Jennifer 8. *The Fortune Cookie Chronicles.* New York: Twelve, 2008.

Leonard, Jonathan Norton. *The First Farmers.* New York: Time-Life Books, 1973.

———. *Latin American Cooking.* New York: Time-Life Books, 1968.

Lester, Julius. *Lovesong: Becoming a Jew.* New York: Arcade, 1991.

Levine, Lawrence W. *Black Culture and Black Consciousness.* New York: Oxford Univ. Press, 1977.

Levy, Faye. *Jewish Cooking for Dummies.* Foster City, CA: IDG Books Worldwide, 2001.

Lewis, Earl. "The Need to Remember: Three Phases in Black and Jewish Educational Relations." In Salzman and West, *Struggles in the Promised Land,* 231–256.

Lowe, Kate. "The Lives of African Slaves and People of African Descent in Renaissance Europe." In *Revealing the African Presence in Renaissance Europe,* edited by Joaneath Spicer, 13–34. Baltimore: Walters Art Museum, 2012.

Lowenstein, Steven M. *The Jewish Cultural Tapestry: International Jewish Folk Traditions.* New York: Oxford Univ. Press, 2000.

MaNishtana. *Ariel Samson, Freelance Rabbi.* New York: Multikoshereal Press, 2018.

———. *Thoughts from a Unicorn.* Independently published, 2012.

Marks, Gil. *Encyclopedia of Jewish Food.* New York: Houghton Mifflin Harcourt, 2010.

Mellon, James, ed. *Bullwhip Days: The Slaves Remember.* New York: Weidenfeld & Nicolson, 1988.

Melnick, Ralph. "Billy Simons: The Black Jew of Charleston." *American Jewish Archives* 32, no. 1 (1980): 3–8.

Merwin, Ted. *Pastrami on Rye.* New York: New York Univ. Press, 2015.

Michaeli, Ethan. "Another Exodus: The Hebrew Israelites from Chicago to Dimona." In Chireau and Deutsch, *Black Zion,* 73–90.

Moore, Deborah Dash. "Separate Paths: Blacks and Jews in the 20th Century South." In Salzman and West, *Struggles in the Promised Land,* 275–294.

Musleah, Rahel. *Apples and Pomegranates.* Minneapolis: Kar-Ben, 2004.

Nadin, Elvira, and Mihai Nadin. *Jewish: Does It Make a Difference?* Middle Village, NY: Jonathan David, 2000.

Nathan, Joan. *The Foods of Israel Today.* New York: Alfred A. Knopf, 2001.

———. *Jewish Cooking in America.* New York: Alfred A. Knopf, 1998, 2005.

———. *The Jewish Holiday Kitchen.* New York: Schocken Books, 1988.

Newhouse, Alana. *The 100 Most Jewish Foods: A Highly Debatable List.* New York: Artisan, 2019.

Nickles, Harry G. *Middle Eastern Cooking.* New York: Time-Life Books, 1969.

Osseo-Asare, Fran. *Food Culture in Sub-Saharan Africa*. Westport, CT: Greenwood, 2005.

Ottolenghi, Yotam, and Sami Tamimi. *Jerusalem: A Cookbook*. Berkeley: Ten Speed Press, 2012.

Page, Karen. *Kitchen Creativity*. New York: Little, Brown, 2017.

Painter, Neil Irvin. *The History of White People*. New York: W. W. Norton, 2010.

Pearl, Judea, and Ruth Pearl. *I Am Jewish: Personal Reflections Inspired by the Last Words of Daniel Pearl*. Woodstock, VT: Jewish Lights Publishing, 2004.

Peck, Alice. *Bread, Body, Spirit: Finding the Sacred in Food*. Woodstock, VT: SkyLight Paths Publishing, 2008.

Piersen, William D. *From Africa to America: African American History from the Colonial Era to the Early Republic, 1526–1790*. New York: Twayne Publishers, 1996.

Pogrebin, Letty Cottin. "Blacks, Jews, and Gender: The History, Politics, and Cultural Anthropology of a Woman's Dialogue Group." In Salzman and West, *Struggles in the Promised Land*, 385–400.

Raboteau, Albert J. *Slave Religion: The Invisible Institution in the Antebellum South*. Oxford: Oxford Univ. Press, 1978.

Rediker, Marcus. *The Slave Ship: A Human History*. New York: Penguin, 2008.

Roden, Claudia. *The Book of Jewish Food*. New York: Alfred A. Knopf, 1996.

Rosen, Robert. *A Short History of Charleston*. Columbia: Univ. of South Carolina Press, 1982.

Rosenberger, Bernard. "Arab Cuisine and Its Contribution to European Culture." In *Food: A Culinary History*, edited by Albert Sonnenfeld, 207–223. New York: Penguin, 1999.

Rosenstein, Wendi Zelkin, and Kit Naylor. *The Lincoln Del Cookbook*. St. Paul: Minnesota Historical Society Press, 2017.

Rossel, Seymour. *The Holocaust: The World and the Jews, 1933–1945*. Springfield, NJ: Behrman House, 1992.

Salzman, Jack, and Cornel West, eds. *Struggles in the Promised Land: Toward a History of Black-Jewish Relations in the United States*. New York: Oxford Univ. Press, 1997.

Sarna, Jonathan D. *American Judaism: A History*. New Haven: Yale Univ. Press, 2004.

Sax, David. *Save the Deli*. New York: Houghton Mifflin Harcourt, 2009.

Schmidt, Roger. *Exploring Religion*. Belmont, CA: Wadsworth, 2006.

Shillington, Kevin. *History of Africa*. London: Red Globe, 2019.

Shosteck, Patti. *A Lexicon of Jewish Cooking*. Chicago: Contemporary Books, 1979.

Silbiger, Steven A. *The Jewish Phenomenon*. Marietta: Longstreet, 2000.

Silver, Laura. *Knish*. Lebanon, NH: Univ. Press of New England, 2014.

Singer, Merrill. "Symbolic Identity Formation in an African American Religious Sect: The Black Hebrew Israelites." In Chireau and Deutsch, *Black Zion*, 55–72.

Sokolov, Raymond. *Why We Eat What We Eat*. New York: Touchstone, 1991.

Soler, Jean. "Biblical Reasons: The Dietary Rules of the Ancient Hebrews." In *Food: A Culinary History*, edited by Albert Sonnenfeld, 46–54.

Southern, Eileen. *The Music of the Black Americans: A History*. New York: Norton, 1997.

Spalding, Henry D., ed. *Encyclopedia of Black Folklore and Humor*. Middle Village, NY: Jonathan David, 1990.

Spiegel, Murray, and Rickey Stein. *300 Ways to Ask the Four Questions*. Roseland, NJ: Spiegel-Stein Publishing, 2007.

Stern, Chaim. *Day by Day*. Boston: Beacon, 1998.

Stern, Lisë. *How to Keep Kosher*. New York: HarperCollins, 2004.

Stone, Emily. *Did Jew Know?* San Francisco: Chronicle Books, 2013.

Strassfeld, Michael. *The Jewish Holidays*. New York: Harper & Row, 1985.

Sussman, Adeena. *Sababa: Fresh, Sunny Flavors from My Israeli Kitchen*. New York: Avery, 2019.

Tapper, Aaron J. Hahn. *Judaisms: A Twenty-First-Century Introduction to Jews and Jewish Identities*. Oakland: Univ. of California Press, 2016.

Telushkin, Joseph. *Jewish Literacy*. New York: HarperCollins, 1991.

Thiam, Pierre. *Yolele! Recipes from the Heart of Senegal*. New York: Lake Isle Press, 2008.

Thompson, Robert Farris. *Flash of the Spirit: African American Art and Philosophy*. New York: Vintage, 1984.

Tipton-Martin, Toni. *The Jemima Code: Two Centuries of African American Cookbooks*. Austin: Univ. of Texas Press, 2015.

Twitty, Michael W. *The Cooking Gene*. New York: Amistad, 2017.

———. "Divine Cravings: Soul Food as Edible Scripture." Unpublished paper presented at "Uncovering Connections: Cultural Endurance Between Africa, the Americas, and the Caribbean," Medgar Evers College, City University of New York, March 15, 2003.

Wallach, Jennifer Jensen, ed. *Dethroning the Deceitful Pork Chop: Rethinking African American Foodways from Slavery to Obama*. Fayetteville: Univ. of Arkansas Press, 2015.

———. *Every Nation Has Its Dish: Black Bodies and Black Food in Twentieth-Century America*. Chapel Hill: Univ. of North Carolina Press, 2019.

———. *Getting What We Need Ourselves: How Food Has Shaped African American Life*. Lanham, MD: Rowan & Littlefield, 2019.

Walter, Eugene. *American Cooking: Southern Style*. New York: Time-Life Books, 1971.

Wex, Michael. *Rhapsody in Schmaltz*. New York: St. Martin's, 2016.

Williams, Elizabeth M. *New Orleans*. Lanham, MD: AltaMira, 2013.

Williams, Joseph J. *Hebrewisms of West Africa: From Nile to Niger with the Jews.* New York: Dial Press, 1930.

Williams, Patricia J. "On Imagining Foes, Imagining Friendship." From Salzman and West, *Struggles in the Promised Land*, 371–384.

Williams, Susan. *Food in the United States 1820s–1890.* Westport, CT: Greenwood, 2006.

Witt, Doris. *Black Hunger.* Minneapolis: Univ. of Minnesota Press, 1999.

Wolfe, Linda. *The Cooking of the Caribbean Islands.* New York: Time-Life Books, 1970.

Wolfson, Bernard J. "African American Jews: Dispelling Myths, Bridging the Divide." In Chireau and Deutsch, *Black Zion*, 33–54.

Yentsch, Anne. "Excavating the South's African American Food History." In *African American Foodways: Explorations of History and Culture*, edited by Anne L. Bower, 59–100. Urbana: Univ. of Illinois Press, 2007.

Yoskowitz, Jeffrey, and Liz Alpern. *The Gefilte Manifesto: New Recipes for Old World Jewish Foods.* New York: Flatiron Books, 2016.

Zafar, Rafia. *Recipes for Respect: African American Meals and Meaning.* Athens: Univ. of Georgia Press, 2019.

Zamore, Mary L. *The Sacred Table: Creating a Jewish Food Ethic.* New York: Central Conference of American Rabbis, 2011.

Ziegelman, Jane. *97 Orchard: An Edible History of Five Immigrant Families in One New York Tenement.* New York: HarperCollins, 2010.

ABOUT THE AUTHOR

Michael W. Twitty is a culinary historian, living history interpreter, and Judaics teacher. He is the creator of *Afroculinaria*, the first blog devoted to African American historic foodways and their legacy.

Michael is the author of *The Cooking Gene*, winner of the James Beard Foundation Book of the Year Award as well as Best Writing 2018. He is a highly sought after speaker and consultant on issues of historical interpretation; food culture and politics; intersections between food and spirituality; and issues related to Jews of color, the history and legacy of enslavement in America, Jewish foodways, and Black-Jewish relations.

He has appeared on programs with Andrew Zimmern (*Bizarre Foods America*), Henry Louis Gates (*Many Rivers to Cross*), Padma Lakshmi (*Taste the Nation*), Michelle Obama's *Waffles and Mochi*, Netflix's *High on the Hog*, and, most recently, his own MasterClass on preserving your family's food heritage, as well as partnering to present online seminars with Atlas Obscura. He is the first Revolutionary in Residence at the Colonial Williamsburg Foundation, a TED Fellow, and a Smith fellow of the Southern Foodways Alliance. He was named to the Forward's list of influential American Jews in 2020. He was named a National Geographic Emerging Explorer in 2021. His line of personal spice blends with the boutique supplier Spice Tribe regularly sells out. He lives in Fredericksburg, Virginia.